ROMAN DAZE
LA DOLCE VITA FOR ALL SEASONS

Bronté Dee Jackson

M

MELBOURNE BOOKS

Published by Melbourne Books
Level 9, 100 Collins Street,
Melbourne, VIC 3000
Australia
www.melbournebooks.com.au
info@melbournebooks.com.au

National Library of Australia
Cataloguing-in-Publication entry : (paperback)
Author: Jackson, Bronté Dee.
Title: Roman Daze : La Dolce Vita For All Seasons.
ISBN: 9781922129338 (paperback)
Subjects: Jackson, Bronté Dee.
Women--Italy--Biography.
Italy--Description and travel.
Rome--Description and travel.
Dewey Number: 920.72

Bronté Dee Jackson's blog can be found at:
brontejackson.com

This book is dedicated to

Franceschina and Antonio

Grazie infinite

Acknowledgements to
Helen and Arthur, for their constant support
and belief in me as a writer; to Julie and Terri,
for their enthusiastic reading and feedback;
and to Alfredo, for everything.

Contents

AUTUMN

WINTER

How a raffle ticket changed my life

Twenty years ago I had a normal life. Then I bought a raffle ticket. Who knew two bucks was going to change my life forever?

Everything was on track. I had graduated university, travelled a bit locally, gotten married, was contemplating children and a mortgage, had a professional career, all before I turned thirty. But within three months I had lost it all and instead had a free airline ticket to Europe (via the raffle ticket) and a huge redundancy package (via having lost my job). No husband, no job, lots of money and an airline ticket. And still I hesitated. Then my landlord gave me notice.

I was in my late twenties, not the time you give up your life to go travelling. It was the time to buckle down, get even more serious about your career, do a post-graduate master's degree, buy a house, or quickly find a man and start procreating. All of these things I had expected of myself and desperately wanted to want enough, so that one day they might seem like the rewards I had always thought they would be. Even though I couldn't seem to make my life work, I didn't have the will left to figure out a different one.

I spent the first six months of that long ago trip consoling myself on the beach in Greece and Turkey over the life I had lost, and then admitting to myself the profound relief I felt in no longer having to have it. During that time I had no itinerary or even a vague idea of where to travel. I decided to stay a month in Rome, unheard of in backpacker terms. Staying for a month in one city is a lifetime. When I eventually found myself there it took only three days to fall in love with it, deeply and profoundly, like I had found a soulmate.

My passion for wanting to stay in Rome meant that I accepted any job I could get. Knowing that I had no grounds to apply for legal residence, it was therefore hopeless to think about having any kind of career job. At first I was the manager of an illegal *pensione*. Then I was a model for an art class, a job in constant demand. And I lied to get work, which at one point resulted in me staring at around 250 people across the counter of a bar at the opening night of the 'first Australian bar in Rome', along with Phil, the other Australian who had also illegally stayed and needed to lie about his experience, both of us expected to pull beers rapidly for all of them, neither of us ever having actually done it before. Luckily, Italians are not big connoisseurs of beer and didn't seem to notice the lack of foam, or the presence of too much, in their glasses. But even the most lowly jobs are not legally open to non-European citizens for more than a few months and I took the only option open to me. I advertised myself as an English language teacher.

A professor from a university contacted me and offered me two jobs: one where I would teach a subject in English that I knew something about to university students, the other one was where I would accompany him all around Europe on free tours, staying in the most luxurious hotels, meeting dignitaries (as this Professor was the only one in his field in Europe) and not actually doing much teaching. This role required me to be his 'girlfriend'.

But teaching didn't pay nearly enough to keep me in the habit I wanted to become accustomed to, and after two years I started to look around. I noticed that down the street from me was an office where a lot of people who spoke English seemed to exit every evening. Speaking fluent Italian was a pre-requisite for any job in the Italian market, as was the kind of VISA I could not qualify for, so I needed to look at places where English speakers were sought after and where I could work using English as my primary language. One day I walked in with my CV and asked to speak to the HR Manager.

There was no sign on the door or anywhere in reception to identify this building. There was an acronym written across the top of the building – WFP – written in huge letters and surrounded by some circular leaves. This was in the days before the internet, and the only other place where I had seen a similar symbol and acronyms was on the television, marketing the plight of pandas throughout the 1980s. I therefore assumed it was some Italian version of the World Wildlife Fund, with the letters changed to reflect the different sentence structure of the Italian language.

I was asked to come back tomorrow and do some preliminary tests. Here started my career in the United Nations. Buried in the bowels of HR administration procedures, where nobody ever referred to the organisation in full but only by acronym, before the days of branding, websites, email, the need to have a market 'presence' and a corporate identity, I diligently managed tasks and processed documents, wondering why there was always so much reference in them to rice and the costs of shipping, while pandas were hardly mentioned at all. It turned out I was not, in fact, working for the World Wildlife Fund but for the World Food Programme of the United Nations. I was equally happy, however, to be working for the world's largest humanitarian organisation providing emergency food to millions of people in times of natural disasters, war and famine.

A few years after I had been living in Rome, I met a diplomat at a toga party. We were side by side, pushing a supermarket trolley disguised as a 'chariot' and in which rode his wife, around a circular driveway as part of a race against other party guests. It was after the belly dancing display but before the fake human sacrifice. Here started my stint in Foreign Affairs.

I was happy and peaceful for the first time I could remember since I was a young child. The day I realised this, I was walking down my street on the way to the shops and something stopped me in my tracks. I stood on the footpath, wondering what this thing was that I was experiencing, this difference that I couldn't quite put my finger on. I was missing something, and the thing that had gone had been so much a part of me for so long that its absence made me feel something was wrong. I realised that it was the absence of anxiety. *So this is what peace feels like*, I thought.

So the man who took my breath away the first time I ever set eyes on him was kept at a distance for six more years before I was sure that giving up my singleness was going to be worth it. And it was. Like winning the raffle ticket all those years before, marrying Alfredo felt like I had won first prize again.

My heart responded to Italy's maternal character, the firm agreement that everyone needs to be cared for and forgiven. The greeting of each other every morning, the time taken to chat for a few minutes before serving the customer, the acknowledgement of each other as humans that have good days and bad days. And, as we all have bad days, the forbearance of someone who is having one, not expecting too much of them, giving them time and space, frustrating as that is if you are waiting for them to cut your hair, cash your cheque, make your sandwich or answer your call. You know that it will be the same on the day you need others to wait for you.

Twenty years here has included setting up my own practice working as a Management Consultant for international foreign affairs organisations and flying to over thirteen different countries across Europe, Africa and the Middle East; working for the United Nations emergency response, development and health organisations in Geneva, Rome, Budapest, Barbados, Bonn and Dakar; hearing Fidel Castro speak live on May Day in Havana, Cuba, and having my hire car commandeered by his soldiers with me as their designated driver for the day; taking a train back to Australia via Russia and Mongolia; co-driving a hovercraft to Capri; and never ever having to own a car.

I have had the chance to get to know Rome, my love, very well; its history, its failings, its short-sightedness, its arrogance, its self-doubt and its secrets. I have had the chance to give tours of it, write about it and apply my natural curiosity as a social anthropologist to its inhabitants, its myths, beliefs and identity.

This book is a personal guide to a city seen from the inside. It is an insider's experience of the mystery, misery and magnificence which is modern-day Rome. It includes important facts, such as why Sunday is a re-enactment of the Middle Ages, what 'The Changeover' means and when to do it, when it is okay to go calling in your pyjamas, what to do on a day off in Rome, tips for how to survive the blistering heat, and how to recognise and take advantage of a money laundering enterprise.

Like all infatuations, I expected my feelings for Rome to wear off and decided that I would leave when I no longer noticed the Coliseum, when I treated it as just another roundabout for traffic, the way the locals do. I am still waiting.

SPRING

Chapter 1

Liars, food wars and spring in Italy

I've had the opportunity to host a lot of visitors during my seventeen years in Rome. It is always difficult, mostly because they think you are constantly lying. Like when you tell them that if they plug the hairdryer in at the same time as the washing machine there will be a power blackout. Sometimes for hours. Sometimes in the whole apartment block, even though Italy is one of the seven most industrialised countries in the world.

Or when you tell them about springtime. That just a few short weeks before April the city is bare and freezing cold and that in a few weeks, just after April finishes, the city will be sunburnt and exhaustingly hot. It is hard amidst the lush, cool, waving green foliage and brilliant flowers to imagine the city bare, or that the air could ever warm up so much that you don't want to be outside.

But both are true. Rome's electricity grid was built for another time. The amount of electricity allotted per household is not usually enough for more than one or two electrical appliances. Fridge and washing machine, okay. Fridge, washing machine, hairdryer, not okay. Fridge and hot water heater, okay. Fridge, hot water heater, DVD player and several lights, not okay. There are many different combinations. Most of them I have learnt well by now, but guests take about two or three days, and several power cuts, before they believe me.

Guests are often also intrigued by the electric sockets in our apartment. Each one is an individual, like a snowflake. Some have two thin holes, some have two thick holes. Some have three thick holes, some have three thin holes, and some have two thick holes and one thin hole in the middle. They each require a different kind of adaptor. It's okay though, most hardware stores sell many kinds of adaptors. It seems to be easier to make an adaptor than standardise electrical sockets in Italy.

The electrical sockets in my apartment are, for my guests, a good introduction into Italian society. If guests can accept that within the parameters of electrical sockets there may be a world of difference, that no two sockets may be alike, and that you need to adapt to them rather than vice versa, then it helps them to understand Italian society. Italy as a society is rigid with rules, bureaucracy, rituals and traditions that are slow to change. It is therefore important that within these structures that keep Italy essentially Italian, individuals be allowed to express themselves and flourish. This means that room is made for everyone to be different in their own way.

This is reflected in the traffic and in Italian politics. In spite of the enormous amounts of congestion and time it takes to get anywhere, if someone wants to stop or slow down and have a conversation with a person on a *motorino*, a moped, driving next to them, everyone waits. If someone wants to cross three lanes of traffic at the last minute everyone lets them do so, without tooting. If someone is in a hurry and doesn't want to queue at the toll booth they just drive up to the front of the line and someone will let them in.

In Italian politics, the ruling party is usually made up of a spectrum of smaller parties all joined together from the full breadth of left to right. It explains the constant elections and referendums at a State, province, and city level, and the occasional dissolution of the government due to a lack of a quorum.

Individual rights to opinions, at whatever the cost, is highly tolerated as a collective principle. Each person is made room for in their uniqueness, while being supported by communal traditions and lifestyles. If you all have to be electrical sockets, you can at least be different kinds of electrical sockets.

Spring in Rome is an easy thing to adapt to. Foliage bursts out of every possible space available in a concrete-covered city. Where there is a space between wall and sidewalk, there is a sprig of green bursting out of it. The trees, which sit in tiny squares of soil carved out of the concrete sidewalks, are laden with pink blossoms. Not the fly-away, fairy floss pink kind, but the heavy, fuchsia kind with serious, sensuous petals.

Rome glistens in spring; it glistens with new life and with the magic that comes with birth. It is all the more spectacular because Rome sheds everything in the autumn. In winter the city is foliage-free; not a leaf or shrub remains to break up the concrete grey that is everywhere. Luckily, the sun shines valiantly all through winter, although you get used to stark branches everywhere and increased vision as suddenly all the leaves disappear and all that is left are the buildings.

Then suddenly, after a long absence, the colour green is everywhere and envelops everything it can. Tiny daisies with perfect, egg-yellow centres and bright, white petals are present in every stretch of wild grass. They come out to carpet everything with their cheeky presence and their uncontested right to be here every year in April, for only a matter of weeks, just to herald in spring.

* * *

The air is soft and warm and laps at my skin. Everywhere, above and below me, are the new flowers of the season. It has been spring for a month now and the transition is almost complete, from bare grey twigs to soft coverings of bright greens, dark greens, and delicate frostings of white and pink blossom. The delicate baby pink blossom that trumpets the arrival of spring has almost gone. In its place are the heavier white clouds of blossom, the heady white magnolia flower, the highly perfumed white jasmine flower. When the wind blows it rains white petals.

Here, spring is all the more precious because it is brief. In practice it only lasts a month or two before the summer heat overpowers the gentle air and the green foliage's glare begins to hurt my eyes under the burning sun. The air becomes hot and heavy, the radiance is only present in the very early morning and, like in winter, shelter has to be taken from the outdoors.

Just before leaving Australia seventeen years ago I saw a film called *Enchanted April*. I went with my grandmother. We both loved it. It was a tale of four women, set in the 1920s in London. They hire a villa in Tuscany for the month of April. They don't know each other, and share only a desire to escape the cold and wet London spring. They experience the magical powers of April in the Italian countryside and their souls are refreshed, each life changed a little for the better.

I went home in a trance after that movie. It was raining in Australia. The only piece of nature in my inner-city backyard was a strip of mud that must have once been a flower bed. I took off my shoes and slid my feet into it up to my ankles, under the rain, slowly raising each foot, one after the other in order to feel the earth. I sat for a long time under our one tree – that came over the fence from someone else's backyard – and marvelled at the knowledge that I too could go to that magical place called Italy, and that maybe it could be as refreshing for my soul too.

I think of that film every spring. April truly is enchanted here. The green of an Italian spring is a soft, succulent kind of green. It gently draws the juices up into the veins like sap, causing a feeling of coming back to life after a long, cold winter. It shows that life can be trusted to begin again no matter how long and dark the winter has been and in spite of the fact that everything looks like it has died.

It is April here, now. Enchanted April. And it is possible to be outdoors for as long as you want to in perfect and benign temperatures.

The birds are a riot of noise as I jog around my neighbourhood today, trying to jolt my body back into its new time frame, to stave off the jet lag that I know will soon engulf me. I have just arrived back from a visit to Australia and must get ready for visitors who are arriving tomorrow. The noise, the vibrant colours, the sunshine all help tremendously to keep me awake and stimulated. Everywhere I look there are flowers. Wisteria melts its way along wire trellis and fencing and stops me in my tracks with its perfume. White blossoms weigh down bushes and everywhere there is new foliage. It has the shininess of new born babies and it shyly pronounces itself, pokes, unfolds and sways everywhere. Shades of green, from deep sea to lime, coat the tiny streets and old stone houses. The air is warm with promise.

I run past two women speaking and I take in their conversation. The conversations are always the same and I can almost predict them by now. At mid-morning, which is when I am running, they will be about what the speaker had for breakfast and what they are planning to have for lunch.

When someone told me many years ago that Italians talk about food a lot, I thought they were exaggerating. But they were not; most conversations I overhear in my neighbourhood, at any time of day, with any amount of people, are about food. What someone ate recently, what they are about to eat, how to cook something, where to buy it from, variations on cooking it. Italians are the only race of people I know whose topic of conversation while eating a meal is commonly about what they will eat for their next meal.

Shortly after moving in to my current apartment block, as I was coming home one day, I could see a group of women sitting together at a communal doorway, gesticulating and yelling wildly at each other. I was a little concerned. This area was new to me and still carried the slight stigma of once being one of Rome's poorest and most crime-ridden areas. I was slightly worried that such an argument might escalate and lead to blows, given that the content was obviously serious and passionate. As I walked timidly past with my head down, I overheard one of the women say, 'Well the way I make a *mozzarella in carozza* (mozzarella cheese deep fried in bread) is very different from that. I would first start with frying the bread in extra virgin olive oil from the Sabine region, not from the Piedmontese region.'

Food discussions in Italy are across genders and inter-generational; there is no limit to participation based on sex or age. The best bonding experiences I have with new Italian work colleagues or clients occur when food is discussed. All barriers go down, everyone is equal, and social hierarchies coalesce and form before my eyes. I often find it easier to get people to accept my advice after I have discussed food with them. I once worked with a team of people who started off every morning discussing what they had eaten or cooked the evening before, in detail and with recipes. Not only did I get paid for that time, but I came away with a vast array of culinary skills and knowledge.

So as I run by I hear the women discussing what they will prepare for lunch and how it will fit in with what they will have for dinner, and how it will contrast with what they had for breakfast. I am reminded also of the reason why I think I am in Italy: to learn to live like that. To learn to live one day at a time, with nothing more on my plate – figuratively – than I can handle in one day, and reasonably spaced around three fantastic yet simple meals. I still struggle with it and at this rate will be here for the rest of my life learning how to do it. Not a bad life task.

* * *

I make it to the end of the day without succumbing to jet lag by bribing myself with the promise that if I make it to 8pm I will take myself to my favourite restaurant for a bowl of the world's best *rigatoni amatriciana*, a type of pasta with tomato and bacon sauce. After having sampled far and wide, and seventeen years' worth of Italy's *amatriciana* recipes, this one is by far the best. In fact, everything that this woman cooks is unsurpassed. This is attested to by the fact that everyone I have ever taken there is now as addicted as I am. And the best part about this restaurant is that it is across the road from where I live.

Being such an amazing restaurant you may assume that it would be hard to get a table on such short notice. It probably would be if it was easy to see, find or even identify as a restaurant. It is located at the bottom of an apartment block, the kind that is everywhere in Rome. This particular apartment block, however, was built as part of an architectural competition and is well-known in the area – it was built and is used as public housing. It has the usual washing hanging from many of the windows and the occasional yelling match being conducted in or around it. Yet down a circular drive, off the street, almost into the bowels of the building, there is a small, average-looking door that you may not immediately recognise as a restaurant.

You will only find it if you stop while walking past one day and notice there is a small sign on the fence of the public building that says *Er Timoniere* (Roman dialect for 'the boat driver') and then you ask your husband what it means, and your husband tells you, and then you wonder why there is a sign saying 'the boat driver' on the outside of a building. Unless you walk towards a door at the bottom of the building that is lit up, even though your husband is dragging you back, saying, 'Don't go down there, it's probably someone's house', then you would probably never find it.

This has been confirmed by the fact that several neighbours who have lived across the road from it most of their lives have never heard of it, and that most Saturday nights, if out walking, my husband and I get asked for directions from people who are standing in front of it.

So we book a table and head to *Er Timoniere* as my reward for fighting off jet lag. Inside, it first strikes you as a dining room in a private house. If you arrive at 8pm, which we mostly do even though it is considered incredibly early by Italian eating standards, the cook's husband and co-owner is usually still eating his meal in front of the television, on a sofa chair with a tray in front of him. We are generally the first there if we book for 8pm, and we spend time exchanging a few friendly words to our hosts, who know us well by now. The restaurant is partly underground so there is not much natural light, the décor stems from around the 1960s and there are no matching plates or cutlery. It is brightly-lit and small. There is an original restaurant beer fridge from the sixties along one wall, ancient prints and photos on another wall, a display of fruit and vegetables in front of a large mirror and a kitchen the size of a small fishing vessel.

The co-owner/cook, and her family who wait on you, prepare every meal individually, which means the food doesn't come out at the same time. The wine, water and delicious bread tide you over though. The restaurant fills up quickly and stays full until midnight, with patrons that range in age from eighteen to seventy. Loud conversations and big groups are the norm here and they are all welcomed and treated as though they are family.

I order my *rigatoni amatriciana* and the waiter jokes with me, 'Just for a change huh?' When it arrives, before my husband's dish, I enfold the bowl in my arms, croon to it and sniff its wafting odours, anticipating the goodness it will instil in me once I can no longer see it. It is my 'welcome back to Italy' present, my jetlag/hangover cure-all, my tonic for the heartaches of modern living. I have tried to analyse it, to take it apart bit by bit and study the ingredients, to isolate perhaps a key one, to logically be able to answer why it has these effects on me.

Is it the warm, tangy olive oil? Is it the bite-size, chewy chunks of cured pork from Tuscany? Is it the liberally sprinkled, aged sheep's cheese, or the home-dried chillies that I can faintly taste? I don't know which it is, but all together they sate my soul and remind my body that the earth is full of good things. Whenever my mother-in-law cooks for me it has the same effect. I think that these women cook with love, that you can taste it in the food and is the reason why you feel so exceptionally good when you eat it.

Rigatoni are short cylinders of pasta. They are cooked *al dente*, meaning that they are quite chewy and not at all soft. They are ribbed and hollow, perfect for the tomato-based *amatriciana* sauce to cling to. The tang of the tomato in the sauce is so deep that it almost tastes of the earth. Its concentrated flavours go right to the bottom of my stomach and start warming me from my feet up. My ills and worries start to float away and I emit little groans between each mouthful, to my husband's curious delight. My worries now are new. Do I eat one *rigatoni* at a time to make it last longer or do I put two on my fork and have a double delight each time? How can I scoop up enough oil and at least one piece of deliciously salty smoked *guanciale* (pig's cheek) with each forkful? How can I stop my husband from nabbing any, poised with his fork, watching me from across the table?

A typical Italian meal includes a course known as an *antipasto*, a pasta dish (*il primo*), some meat, fish or cheese (*il secondo*) and vegetables (*la vedura*), and some dessert (*dolce*) and possibly some fruit or cheese (*frutta o formaggio*). In my youth, when I first came to Italy, I could do it all, all five courses. I was a lot lighter and generally a lot hungrier, having often to ration my food intake due to finances.

* * *

The second dish of my welcome back to Italy meal is only a vegetable dish, as it is all I can fit in. Luckily, here in Italy vegetables are never disappointing or boring. I order *cicoria* which has no equivalent in English and which I have never seen in Australia. It is a dark green, bitter, leafy vegetable which one elderly Italian gentleman once described as 'medicinal'. The cook here prepares the *cicoria* 'ripassata', which means that after boiling it, it is re-cooked in a saucepan of hot olive oil, shot through with garlic and chillies. It comes to the table soft, salty, caressed by oil and with the flavours of garlic and bitter greens being borne upon a faint sting of chilli. This time bread must be used as well. It may seem strange to order nothing but a plate with one type of vegetable on it, but eating this *cicoria* feels as decadent as a freshly baked chocolate lava cake.

There is no room or time for dessert. I have reached the limit of my boundaries. I stumble back across the road, almost blind from jet lag, but with the rest of my body zinging from the absorbed love of the meal. The indigo spring air greets me and I raise my head to take in the twilight scent of jasmine. The first long, flat surface to lay down on I have seen in two days awaits me, and I am guided into sleep by *Er Timoniere*, the boat driver.

Chapter 2

Cara Garbatella, darling Garbatella

You know you've been in a city a long time when you can tell, just by the way the wind blows, that rain is coming. I realise I have been here a long time when this happens to me one day.

Romans often ask me how I came to live in Rome. I am always slightly apprehensive about the answer because it doesn't include having a job to come to, Italian heritage, a man or being shipwrecked. In short, none of the rational or more commonplace reasons for ex-patriots choosing to live here. The reason I came to live in Rome is that, during a visit, I fell in love with it. It was actually love at first sight. I had no warning or prior inkling, and within three days of arrival I was making plans to enable my love and I to remain together, for at least another month. I was prepared to do anything to remain, to experience even just a few more glorious days together. That was seventeen years ago.

I never need to be apprehensive, however, when I answer the question about how I came to live in Rome. Generally, Romans just nod their heads understandingly. I live in a community of people who are passionately in love with their city and proud of it. It is a community that thinks it completely natural for someone from the other side of the world to fall in love with it too. I know it does not have the same effect on everyone, though. I put the world into two categories: those who fall in love with Rome within three days and those who do not. I cannot relate to the second category and prefer not to know those people.

Like many backpackers I had met en route to Rome during my five months of travelling around the Mediterranean, I had become feverish and desperate. I had spontaneously and ridiculously found love, my other half, my soulmate, and a million miles away from my proscribed home. Of course, most of the feverish and desperate backpackers I had met in similar circumstances were having this reaction to a person. But being quite determined that my life would be spent single, and knowing that I enjoyed my own company immensely, I was quite content for my passion to be spent on a city. Many years after this decision had been made Carrie Bradshaw, the lead character in the television series *Sex and The City*, echoed my sentiments exactly when she continually rhapsodised about New York and it being her love. I understood completely how you could go out and have a date with a city.

Like any infatuated lover I never, ever tire of my beloved. I never tire of looking at her buildings and monuments, her galleries and museums, her ruins and her shops, her windy streets and long placid boulevards. At first I told myself that once I stopped gaping in awe at the Coliseum every time I saw it then I would go home. It has now been seventeen years and I am still gaping.

The difficulty with determining when enough is enough is that the longer you are in Rome, the more it reveals itself to you. Like a lover that does not want you to leave, it throws ever more tempting situations at you. It shows you deeper and deeper layers of itself, layers that are not noticeable as a tourist. It reveals itself in ways you can only begin to experience once you stop moving. Rome can thrill and impress anyone at a glance, the way Sydney Harbour can. Who isn't impressed by either place at first glimpse? But once you have shown your commitment, once you have demonstrated you are willing to dedicate time to her, there is layer upon layer of further magic, mystery and take-your-breath-away beauty, for as long and as often as you care to look for it.

* * *

I have been dating my love for many years now and we are definitely 'going steady'. Which is how I can tell it is about to rain. I know her many moods and temperaments because, like any good girlfriend, I have spent many hours observing her.

I am sitting at this moment in a tiny cobblestone piazza about the size of a handkerchief, just down the road from my house in a Roman suburb, well away from the tourist haunts. I am shaded, believe it or not, by gum trees – good for soil drainage, or so I am told – on a park bench made from strong old wood and wrought iron. I am gazing at a small fountain. A woman's head sculptured in stone juts out from a pillar. From her mouth a continuous stream of water flows, via ancient Roman aqueducts, into a tiny stone pool below. It is cold, clear and drinkable. There is a steady flow of humans and birds that come to bathe and drink from it, some carrying it away in their water bottles (only the humans do this).

The pillar is topped with a sculpture of a gigantic stone egg, the symbol of this neighbourhood, and repeated throughout it at various entrances to piazzas, buildings and staircases. The pillar also forms the beginning of one side of a very wide and long staircase leading up to another piazza at the top of a hill. The steps are shaded by overhung trees and at the moment a couple is having lunch on them, in between long bouts of kissing. At the piazza on the top of the hill there are four stone archways on either side of the square. They open up onto a series of gardens, walkways and semidetached houses which spill all the way back down the hill until the lowest of them ring the piazza in which I am sitting.

I love this spot and come here regularly. It is five minutes by foot from my apartment. It is quiet, peaceful and full of birdsong. It is a forty-minute walk south of the Coliseum. This suburb dates back to early last century and was purpose-built by the Italian government as a social and architectural experiment in community development. It took the form of a small, self-sufficient town, sitting well outside the walls of Rome at that time, in the midst of muddy fields. The Italian authorities then transferred the poorest of inner-city families, some against their will, to live in these quasi-rural idylls. The idea was that these families would then have lifelong public housing at reasonable rates and not be at the mercy of landlords, unsafe housing or homelessness.

The fact that it was far away from their previous neighbourhoods and communities was hoped to be offset by the provision of semidetached, single-storey houses, set in communal gardens and surrounded by space. It was not something the average Roman, or in fact any European city-dweller, could usually hope to live in. High-rise apartment blocks with front doors that opened directly onto the street and hanging washing out the windows or across balconies were the average city-dweller's prospects. Gardens and green space was for royalty.

This suburb was therefore considered the height of excellent social planning at the time, and in fact still is, in providing housing for the poor. Even Mahatma Ghandi toured the fledgling suburb during his trip to Europe in the 1920s to learn how other cities dealt with housing their poorest families. The rents were, and still are, peppercorn. The town came complete with schools, theatres, churches, communal baths, parks, shops and restaurants. Many well-known architects of the time lent their services and entered into the architectural competitions that produced designs for the buildings. As a result, many of these buildings are icons today. There is an emphasis in the architecture on open, round piazzas and communal spaces, all of which are still in use today. Arches and rounded buildings are also a common feature and were designed to produce an atmosphere of openness and community between the new inhabitants.

One hundred years later and the suburb is a small island surrounded by kilometres of apartment buildings, as the rest of Rome has engulfed it. Rome still consists mostly of apartment blocks without gardens, and although there are now sidewalks between most front doors and the street, there are no nature strips and trees are rare. These one- and two-storey houses set in their own gardens, therefore, create a rare setting. They provide a quiet refuge and the feeling of being in a small country village rather than in the centre of Rome which, because Rome has grown so much, it now is. The gates are always open and anyone from the public can walk into the gardens and communal spaces. I admit it is only because I am a resident that I dare to.

It is a close-knit community. Many generations of the same families live here and Roman dialect is spoken rather than Italian. The Roman football team is so revered here that people often paint their houses in the colours of the team, which are bright red and yellow just in case you were thinking they were taupe and sand. One house has a mural covering the entire front wall that shows all the faces of the team members and their coach. It is a bastion of traditional, fiercely proud Romans. There is a strong sense of identity among the families from this area and it is easier to feel like an outsider here than in other parts of Rome. The architecture that was designed to create an openness among the residents worked, and resulted in a fiercely proud and strong community.

The communal garden areas are immaculately kept, not by the authorities but by the residents, even though this is still all government, or public, housing. Bowers of roses frame makeshift wooden seats and arches, planters hang off the back of park benches, low planters bloom with flowers and herb gardens, and fruit trees nestle between stretches of lawn and pathways.

Traditional Roman cooking and small *trattorie* (informal, often family-run restaurants) abound in this neighbourhood. It has become famous for it. They are hidden in basements, under stairs, behind shutters and in archways. They often do not have menus, signs or vacancies, unless you book or they know you. They are often bare in décor, use plastic sheets instead of tablecloths, have harsh lighting and televisions blaring loudly. They produce food that is cooked daily by the *signora* of the team, which is usually a family, from ingredients procured that morning, so there is not much possibility of a pre-prepared or pre-cooked menu. They are, in my humble opinion, as yet unrivalled by any meal produced within *cooee* (Australian term, meaning 'shouting distance') of an historic monument or in the centre of Rome.

* * *

It is now just after 1pm and a peaceful silence has descended over the neighbourhood. If you want to go for a quiet walk in a park, pick your nose in public, somersault naked in the street (just in case you lost a bet), go to the post office or a supermarket while visiting Rome, do it at 1pm during the sacred Roman lunch hour (or two). The streets are deserted. The more deserted they are, the better you know the restaurants are in that area.

In my neighbourhood, from about 11am onwards, delicious smells start to waft out of windows and onto the streets. Although I generally make it a habit to go out and walk during the quietened Roman lunch hour, I can usually only make it until about 2pm before I have to rush home and make myself some pasta. I march myself quickly past the aforementioned *trattorie*, as I know there will not be a vacancy at this hour and if there was I would not leave them without having had three courses of delicious traditional Roman home cooking. After being a resident in this suburb for twelve years I have no more leeway when it comes to my waistline and I have to keep myself in shape for my love.

And so today I saunter home. But where is this idyllic spot? I'm not going to tell you. I don't want anyone coming here, unless they are invited by me and then the second rule of Fight Club applies. Suffice to say that if you stop and pay attention the city will – slowly – reveal its more subtle delights. But only if you show it true homage, only if you woo it properly, demonstrating your commitment and dedication, just like in any relationship.

I should explain at this point that rather than being in a monogamous relationship as I was when I first lived in Rome, I have now been in a committed threesome for about ten years. My husband, who had separately fallen in love with Rome and who was also dating her, seemed like a perfect candidate when our first few hundred dates consisted of just walking around the city together.

Chapter 3

Francesca and Rita

Francesca and Rita are our neighbours. Were our neighbours. Today is a sad day, as it is the first day without them. They moved out yesterday, after renting here for fifty years. It is the end of an era and everyone in the whole apartment block is sad.

Francesca moved here with her parents when she was nine. Her playmates are still mostly living here too. Their parents all knew each other, and she and her playmates stayed here even after they were married, with their husbands and wives. They had their own children, who are now also friends.

Antonio and Gianni played together as small boys. Antonio still lives in the same apartment underneath us and has lived to see Gianni marry Antonella, who became Francesca's best friend. Marianna's mother and Francesca's mother were best friends when Marianna and Francesca were children. Marianna helped Francesca nurse her dying husband, who introduced Marianna to hers.

We live in a tightly knit neighbourhood. It is unwise to get annoyed at anyone, as they are usually related to someone you know quite well or depend on: the pharmacist, the mechanic, the owner of the local *trattoria* (Antonio's brother owns ours). Many people live within walking distance of where they grew up and where their extended family lives. The inhabitants of this suburb are polite to, though a little wary of, outsiders. They are fiercely proud and protective of their suburb, and find it a little unusual that anyone would voluntarily come to live here.

For generations the traffic has been going the other way.

It probably explains why I get stared at a lot. If I lived in one of the suburbs that are popular with foreigners I wouldn't get a sideways glance, but here people have the look of 'but *why* would you choose to live here, with us?!' It explains partly why, when your neighbours do get to know you, they embrace you with the fierceness of a mother about to be separated from her firstborn. In fact, you can't get away from them ever again.

We have a well-kept, shady garden area as part of the apartment complex we live in. Our apartment complex is not public housing but was built for employees of the post office just up the road. Marianna is one of the only post office employees that still lives here. The communal area consists of a rather large space surrounded by trees and grass, shaped by hedges and containing three separate sitting areas, complete with benches. It is astounding to have this kind of facility in Rome. Most apartment blocks are built one right up against the other, with barely a wall between them. The last one I lived in I didn't need an alarm clock – the man on the other side of the wall had one and it always went off at the time I needed to get up.

I was overjoyed when I first saw the garden. I imagined myself sitting there at any time of the day, relaxing in my own bit of green space. But the reality is I go there stealthily. First I scout from my balcony to see if anyone is sitting in it, then I run there as quickly as possible to avoid being spotted by anyone else. I sit in the part farthest away from the buildings and bury my head in a book, scowl or close my eyes and chant if anyone comes close.

This amount of preparation and strategic planning is necessary. I discovered early on that sitting there by myself was a beacon for anyone else in the apartment block to come down and join me. Apparently, what I am communicating by sitting by myself in the garden is, 'Help! I am lonely and would like some company, please come and talk to me.'

Francesca often watched me when I was in the garden, waving and smoking from her balcony. She folds boxes for a living and is also a *sarta* (dressmaker). The boxes are the staple part of her income in a country where there are no unemployment benefits or pensions for widows. Her husband knew the man she folds boxes for. Out of charity, the work was passed on to her after her husband's death. She is a woman who always manages to look elegant, from her fingernails to her hair. She has a rasping cough, never walks anywhere and has laughter always on her lips. She is a chain-smoker, so there is always a cigarette on her lips as well. The entire house smells of smoke. She is always at home, as is her twenty-five year old daughter, Rita. Rita is tiny, like most Italian women at that age, and could pass for fifteen. She is beautiful and has the dark features of her Arabic father.

As I often worked from home, Francesca was always coaxing me over for a coffee or a chat. It was a welcome relief for me, from a day spent concentrating in front of a computer. Nothing much happened in their lives from one day to the next, or in mine, so our conversations went like this:

Francesca: Well then, what have you got to tell me?

Me: Well, nothing much.

Francesca: Is everything okay?

Me: Yes. Is everything okay with you?

Francesca: Yes. Well that's good then. It is better that way. What more can one ask for?

Smoke, smoke, sip, sip.

Francesca: Yesterday I ate [name of dish] for dinner.

Me: Did you? I had [name of dish].

Francesca: Yes, I cooked it in [method of cooking] way.

Me: Well I always cook it in [method of cooking] way. How was it done in [your method of cooking] way?

Francesca: Well, you know, okay I suppose. It was missing [ingredient]. Next time I will put in more [ingredient].

Me: Ah yes, [ingredient] is often missing. Apart from that is everything okay?

Francesca: Yes. With you?

Me: Yes.

Francesca: Well we can't ask for more then, can we?

Smoke, smoke.

Francesca: More coffee?

What first attracted me to Francesca was that she would often ring my doorbell wearing only her pyjamas. At midday. I would usually still be wearing mine, and the relief to find someone else that not only thought that was okay, but that it was okay to go calling in them, was enormous. Sometimes Rita would poke her head out of their door and she would be wearing only her pyjamas too. Sometimes we would spend quite a bit of time chatting together from our doorways, drinking coffee, in our pyjamas. Francesca would always invite me in, but I refused to cross the threshold of my house wearing only my pyjamas. I find it hard enough to get dressed some days as it is. This never stopped Francesca though, or Rita, who would regularly come visiting in their pyjamas, dressing gown and slippers. It was a private, female world we had on the top floor of our apartment block, where we knew no-one would ever appear unless we knew about it first.

I first met Francesca and Rita a few months after my husband and I had moved in, during a violent rainstorm. Water had come streaming down the stairs from the roof and was forming a small lake in the entrance hall of our apartment. Both my husband and I stood helplessly in the corridor outside our apartment, watching the flow and not knowing what to do. Next thing I knew, two women had run out of their apartment and were in mine, mopping the floor and laying towels on the stairs while shouting for the man downstairs to come and unblock the drains on the roof. They mopped and sopped and then went back into their apartment, leaving my husband and I staring at each other and wondering what we would have done without them. We had met them once before.

* * *

Yesterday, we helped Francesca and Rita pack and said goodbye to them as they drove their car out of the compound one last time. We were all crying, and smoking. Many of the residents had come out to say goodbye, and for each hug there would be fresh tears and a fresh cigarette. Francesca did not want to go. The landlord wanted to sell the property and had offered her a substantial amount of money to move, two years before her lease was up. It was more than she could hope to earn in a year. She was entitled to stay in the apartment, even if it sold, for another two years but then she could be given notice without any compensation. So Francesca had chosen a new rental place in a seaside town about an hour south of Rome. She would be close to her brother, who also lived there. She could not afford to rent in Rome any longer. With the compensation she could afford to furnish the new rental place, and the furniture would be hers and not the landlord's.

Although I often declined Francesca's daily invitations over the years, it was comforting to know she was there. If I ever wanted company, a cigarette, an egg or to know that someone would hear me scream, she was there. I had lived some hard and sad times in this apartment and spent a lot of time alone as a result.

I rarely spoke that much when I visited, as I usually found it a stretch speaking Italian, let alone the Roman dialect that she spoke. I rarely offered much of myself, and gained a lot from being with her. Hanging out the washing together on the roof, talking about whether it would rain or not that day, whether the supermarket was open, what kind of tomatoes were in season, what I was going to eat for dinner, gave me a well-needed sense of normality. Having a two-minute connection with someone living in the same space and time as me was grounding, and somehow kept me connected to life at a simple and basic level. I felt not alone.

I wasn't really on my own; I had my husband, I had friends. But in day-to-day living, Francesca made me feel not on my own. I understood then how all the women in the *palazzo* got on with things. Antonella, who worked two jobs and never had money for luxuries, such as annual holidays. Marianna, whose husband left her after childbirth nine months after they were married, twenty-five years ago. Rita, Francesca's daughter, who could not find work. And Francesca, whose husband died after a few short years of marriage, who eked out a living and who was never going to be able to afford her own home. They were always together, the women of this *palazzo*. Those daily visits of minutes at a time made sure none of them felt on their own.

In the weeks leading up to their departure we spent most evenings with them, eating with them, going over for a chat or just sitting together. One evening, Rita read out a letter which was addressed to my husband and I. In the letter, she told us that the thought of leaving her home where she was born and where she had nursed her father until his death, had been continually traumatic and at times paralysing over the past few months, but that throughout it all she had not felt alone because of us. She told us, through her poetic writing, that just our presence across the hallway, our hellos and other greetings, and our smiles, had helped ease the burden for her and that she was grateful.

* * *

We didn't see Marianna the day that Francesca and Rita left. We saw her the next day as we were driving our car into the compound. Her face was haggard with grief and when she saw us she lurched towards us, almost slamming herself onto the windscreen, like a leaf in a tornado. Luckily, my husband had seen her and wound down the window in anticipation, so she did not have to bang on the glass with her fist.

'They've gone, they've gone!' she bellowed. 'It is the end of an era! It is not just them, it's the end of an era. Our mothers were friends; they knew each other. Who is left to remember my mother now? We left these apartments as brides, both of us, and returned as wives. It's a piece of our history that has gone. That bastard that kicked them out, he's a criminal without a heart! It's a piece of our shared history that has gone!' I didn't get the rest as she subsided into tears, leaning on our car door.

They call Rome 'The Eternal City'. It refers to the fact that it is timeless, changeless, always there. It has indeed, in many ways, resisted much of the change that has occurred in other post-industrial, European capital cities. Maybe that's why, when it comes, it is such a shock and so hard to adjust to. It seems that when things change in The Eternal City, they do so in a big way.

Chapter 4

Il Cambiamento, **The Changeover**

I never tire of that delicious feeling I have every Saturday morning upon waking. The feeling that I could go to Piazza Navona for coffee if I wanted to, that I could sit there all day if I wished, experiencing *la dolce vita* (the good life) without having to pay for an airfare or having flown for twenty-four hours. Piazza Navona is not the latest in a chain of new coffee shops, but one of Rome's lovelier squares. It is full of flowing fountains, sculptures by Bernini, a magnificent church designed by Borromini, modern-day painters selling their wares, gorgeous Romans taking walks and, of course, fabulous coffee.

It is a lifestyle choice that I never tire of or regret. It is an option that I insist always be present. It is a deal-breaker when it comes to deciding where to live. 'Will I be able to go and have coffee in Piazza Navona whenever I want to?' is the deciding question. So Rome, as a choice of dwelling place, always wins.

The principle that 'if it is for free it is not appreciated', slavishly adhered to in my consulting business, or the truism 'if you live near it you never visit it', reigns supreme no matter where you live. Maybe that is why, despite spending just under half of my life in Melbourne, I have never been to the Melbourne Cup (an international annual horseracing derby) or to Bali (one of the most popular overseas destinations for Australians). Although I can say, probably because of my shame of never having been to the Melbourne Cup or to Bali, that I have sat in Piazza Navona and had coffee on numerous occasions, despite being a resident and not a tourist.

Unfortunately, as I actually am dwelling in Rome rather than visiting it, I rarely have time to go and sit and while away the hours in Piazza Navona on a Saturday morning. It remains a rather nice idea upon first waking but never seems to quite fit with the reality of my life because I always have things to do.

Today, like most Saturdays, I may not get the chance. We residents have things to do, things like *Il Cambiamento* (The Changeover). When I first came to Rome and heard people saying they spent their weekend doing 'The Changeover', everybody else nodding sagely and expressing understanding-type noises, I was a little daunted. It seemed to be a ritual that took all weekend and got such approval when you were the first in your group of friends to do it, and was always followed by a discussion about when the other listeners were going to do it. It did not seem like something people looked forward to.

Although I am a pretty good guesser, and in fact learnt a lot of the language that way, the words themselves gave me no clue. It was always followed by discussions about the weather, so I knew it was connected somehow. Did people change their partners or lovers with the seasons? Did they have one type of partner for the summer and one for the colder weather? It sounded like a big job. Did they change apartments or décor to suit the seasons? I am talking about a population who put on make-up to go to the gym and can change their clothes from morning to afternoon, so I thought anything was possible.

I soon discovered that *Il Cambiamento* means something quite different. It is a serious and laborious Roman ritual that takes place at the beginning of spring and autumn each year and can take up to a week. The Changeover involves taking all your winter and autumn clothes out of the wardrobe and replacing them with your summer and spring ones.

This changing over of clothes is necessary for several reasons.

Firstly, Italian apartments are not large. They do not come with built-in, wall-to-wall robes or dressing rooms, and one or two seasons at a time is definitely the maximum that can fit into an average Roman wardrobe. Storage space is usually provided but is in rooftops or cellars, or a small 'walk-in' cupboard provided for the entire family's needs.

Secondly, the temperature ranges from zero, or below zero, in the winter, to high thirties with high humidity in the summer. You can get frostbitten in January without wool from head-to-toe and pass out from heat exhaustion without appropriate coverings in July. You need cashmere to cope with the first instance and linen in the second. Of course, cashmere and linen require completely different sets of lingerie, accessories, shoes, bags, scarves and hats, which take up quite some space in the wardrobe.

Thankfully, another feature of Roman weather is that it is not changeable within seasons. It is predictable; you can tell the temperature by the month. Once the temperature soars in May it does not change for the cooler until October. Therefore, there is no possibility that any of the opposing seasons' clothes would ever be needed. When the temperature does change, however, there is often up to fifteen degrees Celsius difference from morning to evening. Sometimes this change of temperature can happen in the middle of the day. When you enter the office it is summer, then it rains and when you leave it is autumn and you barely make it back to your apartment in your sandals and linen blouse.

Il Cambiamento must be cleverly timed, or you risk having to scrabble around in boxes hidden in your roof or deep at the back of the storage cupboard before work in order to be able to leave the house. Of course, this only happens to novices who either do not know that they need to do *Il Cambiamento*, who have not done it in time, or who do not know that Rome's temperatures change by the month and who are still wearing sandals in October.

I do understand those who leave it until the last minute because *Il Cambiamento* is a laborious task. It requires unpacking boxes of summer or winter clothes and packing them away in drawers and in wardrobes. At the same time, you have to remove the previous season's clothes from the wardrobes and wash or dry-clean the clothes before packing them away. As everyone else is doing the same thing at the same time, it usually takes over a month to get your clothes back from the drycleaners. After your clothes, boots, coats, scarves and hats are cleaned, washed, ironed and stored, you can then assess your current season's collection for gaps and proceed to do *Il shop*. Okay, I just made that part up, but that is what I do.

* * *

As my husband and I cannot face the idea of doing *Il Cambiamento* first thing on a Saturday morning, especially when it is being compared with sitting in Piazza Navona all day over a coffee, we go to *la pasticceria* (the cake shop or bakery) for breakfast and to fortify ourselves for our task ahead. Rome is littered with divine pastry havens that serve excellent coffee and freshly squeezed orange juice, as well as sandwiches and freshly baked sweet and savoury treats. Most Italians go to a *bar* (café) each morning for their breakfast or at least for a coffee and have their breakfast pastry, supplied by the local *pasticceria*, there. However, the best of both worlds is to go directly to the *pasticceria* and have your coffee there.

The taking of good coffee and breakfast pastry in a leisurely fashion while sitting down is a Saturday morning treat for my husband and I. It rewards us for the work week we have completed, helps us shift down a gear, lets us catch each other up on our previous week and plan our weekend. It usually takes hours, depending on how big our week was or how much we have to do on Saturday. We often use it as a joint procrastination technique which we willingly enable each other to carry out.

We have our regular cafés, but today we decide to try a *pasticceria* near our house. The best thing about a *pasticceria* is the range of baked goods available. There are light, flaky filo pastries and dense shortcrust pastries filled with cream, jam, custard, Nutella, honey, chocolate, cherries or apple in just about every size and shape you can dream of.

'Are there any of those cream-filled pastries left?' a woman asks me, straining to see past me as I stand at the counter. She has just run in wearing the uniform of a public street cleaner.

'Oh *Dio* (Oh God), I really hope they have them left!' she says.

She is satisfied and leaves with a finger bun filled with a Piazza Navona-sized amount of cream. I order a piece of shortcrust pastry, thin and crisp, biscuit-sized, topped with sour cherries cooked in their own juices until they form a type of jam. My husband has his usual custard-filled pastry. We sip our *cappuccini* and, after a decent amount of conversation, ask each other if we happen to feel like another, knowing that both of us will always say yes. This time, we split a flaky pastry base topped with thin slices of apple and glaze. We sip our coffees slowly and put off *Il Cambiamento* for another hour. Eventually, there is no more putting it off and we head home to begin.

* * *

After labouring all weekend, on Sunday evening we admire the fruits of it in our 'changed over' warm weather wardrobes. The next time I am in company, I too will relate the fact that last weekend we spent the whole time doing *Il Cambiamento*. I too will bask in the admiring glances and understanding nods. I too will feel smug that I have finished it so early in the season and gain satisfaction from being part of an inner circle, in a tradition I once thought of as bizarre.

Chapter 5

Why I regularly need to leave Rome

I feel like getting out of Rome for the day. It is a common feeling, associated with the need to see nature and have physical space around me. This is one of the hardest things for an Aussie to get used to, living in the beautiful city of Rome – the lack of space and greenery. These are things that we see and experience every day in Australia, which Romans do not. Every part of Rome is paved, there are no nature strips, there is no housing that provides private individual gardens and there are millions of people who live within in a small area. There are more people living in my apartment block, about the diameter of two double-fronted houses in Australia, than live on the whole residential block of my former suburb in Melbourne. At least weekly I get an overwhelming urge to go somewhere where I can see the horizon, where there are few people, not much noise and a lot of trees.

Often we spend the day in a large Roman park. Most parks in Rome were once the grounds of substantial royal or aristocratic palaces and now consist of wild woods for hunting, man-made lakes or streams, manicured gardens, tree-lined avenues, pleasure parks for kids, playing fields for football, running tracks, shady grottos and grassy, statue-filled picnic areas. They are a haven for Romans, as they are right in the middle of the city and provide them with a welcome green space to walk, run, play and relax in. Although this makes them eminently qualified in the 'lots of trees' category, they sometimes fall short of the 'few people' category, particularly on weekends.

Romans also like to get out of the city on a weekly basis. Wherever you go – beach, mountains, ski slopes, parks, forests – it takes hours of sitting in traffic and is always crowded. We have worked out a crafty plan, however, after years of experience. The other thing that Romans do every Sunday is have a big lunch at 1pm. On Sundays, lunch is from 1pm until 4pm, including siesta. So we generally leave our house at 1pm, then leave the park, beach or forest at 4pm. It means we have a relatively, but not completely, people, dog and football free time.

One of our favourite parks is called the Villa Pamphili. It is the grounds of a former aristocrat's home and includes a stately mansion and art gallery, which is open to visitors. The grounds are miles wide and deep, and there is the possibility of getting lost in them. It consists of walking paths ringed with magnificent laurel trees, an entrance park that is cool and windy even on the hottest days, a formal garden filled with rockeries, fountains, marble-carved benches, a lawn, running tracks with outdoor equipment for exercising, long wild grass and pine trees.

The deeper you go into the park the less people there are, but by Australian standards it is still packed to the gills. Every ten or so metres sits a small clump of people, complete with blankets, food, footballs, bikes, books and music. Some loners are set up with beach towels, bikinis and suntan oil, and some couples are in the long grass and do not want any attention.

I am still mesmerised when I come across this – naked or semi-naked couples on a blanket hidden only by long grass or behind trees so that you don't notice they are there until you are nearly on top of them and have to quickly look away. When this happens, my husband calmly steers me in the other direction while I am left gaping and pointing and switching quickly to English so no-one understands me.

'Did … did you see that?' I always stammer, pointing.

'Yes, yes, leave them alone,' my husband always responds.

'But ... but how can they do that out in the open like that when anyone can come across them?' I say.

Then he patiently explains to me that because most people who aren't married, and some who are, still live at home and share bedrooms with siblings, couples don't have anywhere else to go.

This use of a public space for very private couplings is a timeless Italian tradition; it is respected and understood. Couples rely on people turning their heads rather than gawking, thereby ensuring their relative privacy. I am constantly amazed by it, however, and amazed at my husband, who notices these things usually before I do and whose reaction is to not look any further. My reaction is to clarify, by repeated attempts at sighting, what I think I have just seen.

Cars are the most popular alternative venue for couples, and old-fashioned 'parking' occurs most Saturday nights and all day Sunday. It is common to see cars with newspaper covering up the windows on the inside, thereby assuring a modicum of privacy, while at the same time announcing to all what is happening on the inside. One Sunday, as we were driving past a small field in the countryside, we saw a mini cooper parked in the middle of it. It was completely covered by a floral bedspread, flung over it from the outside.

My husband's favourite pastime as an adolescent was to go to the local parking lot by the sea on a Saturday night, when cars were parked bumper-to-bumper in the dark. He and his cousin would creep alongside one, then jump up and shine a torch through the window and run away, usually to the sounds of threats and screaming. It was not long, however, before he was joining the rows of cars 'parking'. He told me that sometimes he would have to circle for ages to find a space.

* * *

This Sunday, instead of going to our local park, we feel the need for more than just the usual respite from the city. We feel the need to actually leave the city. We do not want to drive very far, firstly because that would necessitate getting up earlier, and secondly because we do not want to sit in traffic jams for hours, thereby negating the benefits of the relaxation gained from leaving the city. So we head for a place called Veio, which does not exist any longer. I am intrigued by the fact that I can choose to go and visit a place that is not there anymore.

Although indicated on our map of Rome, the actual city and the culture it once represented has long since gone. Veio was an Etruscan city, founded by an ancient civilisation that inhabited much of the local area for centuries before Romulus and Remus arrived. Veio was once a thriving town and farming community, complete with complex irrigation systems and a cemetery, the only things which are now left standing for the twenty-first century eye.

The expansion of Rome from the seven hills surrounding the River Tiber in the middle of the third century BC, to all of the then-known and 'civilised' world by 1400, began with the Romans first annihilating Veio. It was the first town in their path to world domination. Countries such as China and Australia were not considered part of the 'civilised' world back then. This is in spite of the fact that at the height of Rome's world domination, China had been making paper and printing on it for decades while the Romans were not even up to using it to wipe their behinds.

Nowadays, Veio is just outside a bustling modern suburb of outer Rome. It is indicated on the map as being a little way past the Grande Raccordo, the ring-road that circles modern-day Rome. It is also quite close to a surviving medieval hilltop town. I find it quite symbolic that modern-day Rome has just extended out and engulfed the area the city once lay in, as it did in 396 BC.

We drive through this outer Roman suburb, about an hour from the centre of Rome, and just at the end of it we see the sign to the extinct Etruscan city. We follow the small road down into a ravine and arrive at the National Park that now protects a great tract of land, cleared fields, ravines and an ancient waterway that is the remains of Veio. We make our way by foot to a huge open space full of calf-high green grass, a few trees sticking out against a sky swirling with puffy silver-grey clouds. It has recently been raining and the ground is soaking. The space is endless, the green is striking and I can finally see the horizon. There are no people within sight, no noise except the wind, and there is nothing left of Veio except this huge expanse of preserved hills and green pastures.

We take the path to the Necropolis, the ancient cemetery, to see the tombs of Veio. Our walk takes us past high trees and through bramble-coated paths. There is blossom everywhere, its delicate white petals holding the last drops of the shower. All is silent, quiet and green. The paths are muddy and the air is still and heavy with nature. There are no other humans near me except my husband and the remains of Veio's dead.

It fills me with peace. It restores in me faith that nature is always here – growing, renewing, alive – in spite of what we do to stop it. The petty thoughts and fears of the work week fade away and in their place there is awe at the strength of the energy of nature that keeps everything growing.

We walk in silence and admire the tombs of a civilisation that existed over two-and-a-half thousand years ago. We come again to the wide expanse of nothing where the city once stood, and see in the distance the medieval town and the modern buildings that surround it. I think of the people, the children, the lives that were once lived in this spot and wonder if they could have imagined me. I wonder if, in two-

and-a-half thousand years, another woman will walk on the spots that I once lived and think about me.

We walk back to the car, past the ruins of the Etruscan temple to Apollo and the ruins of a medieval grain processing plant, a mill. The waterways crafted to support the grinding of the wheat thousands of years ago still flow unabated over huge stone mills and into the ravine below. All is green, even the tree trunks, an eerie, glowing, mouldy green.

I have seen the horizon from an extinct civilisation's dwelling spot. I have felt space around me. I have been immersed in the deep, energising green of nature and I am ready to live for another week within the complex, competitive, concrete monolith that is Rome.

Chapter 6

A day off in Rome

My heart is singing upon waking because of the knowledge that I am giving myself the day off to see the Renoir exhibition. It is that delicious feeling I used to get on Royal Melbourne Show day as a kid when I knew that even though it was a weekday I was going to use it to do a 'weekend' activity.

This particular day off is not an Italian public holiday, but a much needed day out to restore my mental health after too much study and work. In my view, there is nothing as frivolous or indulgent as going to see an exhibition of paintings. It won't restore world peace, provide food for the hungry or help others, all of which I see as undoubtedly my responsibility. On a more practical note, how does it pay the rent, get my assignment finished, increase my marketability as a consultant? The point is that it doesn't and I badly needed a day off from all of that.

Once outside, the day begins incredibly well with a lovely *cappuccino* at my local *bar*. It is such a nice day and I ponder whether I don't just want to sit in the park on my day off and enjoy the sunshine rather than be inside. I comfort myself with the thought that I will have my *cappuccino* outside and read my book to get some sunshine. But for the first time in the two years since I have been going to my local *bar*, the *barista* is in a good mood and actually says hello to me, and then begins chatting to me. I desperately want to go outside and sip my *cappuccino* but do not want to miss the opportunity to befriend the *barista*, which is absolutely vital to your wellbeing here in Italy.

Any minute now I expect her to regroup and become her usual surly self, but she is talkative and smiley, and I keep the conversation going like a new juggler, amazed at how far it has gone and desperate to try to keep it going. We talk about Australia and how much she would love to go. I go through the paces. It seems everyone wants to live in Australia except me, and I have to answer the usual reasons about why I am not living there when everyone else wants to. If I had a euro for every Italian who said 'it is my dream to go to Australia' I would be rich.

I try to do it without sounding like a bad stereotype – I married an Italian man, I work for the United Nations and I am here for my job – or a bad advertisement for Australia, but some days I dismally fail and just draw blank looks. These are the same blank looks I draw from Australians when I tell them why I love living in Rome so much. I am overwhelmed by the fact the *barista* and I have chatted, however, which bodes well for my future wellbeing.

It is difficult when the absolute best coffee in your neighbourhood is served by someone who mostly tries to ignore you when you order, and then acts like you are a great inconvenience to her life when you do. Every now and then my husband and I get fed up. We have a few backup places when our weeks have been particularly bad and can't handle feeling any more inadequate than we already do. However, we always come back here; the coffee is just too good.

'Why is their coffee so damn good?' I once asked my husband.

'It's because they take their time to make it,' he said.

That certainly explains the long waits, the hundreds of people jostling and the mood of the *barista* as she tries to deal with many orders at the same time. It's a catch-22 situation, though. They take their time, so their coffee is good, so they attract more customers, which annoys them, which makes them slow down, which makes their coffee good. Someone should tell them.

* * *

Even the bus is on time today, and I bounce and jostle my way to the doorstep of the museum. I am not sure if it will be open, as Italian museums and exhibitions can be closed for no reason on any particular given day. Websites are few and far between, and even then are not always connected to the reality on the ground. 'Oh, we forgot to update it' or 'I don't know, I only work here, I don't take care of what the internet says' are two responses I have had when politely asking why something is not as advertised. Therefore, it is always best not to have too firm a plan when having a day off in Rome and to have at least two or three other alternatives.

Most Italians are adept at this; I as an Anglo-Saxon still rely a little too much on planning for living in The Eternal City. My husband never says, 'We are going to do X on Saturday,' even though we are, according to me. I know it is because he has been trained to think it's bad luck to pre-empt things and that you can never really rely on your planning to be the whole answer. It is also the reason that baby showers are not had in Italy. It is considered bad luck to celebrate before the baby is actually born; the cot and baby clothes are hidden until the moment there is a baby to put in them.

I walk up the magnificent stairs of the Campidoglio to the official Town Square of Rome, avoiding the many excited Spanish teenagers who are there for the day to visit the Capitoline Museums. I wander lazily through the square, imagining how amazed those visitors will be at Rome's magnificent squares, statutes and history, just as I still am after so many years of living here.

I am not sure exactly how to get to the entrance of the Vittoriano Museum that houses the Renoir exhibition, but I spy a delicious and fresh-looking garden that gives a magnificent view over the Forum, the

Coliseum and from which I judge I will be able to see the entrance. The view over the Forum is spectacular and the garden is quiet, sun-filled and has seating, a rare treat in Rome. I walk over to the edge and on my way spy a backpacker who has taken an interest in me.

From my solo backpacking days, I can spot a man longing for company from a hundred paces. Solo backpacking is lonely – great but lonely – especially in big cities, where most other backpackers are just moving through and you don't get the groups that stay for weeks who get to know each other. It's also lonely seeing some of the world's greatest monuments on your own and having no-one to go 'wow' with.

This is probably why sex and backpacking go hand-in-hand. Firstly, because you're often frightened, sometimes a lot, and sex is a life-affirming activity that calms you and convinces you that you are closer to life than death. And secondly, the feeling of danger and of being alone and in a strange place increases your sex drive. Backpacking is also incredibly romantic. Meeting attractive strangers in beautiful cities, neither of you knowing anyone else, both of you only passing through, both of you with travel stories to tell, you therefore share more in common than with any other person on the planet in that moment. So I feel the interest as the backpacker comes to rest by me on the ledge, gazing out over Rome.

Since my backpacking days are long over and I have a wedding ring on my finger, I march smartly off, run down the stairs and into the museum. I feel his eyes on my back the whole way and I am surprised and flattered that I can still get this attention, even though it has been many years since I hung my backpack up.

I am so delighted that the museum is open, that the exhibition is actually on, that I can leave my bag in the cloakroom, that I can indulge in as many hours of frivolous and indulgent painting ogling as I like.

Italians know how to do galleries and museums. The setting is always magnificent – large marble staircases, huge stone columns and beautiful sculptures at every turn, and just for decoration. The building is very classical and has been modernised for the exhibition. The two-storey high columns are encased in wood and glass, the walls repaneled with light yellow wood to make false walls and barricades of glass, transforming the room into something that will better frame the exhibition.

First off, there is a film about the life of Renoir that runs continuously in a small dark theatre at the beginning of the exhibition. I feel my whole body relaxing as I experience the effects of doing something for no purpose at all except to enjoy it. What a fitting subject: a painter who had almost no public recognition in his lifetime, painted things no-one wanted, but painted solely for his own pleasure. I feel a freedom in hearing about this life which so contradicts my regimented, over-achiever, goal-oriented one, and I suddenly know why it is so important that I am here today. This is my homeopathic remedy: take one day's dose of your worst nightmare, living without a specific purpose, and just please yourself. This should help me mange the symptoms of my disease better.

I know from experience that painting ogling is a limited activity for me and that I can only spend about two hours on my feet before they start to ache so much that I don't care if I am looking at the Venus de Milo, I want to sit down. I also know that I have loads of energy at the beginning and spend an inordinate amount of time on introductions and 'first attempts' but can suffer from the Venus de Milo syndrome by the time I get to the main event, so I usually try and start where the important stuff is.

So I quickly take in two floors, then go to the nearest security guard to ask if these are all the rooms the exhibition is in, or whether there is another room with all his most famous pieces at the end. He is about sixty-five and a snappy dresser, as many older Italians are. He tells me that these two rooms are the sum of it and then goes on to try and make conversation as I am turning away. I am puzzled; most officials act as though you are disturbing them while giving birth if you ask for information. I am not used to one wanting to engage me in conversation.

I begin my tour and am absolutely entranced. I cannot get enough of the paintings. I stare at each one a long time, first up close as I admire the brushwork, then from a distance to marvel at how magnificent the image is. I also marvel at the type of images. They are mostly nudes and hugely fat, according to my standards, the category of which I fall into myself. I am so happy to see women who look like me, who have out-of-proportion bottoms, hips and thighs that are displayed so proudly, and painted so lovingly and tenderly. It makes me feel better being surrounded by these images rather than with the daily barrage of images of women who have slender hips and no-carb thighs. Life for me would just be better in general if we could have less of those images and more of Renoir's.

I feel a presence. It is the security guard looking at me; not just looking but watching. From years of experience of being ogled at, mostly because I look different and am doing odd things like walking along on my own rather than because I am anything special to look at, I can immediately feel it. Also, women-watching seems to be the hobby of the Italian male. I used to comfort myself with the fact that one day it would all be over, that I would get old and not be worth looking at, and I could go back to enjoying walks by myself. However, it has never stopped; the men just get older.

I know the dance well. He remains just out of my direct eyesight; it would be unsophisticated to be directly in front of me. By being in my peripheral vision, when I change position he will be there, smiling and making 'accidental' eye contact, which means I will have to acknowledge him and which will give him an opening to start a conversation. He is patient, as I studiously avoid making eye contact with him about forty times while I work my way around the room. Sometimes he comes quite close, as though studying another painting himself, but although he is good, I am better. After years of studying the art of avoidance, I manage to blithely pretend that I miss him in my peripheral vision, over and over again.

This is important, as to openly ignore him would be rude and provoke a negative reaction. However, to confront him and ask him to stop would result in him innocently protesting he was doing nothing, though in fact he was, and could possibly result in making a scene with me at the centre of it. Although he has annoyed me by being so assiduous in his attentions that my attentions have been focused on him rather than the paintings, I know that he can only persist for so long, and I am used to winning. It is a competition of Masters.

Again, my backpacking experience comes to the fore. Years of travelling the world alone and seeing places for maybe the only time, yearning to take them in and fully experience them, memorise them and capture my own unique experience of them rather than be chatted up, sold something or given a tour I did not want, has enabled me to zone out distractions. Backpacking in a couple or with guys in your group halves these distractions. Backpacking in a group of girls, we would always designate a 'deal with the distractions' woman for the day, place or monument. That way, the rest of us could view it in peace. We would then change designated dealers and go through the place again. Travelling solo puts a whole load of responsibility on the individual. While for you the event is a once-in-a-lifetime opportunity to experience something, for them you are a desperately needed distraction or dollar.

After the guard has given up, I do the room again, this time focusing more on the paintings. I am aware that he has spoken with all the other guards in the room and now they too are watching me, but it is from a distance and I can easily zone out their presence. It is the same in any arena of Italian life, but I must admit I have not experienced it quite so intensely in a museum before. I am mostly protected these days by my husband, who makes a habit of scowling at any male in our neighbourhood, which means that when I go out by myself they never dare look at me twice.

As I finally turn to leave the exhibition I stop and ask another museum attendant, one of the ones who has been keeping an eye on me for his friend, for directions to make sure I am heading out of the building. He answers me in newly-learnt English and in a last-ditch effort, on behalf of the museum guards that have been watching me all afternoon, says, 'Yes it is that way, and you are a very nice and beautiful girl!'

'Thank you,' I reply and scurry away, amazed and abashed all at the same time. Since when do retirement age museum guards speak English? There was a time not so long ago when even the English teachers in Italian schools didn't speak English. A revolution has occurred since I first arrived in Italy, an acknowledgement that billions of visitors each year speak English and need to know where the exits, toilets, bank and stations are. On the other hand, some things never change, and I laugh to myself at the audacity of a museum attendant using his new-found skill, plus his position, to engage in picking up women.

My day has been a complete success. My mind is off the unimportant stuff and back into wondering about human capacity, beautiful images of the female body, and how surprising and unpredictable life continually is.

Chapter 7

Escape to the hills

It is Sunday again and still spring. It is imperative to leave the house, in fact to leave Rome, for the day. So we join the throng of Romans who leave the city each spring Sunday for the lake, hills and countryside to touch the earth and hear the birds, something that doesn't happen the other six days of the week. I am usually so used to looking at concrete that my eyes hurt if I am thrust into forest too quickly on a Sunday. But this Sunday I need to be deep in quiet, green, wet and lusty nature. So we head to Lago Albano (Lake Albano). It is about forty minutes' drive south-east of Rome and is a part of the area flocked to, ever since Roman times, by those wishing for some respite from the city.

As it has started to pour with rain just as we leave Rome, we decide to take the scenic route rather than head straight to the lake for a walk. Just past the Ciampino Airport you start coming across little towns, one after the other, some with medieval hilltop centres, some existing only because they were papal getaways where the Pope came to rest and relax, and some are newer and cheaper locations to live while enabling a worker to commute to Rome.

Lago Albano is a volcanic lake. After erupting, the crater filled with water. It still has underground connections to other volcanic lakes in the area and is very, very deep. It is also very, very beautiful to look at. It is nestled low in a deep crater, so there are many gorgeous vistas from its perimeter. About half of it is covered with forest that overhangs into it, with no banks, just gently rolling earth covered with shrubbery and then clear lake water. The sides of the perimeter are also covered in vegetation. It takes about an hour and fifteen minutes to walk around the whole lake, two hours if you want to stroll.

The half that is covered with forest has a path, like a green tunnel, that hugs the shore of the lake. The other half consists of a variety of restaurants and outdoor cafés that sit on its green banks, culminating in the main 'beach', which has a flat entry into the water via black dirt. This beach has umbrellas in the summer, and all year round a plethora of cafés and restaurants sit on the road overlooking the lake.

Today is not warm enough to swim and I am just looking for a long, quiet walk through the forest by the side of a lake. We drive around the lake from above, admiring the view. White mist is working its way up the sides of the volcanic crater quite quickly and rolling over its top. We dive in and out of it, catching glimpses of the main town of Albano with its beautiful cupola and palace, directly across the crater from us.

We arrive at the entrance to the walking path, but are unable to walk along the forest track as there has been a landslide. A path has been cleared through it but it is still a thin track in what looks like a river of mud. We brave the track for a while, but every aeroplane going overhead fills me with terror as I imagine another river of mud starting above us. So my husband promises me lasagne instead.

We drive through more little towns in the hills, winding around roads that are canopied with dripping green trees until we get to Genzano, just around the corner from Arricia. My husband has promised me that there is a great *fornaio* (a bakery) there where we can get lunch. Every *fornaio* in Italy produces bread or biscuits. If you are lucky they make pizza and if you are luckier you will get tea, coffee and other drinks. This one has it all, plus homemade mushroom and truffle lasagne. This is a real neighbourhood affair; the radio is blaring, the seating is plastic and you get your drinks from the fridge next to the cash register. One of the servers wears a traditional baker's costume from Genzano over a tracksuit and runners.

The pasta is delicious and costs ten euro, with a bottle of water, for the both of us. I constantly marvel at such out-of-the-way places, that place no importance on the comfort of the diner, yet have the most remarkable standard of food. There is almost no attention to service or presentation and I never would have chosen to eat here it unless my husband had heard it was great. Yet this is so typical in most of Italy.

A few years ago, as a result of not being a backpacker any longer and therefore being able to choose a restaurant based on anything other than its price, I set about sampling the haute cuisine of Rome. I tried about half of the restaurants commonly found in all guidebooks and presented as the top of Roman dining. After three extremely disappointing meals that cost over 200 euro (around AUD$370 at the time) for two, I felt I had done enough investigative research. It wasn't just that they were bad meals, it was that they were stunningly and embarrassingly bad. These same kinds of dishes you could literally get around the corner for a tenth of the price and which were infinitely better. Also, the service was utterly snobby and unwelcoming. Your seating allocation depended on how expensive you looked, and the ambience was tired and touristy.

In Italy the best food is served with the least fanfare, far away from famous piazzas and landmarks. In fact, I find the less obtrusive the establishment, the brighter the fluorescent lighting, the more plastic the chairs and the louder the television or radio, the better the food will be. This is because it is catering to the local, discerning population of Italians who know how the food should taste and who will only eat out if the food is as good as they can get at home. They also usually want to watch the football match and talk to each other, so the ambience is not fundamental. Entertaining at home is much less common than for other nationalities and is reserved for family and formal occasions, such as baptisms or small children's birthdays.

There are, of course, exceptions to every experience and I have not eaten in every restaurant in Italy. I have even once been coerced into eating close to a monument, due to the power small children have when they whine nonstop, and was pleasantly surprised. Also, some foreigners have been working in restaurants in Italy so long that they are very good Italian cooks. But if you are here for the real deal or for a short time, then I recommend sticking to those Italian restaurants run by locals and eaten in by locals, otherwise you might as well be eating Italian in your own country.

* * *

After snuffling down our truffle and mushroom lasagne, my husband having wisely put a stop to me ordering the crumbed veal and vegetables until after we had finished our *primo*, we reluctantly decide that we have to go straight to dessert. We both choose a sponge roll, one filled and coated with chocolate and one with white chocolate and cherries.

I am not a big fan of Italian desserts. Italy comes a poor second to my own country and many other European countries in the dessert category. I like to think it is because everything that comes before it is just so damn good that no-one notices what dessert is like, or no-one has room for it.

The traditional use of flours made from almonds, chestnuts, walnuts and grains other than wheat, as well as a lack of raising agents, means that there are no light fluffy cakes here, or butter-soaked puff pastry. Icing is nowhere to be found and cream is only used in January, sparingly. So desserts have a tendency to be ice-creamy and, frankly, why would you bother being good at anything else when you have the world ice-cream market cornered?

Whenever I spy something a bit different I always like to try it and it is usually at my peril. Like today, I realise, after my first bite into my white chocolate and cherry 'sponge'. They weren't kidding about the white chocolate part. The hard and crumbly sponge, or *pan di spagna*, is wrapped around semi-dry white chocolate that is so sweet I can't eat more than a mouthful and which drowns out the occasional cherry. I put it aside for my husband to finish after he gets through his dark chocolate one and ask for the chocolate and pear *torta*, a flat, dry-looking tart. But before doing so, wary of the white chocolate and cherry roll, I ask, 'Is there much chocolate in the pear and chocolate tart?'

'No, it's chocolate tart, not a tart of chocolate,' the waitress says.

It is delicious, bitter in its chocolaty, crumbly pastry form, the sweetness coming from the syrupy pears.

We buy some Genzano bread to take back with us to Rome, which is apparently well-known as being great bread. We also have a selection of biscuits made from almond flour, nut flour, chestnut flour and flavoured with chocolate and orange, and a few slices of *porcetta* for our dinner. *Porcetta* is another wonderful speciality of the hills surrounding Rome. In many of these little eateries you will find a nearly whole cooked pig body, with no legs, resting under a large curved Perspex container. It has been roasted and stuffed with herbs. You order it by the gram or the slice. The lid is raised up and a sharp knife slices off delicious rounds of crackling, fat, roasted pork and herb stuffing. It is divine eaten by the slice from the paper it is served on, on a piece of bread as a sandwich or with vegetables.

It is time to head home. It is still raining and although I have not thrust myself into a whistling, dripping, green forest this Sunday, I still feel I have been refreshed.

Chapter 8

La Liberazione, **Freedom**

Today is April 25, a big day for Italy. It is a holiday that celebrates the day Italy was liberated from German occupation during World War II, the day that was also the beginning of the end for the Italian Monarchy, and the day that was a precursor to Italy becoming a democratic, voting, independent republic. My husband explains all this to me on the way to our local *bar* to have our usual Saturday morning *cappuccino* and *cornetto* (breakfast pastry).

'That is an important day,' I remark. 'No wonder it's a holiday. All of that happened in one day?' I ask, incredulous.

'Well, maybe not all in one day,' my husband says, 'but it all started from *La Liberazione*.' It seems they were liberated from more than just the Germans.

Today has the air of a special and sacred day. It is a day that honours Italian soldiers killed fighting for their country, it honours those who lost their lives resisting the German-supported Fascist State, and it honours the partisan, or people's, movement which formed the basis of the movement to become a democratic republic. There are celebrations all over Italy; military parades and ceremonies to honour the living who participated in it and to remember their comrades who died for it.

There are old faces on the news. Old faces accepting with dignity the accolades due to them for activities long forgotten and unwitnessed. Faces that know they deserve this honour for the courage they had, the fear they had to overcome, the secret deeds they had to do. It is hard for me to imagine that kind of sacrifice.

There are other faces too. Faces that say 'I am defeated' and 'I can't stop remembering'. Faces that show that some fear, some pain, some memories never go away. Faces that say 'I cannot forgive, I cannot forget, but I go on anyway'.

Most families have a story about wartime Italy; a loss, a death, a resister, a traitor, a collaborator, a soldier, some of which were women. These were the roles given to the Italian public to play. Everyone had one. My friend's house, just outside of the main metropolis of Rome, was taken over and used as Nazi headquarters. My friend's parents were part of the Italian Monarchy and lived in a huge villa set in extensive grounds. Their groundsman, who I later came to also be friends with, had a brother who was one of the thirty local men randomly selected one day by those Nazis and shot, in retaliation for three dead German soldiers found nearby. Ten Italians for every one German soldier. I drive past the memorial to these war crimes, built on the sight of the massacre, on a weekly basis.

This holiday to remember them all comes a week or so after Easter and a week before May 1 which is, of course, the famous 'workers day'. No-one works on *that* day. I once tried to fly out of Italy on May 1. It is worse than Christmas Day because the 'workers' operate the trains, buses and taxis that get you to the airport, and they are all on holiday. There is no-one on the streets and nothing is open. These workers take their one day a year seriously. The Italian democratic republic State does too.

Not so with April 25. Although there are no shops open and the streets are quiet, you can still get a coffee until 1pm or go to the supermarket, as with most public holidays. Although, you have to be careful; my husband had gone yesterday to check that the supermarket would be open today and saw a sign which said it was open the usual hours. Today, it has changed its mind and is shutting in half an hour, half a day earlier than it said it would.

Except for the fact that I know Italians are brilliant astronomers and engineers, I would assume that they, as a culture, have a problem with numbers. They change depending on who they are being given to, where they are located and the level of convenience associated with them. For example, a set of favourable statistics being requested by the Pope at the Vatican would be easy to come by. However, some unpopular economic figures requested by a mayor's assistant in a small province, that required work during a lunch hour to produce, probably wouldn't be.

Birth dates are another example. When I first met my husband he told me his birthday was on December 29. So on December 29 I wished him a happy birthday and made a big fuss. I found it a bit strange that no-one else seemed to be doing so – no family members, no friends. Imagine my surprise when the next day his family and friends rang to wish him a happy birthday. Yes, he explained to me, he was born on December 29 but his birthday is celebrated the day after because that is the date written on his birth certificate.

'But why does your birth certificate say you are born the day after you were actually born?' I had asked. 'Is it tradition to add on a day?'

'No, it is because the doctor signed it on the day he received the birth certificate,' my husband said. I was outraged.

'Apart from the obvious astrological ramifications,' I explained to my husband, 'the whole point of a birth certificate is to certify that you were born and on what day. Not the day it was convenient for the doctor to sign it.'

'Well, it's better than my niece,' he replied. 'She was born on August 31 but her declared date of birth is September 3.'

August being traditionally the month that everyone goes on

holiday, there were no doctors around to sign the birth certificate, so it was signed when they got back from holidays. Whenever I start this conversation among Italians, there is always someone whose date of birth had to be changed for the sake and convenience of bureaucracy. Some people have up to one week's difference.

So who makes them celebrate the date they are declared to be born and not the actual date? The State does. The Monarchy is dead and in its place is the mighty Italian State. While we are sipping our morning *cappuccini* on the Day of Liberation, enjoying the quiet tranquillity of the holiday, I realise that liberation from one form of social control does not mean there won't be any in its place. It is a matter of having the choice, I suppose, and being able to choose the one that makes you feel safer and the one that you feel is the fairest. When your king runs off as the invading armies enter your country, after enjoying the fruits of Monarchy all his life, it would be galling. I can see how painful it must have been for Italians to experience that. I can see how that would lead to a fierce desire for self-determination and the realisation that the people could probably run the country just as well.

Italy as a nation had not long been in existence before World War II. It was only in the mid-1860s that all the principalities and kingdoms that make up the current landmass of Italy were conquered and forced to become one nation under one king. Before that, there were several kings and local princes that ran each part of it – there was the Kingdom of Naples, the Principality of Florence, the Kingdom of Sardenia, the Principality of Venice, and so on.

It explains why Italy doesn't feel like one country. The language, food, how people look and behave, and the types of housing differ significantly from one part of Italy to another. It is only just under 150 years that they have been referring to themselves as one country. It also explains the fierce identity that most Italians have with their place of birth. If they move locations they are still known as 'the one from Abruzzo', 'the Southerner' or 'the Venetian', even twenty years after they have been living in the new place.

There is also a wariness between northern and southern Italians, that at best borders on suspicion and at worst explodes as judgemental disdain. A few years ago a major political party ran on a campaign for the north to secede from the south. They got enough votes to be part of the government for many years. I once saw graffiti in Venice written in huge letters which ran the length of a wall that said 'Southerners go home'. The word used for Southerners, however, was a derogative phrase, the equivalent of the Western word 'nigger'.

After a concert one evening in Bologna in the north, friends of ours from the south were in the queue to get out of the car park. A woman backed her car out in front of them, only just missing them.

'Watch where you are going, lady!' my friend yelled out.

'Oh shut up you Southern immigrant, what would you know?' she replied, discerning his southern roots from his accent.

My friend, who is a large man from the south and a criminal court judge, was for the only time in his life short for words.

'Come here and I'll show you what a southern boy knows,' he eventually managed to squeak out, on the road one hour out of Bologna.

The Southerners get their own back, though, by instinctively knowing that they have the better deal when it comes to day-to-day living in Italy. They have all the best beaches and the sunshine, which, along with the chronic unemployment, provokes a happy-go-lucky way of life that is much better for the soul. They have generous, forgiving hearts, these Southerners.

Romans, I must add at this point, are a race unto themselves. They don't fit into the north/south divide because they are simply Roman. They have been there far longer than Italy itself, and in fact far longer than any other Italians. Italy grew up around them and they never let anyone forget that. They have nothing to prove, nothing to hide; they just are, and they are unapologetic about it.

When I first went to Bologna for a four-day weekend, I felt that something was wrong. I couldn't put my finger on it. By late Saturday afternoon I realised what it was. It was quiet. In the middle of a major city, it was quiet.

It wasn't just the smaller population, it was the way they behaved. I couldn't hear anyone's conversation. When they spoke into their mobile phones on the street they were not speaking loud enough for everyone to hear, as a typical Roman would be. There was no mad gesticulating as the speaker tried to stop the other party thanking or congratulating them, or asking them for advice. There was no way of overhearing what that person was going to have for dinner or at what time they would be arriving somewhere and why.

And the traffic. It was circumspect and what I would call rational. That is, it went from A to B without any flourishes of Formula One-type demonstrations, no knee-touching-the-road turns by the *motorini* drivers and no horns!

'Why is Bologna so different?' I wondered out loud to my husband. 'Why in Rome do people have the need to announce with symbols and loud sounds that they are there?'

'Because they are Romans,' my husband muttered, 'because they are Romans.'

The Italians chose self-determination, a republic, and from that the mighty Italian State grew. And grew. And grew. And to run such a diverse State you needs rules, laws, documents, processes and people to check all these.

In Italy, bureaucracy reigns. Identity Cards, registering where you live with the local police station, signing up at the local council so you can be assigned a doctor, all these are requirements and seen as common sense by the average Italian. Most Italians are incredulous when I tell them that when I move house back home I don't have to inform my government. Or that I can freely nip to the local *bar* for a coffee without carrying anything that would identify me and where I live.

Nothing in Italy can be done without a plethora of identity documents, which start at birth. Every Italian carries around with them an Identity Card with photo, a fiscal code card, a health card and a licence if they drive, as a minimum. Legally you can be stopped and asked for these by a dizzying array of police – financial police, army police, traffic police, local police – or public transport ticket inspectors who can fine or detain you if you don't have them on you in the original form. And from infancy onwards your date of birth is that which is shown on your official document. You have to repeat it aloud, write it and show it a zillion times; your schooling is based around it, your pension calculated according to it, your medical records reflect it. In the end, you just give up and celebrate this official birth date when the bureaucratic machine that is the State of Italy tells you to celebrate it.

This is why my husband now has a two-day birthday that starts on December 29 and goes until December 30. The person who has a week between their two dates is also very keen on this idea, they tell me.

The other numbers that change due to convenience or, in this case, cultural tradition, are house numbers. When my husband and I rented apartment number 17 at number 20 Pennabilli Street, we were perplexed the first time we checked the letterboxes. All of our mail came with the number 17 crossed out and the number 16b written in pencil next to it. We checked the number outside our front door and the number on our lease; they both said we had rented apartment number 17. However, our letterbox said 16b, and underneath was written the number 17.

I was anxious to get this number correct, as we had given our new address to family and friends, and it was also the address for my business. Finally, we asked our neighbour. The answer, it seems, is based on the fact that the number 17 is an unlucky number for Romans. In order to avoid coming across it and having to associate with it daily, the postman and the administrator of our apartment block – the Italian State at work again; all apartment blocks must be administrated – changed the number of our apartment at the most local decision-making level. It seems they did not need to inform us.

Numbers can also change depending on the consequences of having those particular numbers. A friend of mine was applying for one of the many documents that you must have if you are a foreigner and intend to live in Italy. As per usual, one document lead to another. In order to have this particular document she needed to demonstrate that the bill for the emptying of rubbish by council rubbish trucks was in her name. In order to have the bill for the rubbish in her name she had to register herself at the local office for rubbish removal. It was explained to her that the bill would be calculated based on the size of her apartment and she was asked how many square metres it was. When she replied, the official was amazed; it seemed her apartment was rather large compared to all others in the vicinity, including those in the same building. He asked her several times if she was really, really sure that her apartment was that size.

In Rome it is quite easy to know how many square metres your apartment is, as they are bought, sold, rented and leased based on this number, which appears in the documentation. So my friend was quite sure how many square metres her apartment was.

Her annual bill was then calculated based on these measurements. My friend's face fell. It was a huge sum of money for her. The official quietly asked whether she now thought her apartment was not quite as large as she had first imagined.

'Yes,' she humbly replied, 'yes, I think you are right, it isn't quite as big as I had first thought.' He responded by slowly scrunching up the previous documentation and taking out a fresh sheet of paper to begin the calculation again.

Lastly, numbers can change without any explanation at all. And then change back again. When I first moved to Rome in the mid-1990s, I lived in a condemned apartment block that has since fallen down. My flatmate and I would wait until the very last moment to pay our phone bill. We were both struggling backpackers trying to eke out a living, and times were often desperate. There was only one phone company in Italy, no phone cards, no mobile phones, no competition and we were often homesick for family and friends. It cost $3 per minute to phone Australia back then. The telephone company would send the bill and then it was about three months before they cut off your ability to make calls if you didn't pay. But you could still receive calls for another two months before they would cut you off completely. That always gave us around five months to pay the bill. At the end of three months we would inform our friends that they would have to call us as we could no longer call out. Most people were in the same situation so it was taken for granted that we would all have to do this for each other at different times.

Once we were sure we had used all the time possible and had scraped together enough money to pay, one of us would go down to the main office in Trastevere. Our phone would be working again within twenty-four hours. This system worked well for several years.

One time, however, something went horribly wrong. We had paid our bill and could call out again, so joyously announced this to all our friends. Then we noticed that we weren't getting our usual quota of calls back. We got the occasional person telling us that they had tried but there was no answer. Then we started getting the occasional person telling us that a guy named Marco answered every time they called our number. Then we started getting Marco's friends calling us. We called the telephone company on numerous occasions, telling them that somehow the phone lines had been crossed because our number no longer led to our telephone. They kept telling us we were mistaken.

At one stage, I tried yelling and screaming at the top of my lungs at the main office. I was led quietly and firmly up to the Head Office, where a very nice woman showed me on her computer screen that our number was linked to our phone.

'I don't care what your computer says,' I told her, 'it is wrong. When we dial our number it goes to someone else's house and when they dial their number it goes to our house.'

'There is nothing we can do,' she said, 'the computer says it's all okay.' According to the Italian State telephone company there was no problem, so there wasn't.

Frustrated beyond belief and realising there was nothing we could do, my flatmate and I manned our phone day and night. The next time we had a call for Marco, we explained our situation. We asked what number they had been calling and then gave them our number as the new number on which they could get Marco. We then told our friends and family our 'new' number and got on with life. We continued using our phone as always and were heading towards the usual enormous bill of over $1,500, when one day a sheepish telephone company man knocked on our door. He had come to 'adjust' our phone. Nothing unusual, just routine, but he couldn't quite explain what it was, just an adjustment.

The next day our original number was back, no explanation, no apology, no acknowledgement, but also no bill. Their computer had no way of tracing our bill. Our number was registered against this phone as not having been used because their computer said so.

The same Italian telephone company now has competition, lots of it. I was one of the first people in Italy to take advantage of that. They ring regularly, trying to get my custom back and offering me all kinds of deals. When they ask why I won't sign up with them, I tell them the above story. There is usually a short silence and then they hang up.

In spite of all this chopping and changing that occurs within Italy regarding numbers, facts and allegiances, I am in awe of this Day of Liberation as I sit in my usual *bar* sipping on my second morning *cappuccino*. It feels strange to be in a country that was once occupied and is now celebrating its liberation from that occupation, because I see Italy as the country from which high fashion, divine food, exquisite glassware and furniture come. It is a nation that houses some of the world's greatest art, buildings and Roman ruins, so I sometimes forget that it suffered the ultimate humiliation a nation can suffer, that of being taken over by an enemy. Of seeing them drive down the main streets, circling the Coliseum with their tanks, triumphant in their victory. Of having their beloved buildings and masterpieces adorned with another nation's flag, within living memory of many of the people I am sipping my *cappuccino* with.

All around me are people who can sit and enjoy this day of celebration and appreciate what it means to have your country back. They are people who can revel in the relief and reward of overcoming such a humiliation, and have a sacrifice mean something, even sixty-five years later. I understand that, after that kind of experience, getting a few numbers mixed up every now and then is really nothing to cry about.

Chapter 9

Foreigner

It is a glorious spring morning. Everything is bathed in yellow sunshine. It pokes through the leafy branches of the trees that shade the sidewalks with only a hint of the strength it will slowly gain over the coming month, until its rays sting and burn. It has been raining on and off for weeks and Rome has become overgrown almost overnight. The combination of water, fertile soil and a hint of sunshine has caused anything growing to go into overdrive. Trees that were beginning to get coated in green have become festooned with growth and have joined up, so the sidewalks are no longer open to the skies but have become tunnels of lime-coloured shade.

I try to wade through a thigh-high patch of weeds that was not there a week ago and give up, afraid that they will overpower me, drag me down and begin to feed on me. Our garden seems to have gotten a head start on our gardeners for once, and it seems that the flowers and hedges are winning out over the shears and axes that regularly come to tame our green space.

Wildflowers are everywhere in the parks and green spaces that populate my suburb. They range from brilliant violet to buttercup yellow; they draw attention to themselves with their iridescent colours. A fountain pours quietly in the cool morning air as I run past it. The proprietor of one of our favourite Roman restaurants is sitting in the shade out the front of his restaurant, shelling peas and preparing vegetables for lunch. It is too early for children, so the parks are empty and quiet, the bougainvillea and lush wet grass for my enjoyment alone.

Rome has been washed clean. Even the sky looks freshly blue. The medieval buildings and smooth domes of the churches are set off perfectly by the fresh spring air, the waving fronds of green and bursts of flowers.

There is nothing threatening in the Italian countryside, except the occasional wild boar. It is a soft kind of nature compared to the one I am used to. I am used to watching for snakes in long grass, looking carefully at the ground before I sit on it, keeping vigilant for giant stinging ants and trapdoor spiders while I'm down there. I am used to scanning trees for huge hairy spiders or big black bats.

But in an Italian field or garden you can sink into nature knowing there will be nothing to bite or bother you. This is unless you are in a local public park, in which case it is advised that you avoid the grass, which is used twice daily by dogs to defecate on while their owners watch. This is preferable, however, to the sidewalk, where in my suburb there are giant dog faeces in the middle of the sidewalk every five metres or so. This is despite a recent change in law and the fact we live almost next door to a huge police station.

In Italy there are many kinds of police. There are the *Carabinieri*, who are the State police and an arm of the military. They have black uniforms with red stripes, peaked caps and carry semi-automatic machine guns, which they often use in lieu of lollypops to wave the traffic on. The *Carabinieri* are famous for their looks, but who doesn't look good in a tight black suit? They are often seen on street corners in busy tourist areas, standing next to their armoured vehicle, on guard for something I have never quite been able to work out. After seeing them around for years they blend into the background, and whenever I go to another country I wonder where the men in black uniforms carrying semi-automatic machine guns are.

There are also the local police, traffic police and finance police, all with different uniforms. Some branches have women police, all of whom look gorgeous. They wear a full face of make-up and can often be seen putting on lipstick and fluffing up their hair before they put on their caps and get out of the car. Tight white short-sleeved shirts, cinched-in waists and whistles in their mouths help to create the air of eroticism they have about them.

Italians are big on uniforms. Even the weatherman wears a uniform; he is from a branch of the Italian Meteorological Bureau, a State agency that requires him to wear it.

One day as I was preparing to go out I glanced into the street below from my kitchen window, five storeys up. A special kind of police van had taken up position in the street, the kind that usually carries a SWAT team. It was manned by one lonely *Carabiniere* in SWAT gear – tight navy blue canvas trousers and shirt with matching bulletproof vest, usually accompanied by helmet and transparent shield. It looked rather serious, and as several vans sped by and took up positions at either end of the street I wondered what kind of State emergency could be unfolding in my street just as I was preparing to go for a walk.

As I left the apartment block all seemed quiet, so I thought I would approach the *Carabiniere* sitting in the van and ask him what was going on. I asked the question without really looking at him, only doing so as he answered me very politely and addressing me as *signora*, madam. I immediately regretted having only one question to ask him, one he had already answered. He was so handsome he took my breath away. The darkness of his features belied his southern roots. Forget the transparent shield, I would be stopped in my tracks if he just took his helmet off. With a sigh I reluctantly walked away after he had answered my one question, not being quick enough on my feet to think of a second one.

He had told me there was to be a demonstration, an annual march to recognise the patriots who had died during the resistance of the Nazi Germany control of Rome during World War II. As I sipped my *cappuccino* in the *bar* next to the police station I saw a throng of people pass by, mostly under the age of twenty-five with a few self-conscious looking men in their thirties, all of them dressed in mechanics overalls and workers uniforms. It was generally seen as a march for those with sympathies to the left of politics and with therefore anti-State tendencies.

These days those kinds of tendencies were not hard to have, given that the State was run by those with very right political leanings, headed by Berlusconi, one of whose laws included the clamping down on public demonstrations and marches such as this one. Therefore, the stream of about one hundred students and stragglers, silently keeping the annual vigil to those who died defending individual freedoms, were followed by six vans full of State police in full SWAT uniform and around another fifty officers in the usual *Carabiniere* uniform.

The *barista* and his female employee started laughing as they walked by.

'We thought it was a demonstration of police at first,' they said. 'There are more of them than there are demonstrators.'

A houseguest once said to me while seated at a table in the centre of Rome, 'I can always tell I am in Rome because wherever one is in Rome one can always see someone in uniform, someone eating an ice-cream and someone wearing leather.'

I have lost this sense of Rome. For me it all just is. I wonder why there aren't people in uniform, people eating ice-cream and people wearing leather whenever I travel to another country. I am no longer a tourist here. Uniquely Italian traits don't stand out for me as much anymore. I don't blink an eye when three different types of police turn up at the same event and I am amazed if I ever see anyone pick up their dog's poo. Guests ask me questions such as, 'Why doesn't the Italian government restore the Coliseum, protect it, clean it, put signs up explaining what it is?' and my response is, 'Why would they bother, it is just the Coliseum, what's wrong with the way it is?'

In fact, as a resident I know that many Romans would be happy just to shut the Coliseum up and keep it for themselves. They consider it to be theirs and that they are doing all tourists a favour by even letting them in there. 'Tourist' is also a label given to any Italian who is not a Roman – tourists from Milan are deemed to be the least desirable. This is why making any of their monuments more tourist-friendly is never high on the agenda of Roman politics. Besides, if getting ahead in the Italian system is based on doing favours and pleasing others, why waste that energy on tourists who have no power to grant you anything back? They figure tourists will come anyway, just as they have been for hundreds of years. The tourists have always come of their own volition, starting around the 1700s, and the Italian State has reluctantly put up with them ever since, deciding to at least charge them to see these great wonders and make some money from the inconvenience.

Italians feel they have a heavy burden, with so many of the world's precious art, architecture, monuments and ruins to preserve. They are in a constant battle over funding and deciding whether to make their own city more liveable and comfortable for themselves, or to preserve the remnants of the ancient ones for everyone else. For this reason they gratefully acquiesce when other governments want to help them out. Their thinking is that if most of their sights are of interest to the world then the world should help care for them.

So it is with great amazement that when I take my latest guests to visit the Coliseum, I do not have to hold my bladder for a few hours while we're in there until I can sprint to a local *bar* and order something under the guise of using the toilet. The Coliseum, after being in existence for 2000 years and having been one of Italy's most popular and most visited monument for over two hundred years, now has its first public toilet. In Roman times, men would just pee in front of the wall where they sat and women weren't allowed to attend.

It is Culture Week when I take my guests to the Coliseum, so all monuments and museums are free. In spite of it being free entrance we are still made to queue up and get tickets, which we don't pay for. The queues are long and my guests can't believe that we are still required to do this rather than just walk through the open gates. At the gate where we submit our free tickets, the turnstile keeps getting stuck and an attendant is freeing people up continually, all the while muttering under his breath, 'I am so tired, I am so tired of all of you, I wish you would all just go away or stay at home.'

'*Grazie*,' say my unwitting guests as he frees them from a turnstile when their tickets don't work, not understanding that he is actually cursing them. I want to slap him and say something cutting in Italian like, 'Well if it wasn't for us then you wouldn't have a job and you would join the rest of the twenty-five percent of unemployed people your age sitting at home watching television with their mothers.' But I don't want to ruin the buoyant mood of my guests.

* * *

Although I understand, appreciate and love Italians and their culture it does not make me Italian and sometimes I just want to get away. Sometimes I want my own food, my own humour, my own customs, my own way of dealing with things. So it is lucky that on some Friday nights I get to meet my girlfriends at a place that prides itself on being 'foreign'.

Australians have a well-documented mental pattern called a 'cultural cringe'. It is the feeling that everyone else out there is more sophisticated than us, has been around longer than us, and is therefore more accomplished. But Italians have a cultural cringe too. Theirs is about not being modern, about being held back by eons of history, about only being considered important because of things that happened in their past and not being taken seriously as a post-industrialised country.

I can entertain Italian friends for hours with stories of how my brothers taught themselves to surf when they were just kids, and that I have swum with dolphins and within a reasonable distance of sharks. I tell them I left home at twenty, that I have lived separately from my parents ever since I could provide for myself and that I have travelled the world alone. I tell them that in Australia you can have dozens of jobs in a lifetime, get ninety-five percent of a mortgage loan from a bank, own a credit card (in Italy all the 'credit cards' are actually debit cards), own your own home well before you are a pensioner. You don't have to tell the police where you live or when you move and don't have to carry an Identity Card. I tell them these stories and they are convinced they all live in a strange medieval parallel universe weighed down by bureaucracy, tradition, the Renaissance and a fear of nature.

In an attempt to throw off this cultural cringe, there are a few restaurants in Italy set up to be as un-Italian as possible and as New York as possible. The Perfect Bun is a fairly blatant attempt to copy what Italians see as the best parts of being un-Italian by being as modern and groovy as possible. The interior is a scene straight out of a *Sex and the City* episode. It is airy, modern and unlike any other typical bar or restaurant in Rome. Along one side are low lounges and sofas, a staple in any bar in Melbourne but not part of the culture here yet. It is possible to eat at a high bar in the centre of the room, at trestle tables at the back of the room or upstairs in the mezzanine, which has a glass floor. A bar runs down the other side of the room.

This set-up immediately indicates its un-Italian identity because it denotes a lack of seriousness regarding the food side of things. You can choose to have food, a drink or both and listen to music, all at the same time. Blurring the borders between eating, drinking, lounging and dancing is definitely not an Italian trait.

Music greets me as I walk in and I immediately feel I have left Rome and ended up in London or Istanbul. The menu is comprised of completely foreign food. It is modelled on the Hard Rock Café style, so the menu is hamburgers and Mexican food. I have heard the food is excellent. This is quite important because in my attempts over the years at trying to get foreign food in Rome – and I have tried most places that advertise it – I have discovered it is actually better not to have the food you crave than to have it look and taste completely different from what is advertised.

My experience has shown me that there is not much point trying to advise Italians on how to do foreign food. For example, by advising them that a Greek salad should by definition have feta cheese instead of mozzarella and cucumbers instead of artichokes, the response I got was, 'Well, that's how we do a Greek salad.' Or that chocolate cake is generally considered to be a cake that is chocolate, not melted chocolate on top of a piece of Italian pastry. Or that brunch is not usually made up of cold pasta salad served at 11am, and Devonshire tea is not Italian almond biscuits served with English tea. It is truly better to do as the Romans do when in Rome.

So it is with a fair amount of scepticism that I arrive to meet my girlfriends at The Perfect Bun. Waiters buzz around, eager to serve, more than one for every hundred patrons – another sign I have left Italy. They are happy to serve you or let you go to the bar yourself. They are attentive, playful and polite, eager to be considered as modern and as hip as the countries that many of their patrons are from. I am shown to our table, the first one to arrive. It is on the mezzanine floor above the bar. I struggle to walk on the glass floor and I notice we are under a speaker.

From experience I know that the music will get louder as the night progresses and, liberated on our bi-monthly get together from children, husbands and international careers, we are here to talk. Toni has been to six countries since we last saw her, Jess has moved into her new medieval house with her little family, Susanne has visited family and I have published a story since we last met. I also know from experience that asking for a table change in an Italian restaurant is likely to be met with reluctance and annoyance.

However, as I feel I am in 'international' territory, I am encouraged to be less Italian. My request is met with a quick, 'It will cost you fifty euro,' and I am grateful that I do know enough Italian to be Italian at this moment.

'Is that all?' I quip back. 'It's quite cheap at that price.'

My Italian language skills and the fact that I picked up the waggish Roman sense of humour wins me a table change. The young, hip trying-to-be-American waiter then asks me what I would like to drink, in English. I am surprised, as usually a disruptive request such as a table change would result in being ignored for half an hour. There is also no drinks menu so he patiently tells me I can have whatever I want. I am wary, due to past experience, as to what I will actually get if I order what I want, but go for it anyway and get back the biggest, nicest lime daiquiri I have had for quite some time.

Just as I am sipping, Toni arrives.

'Oh, why are we sitting at this table?' she asks. 'Let's ask if we can have one closer to the edge of the mezzanine so we can look over.'

She is off to ask the waiter if we can move again before I have had time to get the drink straw out of my mouth and warn her not to tempt fate. I am sure we are in for a scolding. She doesn't even bother speaking

Italian to our waiter and addresses him by name. He is delighted to be spoken to in English by such an obviously cool foreign woman. Toni has come straight from work and is in a power suit with a briefcase, and her accent seems American even though she is Canadian. I find myself being swept along to another table while Toni orders 'what you made me last week, Massimo'. She has her own cocktail.

Two Aussies, a Brit and a Canadian. We have gathered together for dinners such as these for over a decade, all of us drawn in and swept along by the magic of Rome in one way or another. We all arrived many years ago for different reasons but all with the desire to taste the adventure that Rome and Italy promised. We met through work or through mutual friends and are the remaining four of a much larger group of Aussies, Brits and Canadians that have all made their way on to somewhere else. The four of us stay because we are lucky; lucky to have careers, husbands, businesses and children in the place that we love being.

Jess is British and came many years ago, following a whim to spend a summer in Rome. Now with her husband Mimo and two children, she works for one of the United Nations humanitarian organisations based in Rome. Her latest child, Luciano, is also my godson. Jess and Mimo currently live in a medieval town just outside of Rome. Their house is made of stone and consists of one main room with a mezzanine and a small room for the children, plus a bathroom. They are slowly restoring an ancient stone house outside the walls of this town to turn it into a B&B. At the moment it consists of four walls, one of them crooked, no roof, no floor and is completely overgrown with weeds. It took three-and-a-half years to get planning permission from the local council.

Susanne came to visit one summer and never left. She was a friend of a friend back in Australia. Now with husband Guiglio and her young daughter Gemima, best friends with Jess's daughter Georgia, she runs a cooking school for international guests. She too lives in the same medieval town as Jess, also in a house made of stone that Guiglio restored almost single-handedly. It has two storeys and a *cantina* (a cellar) almost as large as the house itself.

Toni came over from Canada many years ago for a short assignment with the same United Nations humanitarian organisation that Jess works at, and who I also intermittently work for. She is now one of the directors and regularly flies all over the world, representing them and raising funds. She lives almost in the centre of Rome on top of one of the original Seven Hills, the Aventine, in a huge apartment that we regularly invade for a girls' nights in.

As we talk late into the night, supported by a perfect mix of foreign cocktails and foreign food, speaking in English about things far removed from our everyday lives of work and family, we get a break from the fabulous city we all love, and remember what it's like to be among our own kind.

Although all of us need a break from being a foreigner at times, we are all glad when we step outside and leave behind our Anglo-Saxon experience. It's nice for a holiday but we wouldn't want to live there, in that world.

Chapter 10

Sunday is an Italian day

It is impossible to be anything but Italian on a Sunday in Rome. Whatever small amount of cosmopolitanism or international flavour Rome manages to have during the week, it completely gives it up on Sundays, unashamedly. It is as though the façade of having to be a European post-industrial city all week is just too much, and it gratefully heaves off that burden and rejoicing, returns to the pace of the pre-industrial city it has spent most of its existence being.

One of the reasons you have to be Italian on Sundays, even if you aren't, is that nothing is open. No restaurants unless you are in the tourist part of town, no cafés, no shops, no supermarkets, nothing. Sunday is a day of rest for workers, a day of worship to spend at church and a day to be solely with your family. If you want to work on Sunday, go out to lunch or visit friends like an Anglo-Saxon, you can't. The transport is on a holiday timetable, offices are all locked up and no access is given, restaurants are closed and all your friends are with their families. If, for example, you haven't done your weekly shopping, you don't go to church or you have no family here, you are in for a long, boring and hungry Sunday. This is the kind of Sunday I often spent when I first arrived in Rome.

Back in Melbourne on a Sunday, at least in my suburb, I would roll out of bed at midday, walk out the door wearing what I had slept in and head to my high street, which was buzzing with activity. I would buy food for breakfast, or have breakfast out while reading the paper.

I would spend time leisurely buying flowers, meeting up with friends, going to the laundromat, lying on the beach or going for a walk. Most of the day would be spent doing these activities, with possibly a quiet evening and early bed.

I tried this on my first few Sundays in Rome. I came downstairs in my tracksuit with my bed hair and was surprised to note that the electricians, mechanics and shopkeepers who frequent my street during the week in their overalls, tracksuits and jeans were parading up and down in their Sunday best. Never had I seen so much hairspray in one place at one time. Suits, polished shoes, gold jewellery and coiffed hair were the uniform of the day. People were strolling along, fur coats draped to the ground, aftershave permeating the air; they were there to be seen. In between parading they would stop and form small groups, where cigarettes would be lit and gesticulating would begin in earnest and in jest. A few moments would pass and the group would break up, continue parading and then form a new group a bit further down the pavement.

The other thing that I tried to do on a Sunday in Rome when I first arrived was to buy some bread, milk and other essential items, and to my great distress found that I couldn't. I could go to my local *bar* until around 12.30pm, after which they closed for the day. But as I usually didn't venture out until around then, I often missed out on what meagre supplies (a coffee, a pastry) I could have gotten anyway. There are no convenience stores in Rome, no petrol stations that sell food and other products, no milk bars and no corner shops. It is mostly illegal to trade on a Sunday in Rome, and if not illegal, immoral.

In the past few years an influx of Indian and Bangladeshi migrants has led to the opening of small shops that stock a bit of everything and are open on Sundays. But we are talking very meagre supplies, and they are few and far between. With the opening of these shops due to some relaxing of the trading laws, there has not been an urge by Italians to open their shops on a Sunday and therefore compete with them, or an increase in people doing their shopping on Sundays. Italian behaviour flies in the face of most economic theory.

In Melbourne, Sunday evening was often a low-key event, spent with friends or at home alone chilling out before the week ahead. Soon after I had arrived in Italy an Australian girlfriend invited me over for a relaxed catch-up on a Sunday evening. Our houses were not close and public transport slowed down on a Sunday, so to spend an evening together it was easier to stay over and leave early the next morning. We had just turned the lights out at 10.30pm when the doorbell rang. It was the sister of my friend's Italian flatmate and five of her friends.

'*Ciao!*' shouted the flatmate as she opened the door for them. She only just had time to empty the sweets they had brought into a bowl before the doorbell rang again, and again, until there were sixteen people in our living room. Prosecco was being poured and laughter, yelling and lots of gesticulating added to the general uproar that was our house until just after midnight.

Once I went out to go to the bathroom. The friends eyed me strangely. Was I sick? they asked the flatmate. Why was I in bed at 10.30pm on a Sunday evening? In any event, there was no attempt to turn down the volume, and we tossed and turned until they all left.

In Rome, Sunday evenings are used to squeeze the last drop of the weekend out. It is the last opportunity to be together with family and friends, having already spent most of the day with family, eating and drinking before the work week begins. There is no need to prepare for work; it is inevitable and will happen anyway. With any luck it will rain tomorrow morning and everyone can stay in bed.

* * *

Today is Sunday and seventeen years on I am much better prepared, or so I think. Sometimes I just don't seem to learn. It is a beautiful sunny day and not very cold, the kind that you just have to be out in. It is predicted to rain all week, so every Italian and their dog is outside this morning. The whole of Rome is walking, parading. The parks are full, the sidewalks are heaving and there is a sense of desperation in the air to wring every last second out of this glorious Sunday morning.

The thing about Sunday mornings is that they are the only part of the day you are allowed to parade around. By lunchtime the streets are deserted for the mandatory long and large family lunch. The next time anyone is allowed outside is 4pm, and by then it will be starting to get cold and dark. They all know it is now or never.

I too am enticed out into the warm sunshine. The sun is bright and bathes everything in a new yellow light. The world has been dark and cold for so long. Today it has been washed clean by the sluicing of continuous rains, and so now it is fresh and reflects the sunshine back into the ether like a newly waxed car.

I disguise the fact that I am wearing a tracksuit and no make-up by walking really fast. Exercise has caught on finally in Rome and Sunday morning is a prime time. So long as I don't stop at shop windows, which is easy because there aren't any shops open, and keep a brisk pace it will be assumed that I am exercising and therefore no-one will blink twice at my Fila tracksuit, Nike shoes and Furla sunglasses. I do have the gold jewellery on in any case, so I fit in with the rest of my neighbours.

On my way home I am pestered by divine smells that waft out of every second window. They begin to play havoc with my tastebuds and gastric juices until I can stand it no more. I wildly scan every restaurant in my neighbourhood for signs of life as I walk by. But it is Sunday; you must eat at home. However, in my home there is nothing and no-one, my husband having left to spend the weekend in Puglia with his parents. The quiet omelette I had planned suddenly does not meet the standard amidst the tantalising smells of tomato, sizzling pork belly, garlic, warm olive oil and herbs.

I remember with glee that the supermarket at the end of my street had advertised it would be open on a Sunday morning. *About time*, I think. I race upstairs to get my wallet and come barrelling back down into the front garden of my apartment building, hoping to get to the supermarket before it shuts for lunch. I run into Marianna, who both my husband I have called 'customs', as you always have to pass by her and chat whenever you are entering or leaving the building.

She is usually hanging around the garden while her little dog does its best to dig it up. She chats to anyone and everyone, and a conversation with her is like reading Craig's List, Rome. She is kind-hearted and clearly bored a lot. Her opening phrase is usually, 'So what great and interesting thing are you off to do?' or 'Where are you going looking so beautiful?' Usually I resist these lines and don't stop to chat, but today I need her internet-type knowledge base.

'I'm off to the supermarket at the end of the street to buy some food for lunch,' I say, knowing that if there is an alternative or an obstruction she will let me know of it. My worst fears are confirmed.

'But Bronté, it's not open! It's Sunday, remember?' she says, looking at me with great concern as though she fears I have lost my mind as I can't remember what day of the week it is.

'But I have been there recently on a Sunday,' I begin to protest weakly, hope draining out of me.

'Yes, you're right,' Marianna says. 'It was open on a Sunday around Christmas to make sure that everyone could do all their Christmas shopping and still buy their food. And in a month's time it may start to be open again on a Sunday around Easter, but it is not open now. You could try the small shop down the road where the Indian and his family work. Their shop has a few supplies and is open on a Sunday. What is it that you need? Do you want to borrow anything from me?'

How could I have dared, after all these years, to suppose that a supermarket may be open on a Sunday for no other reason except that it is a supermarket and that is what they do? Perhaps someday I will learn that Rome is eternal, that it ignores the recent fads that proclaim consumerism is the key to a healthy, wealthy and natural life.

Rome knows that others will follow its lead, as they have on and off for the past 2510 years, seen recently in the founding of the Slow Food movement in Italy. I love that phrase, 'founded'. What it actually means is that Italy remained doing what it had done more or less since the Middle Ages, as the rest of the world went through capitalism to post-capitalism. Then the world turned around to find Italy carrying on its slow, medieval way and proclaimed it 'founder' of a 'new' way of doing things: eating seasonally, eating close to the production source, sitting down to eat, taking time to appreciate food and its role in an economic cycle that includes the nourishment of people and caring for the Earth, which is the production source. Italians are now nodding their heads, knowing that they have become the founding leaders of this 'new' movement, like they knew they would be all along.

For this reason, it is almost impossible to argue lifestyle issues with an Italian. It is most tempting for me on a Sunday when I am longing for a twenty-four hour convenience store or some decent television.

'Why can't we have both?' is usually my opener. The reply often focuses around heart disease and stroke rates, levels of drug and alcohol abuse, teenage suicide rates, divorce rates, extended family breakdown rates, murder rates, violent crimes against women rates and splits in families due to generation gaps. Somehow, the fact that Italy is in a better state than my country in all of these categories, and 'my country' usually means any English-speaking country, is always related to the fact that there is nothing else to do on a Sunday except get dressed up and have lunch with your family after church, have a walk together to show off your finery, and by definitely never, ever working.

Really, if you are a foreigner in Rome on a Sunday, the best option is to get invited to eat lunch with an Italian family. That way, you are entertained, fed and are unlikely to embarrass yourself by participating in any un-Italian activities.

* * *

It is with great delight that one Sunday I accept an invitation to lunch from Luciano and Brighton, our Italian/Canadian friends. We are invited to arrive at 1pm, which is the standard, acceptable and not-to-be-taken-lightly invitation time.

For work appointments in Italy it is acceptable to be up to an hour late, and a half-hour is considered usual, mostly for reasons relating to unreliable public transport, rain or traffic. However, a lunch invitation at 1pm is for precisely 1pm. Too early and you are inconveniencing the host, who will still be finishing off last-minute preparations and who will have to stop this in order to be sociable. They will then preface every course with, 'This was supposed to be done X way but I didn't get time to properly finish it.'

If you are later than this it sends a disrespectful message about the host's food, which will be primed and ready to go at half-hour intervals to achieve its freshest look and feel, and which will be ruined if their timetable is put out.

In spite of this knowledge we arrive half an hour late, after having been telephoned by the host to see 'if everything is okay'. We bring the recommended flowers and wine, and are introduced to the other members of the lunch party. There are Luciano's family, whom I have met before. Luciano's father is the principal of a school, his mother a teacher. Luciano's sister studies and Luciano himself has just finished a PhD in economics and works at the United Nations. They have also invited their local fruit and vegetable shop owners and some of the customers Brighton and Luciano always run in to when they are there. It impresses me how Brighton and Luciano have taken the relationship with their fruit and vegetable producer that one step further, pushed the boundaries so to speak, and I am eager to see the results. Do they get the first pick of every new season's vegetable? Do they get special cooking instructions or hard-to-come-by herbs?

Brighton is Canadian and so, like me, has struggled to fit into this 'old-fashioned' country, while at the same time thrived on its lost forms of civilisation, like the Sunday family lunch and the ability to have close relationships with your food providers. In Rome, an invitation to eat with a family for lunch would usually only be extended to other family members or godparents. It is a highly personal and private thing, to eat together at home. To invite non-family members would usually make it very formal, and usually occurs where one party is indebted or is in supplication to another.

In Australia and Canada, an invitation to eat at someone's house is seen as the first step towards making friends. Inviting people for lunch is a way of trying them out, getting to know them informally and an opportunity to sift through large amounts of people quickly so you can hone in on those you really like. I am therefore amused when I am confronted with this cultural mix of uses of a Sunday lunch that for Brighton and I are normal. This kind of lunch is not normal for the fruit shop owner and his wife, and is a cherished and eye-opening experience. For Luciano's family, who gracefully gave up hope of traditional Italian family life when their son told them he was gay and going to marry a Canadian man in Canada where it is legal, this kind of lunch is also unusual.

I have long adored Luciano's parents for the things they represent about Italian culture. It is their tolerance and openness to other ways of life and the fact they were both followers of the Communist Party in their youth. It is their value of education, literature and the arts, and their sense of respect for those who work hard. It is their ability to suffer through drastic changes to the education, their sense of fair play when it comes to allowing disadvantaged migrants to gain a place in Italian society but not at the expense of it, their ability to treat their children with respect and kindness and receive it in return, to talk about the olives and wine they have produced that we are eating, to be a symbol of timeless Italian tradition and values while sitting next to their son and his Canadian husband. For all these things I covet them, and so does Brighton.

Lunch begins with Prosecco, handed out by Brighton at the same time as the introductions. This is to be an entirely Italian-speaking Sunday lunch, as most of the guests do not speak English. My husband sighs with relief; I gulp down more Prosecco and exchange a knowing smile with Brighton. Brighton's struggle with the language has become infamous in our circle. If someone could learn a language through will alone, Brighton would be fluent. However, his continual and valiant attempts have produced results not in keeping with his efforts. The thing that most endears him to those who can speak Italian fluently, Italians and ex-pats alike, is the fact that his lack of prowess in the language does not keep him from speaking it or deter him from conversing in it as often as possible.

When he first arrived in Rome, on one of his first mornings in his new apartment, he received a knock on his door at an early hour. A small, frail, very elderly Italian woman stood in front of him with a wicker basket full of small round things, each wrapped individually in newspaper. She began speaking to him. He answered back. They had a lively conversation during which neither spoke the other's language and at the end of which Brighton found himself with a dozen eggs and had parted only with some euro. As one of his first economic transactions, things did not seem to have gone too bad from Brighton's point of view. As a single guy he did not need twelve eggs, but he could give a few away and had given the old woman some business. He was therefore not as happy when the next day he found another twelve eggs on his doorstep, wrapped individually within a box. The next morning he left the payment on his doorstep and returned to find yet another dozen eggs. This went on until he learnt to say 'no eggs today' and 'just every Monday' in Italian.

* * *

We are called to the table after a decent amount of time has been spent sipping Prosecco and smoking on the balcony, each of the non-family guests getting to know the other and the story of how we are connected to Brighton or Luciano. The *antipasto* is served. There are fresh olives doused in oil, garlic and herbs. These are produced on Luciano's parents' land. There is a mound of fresh goat's ricotta, which Luciano's mother picked up from a local producer on her way into Rome this morning. Luciano has made a large pastry-free pie of eggs and cauliflower, the Italian *torta rustica*. There is hot focaccia with rosemary, crispy and thin, Roman-style. Then the *fritti* start arriving from the stove; small pieces of artichoke, cauliflower, capsicum, onion and fennel which have been dipped into a light batter and fried in olive oil.

Luciano's mother has prepared some soft capsicums in olive oil, which are served cold. The plates of *antipasto* are handed around and around until each is empty and everyone has eaten at least two serves. It is all so tasty that my tastebuds are in heaven and much too occupied to even think about speaking. I am glad the usual cacophony of an

Italian lunch is occurring without any effort by me, which leaves me to languish in flavours, broken only by my occasionally asking who is responsible for which dish in order to give compliments appropriately.

Luciano or his parents answer me, usually distractedly, as though I am asking irrelevant questions. In their eyes I can see the pity which is extended to foreigners when they realise that what for them is a very average lunch, is for us a feast to write home about. Brighton smirks at me across the table and I realise that if I had this every Sunday I wouldn't care if there was a twenty-four hour convenience store in Rome or not. We wash our food down with a red wine Luciano's father buys by the barrel. He decants it into whatever wine bottles are available in order to recycle. Brighton doesn't understand this explanation and thinks he is changing wine by selecting a different bottle. I have juice from Luciano's mother's baked capsicums running down my chin and so cannot be bothered translating. He does not seem to notice anyhow.

The plates are cleared and bowls appear in front of us containing a huge steaming dish of homemade pasta with ragu, my favourite. Individual bowls are filled and the main plate taken away as silence descends upon the table. The pasta is sacred. And hot. No time to talk. The juicy nodules of meat are eaten with the chewy pasta, the tomatoey sauce flicks over everything as pasta is swirled around forks. There are no knives. Freshly grated, tangy Parmesan cheese is passed around and only Brighton and I stop to fill up our glasses during this ritual.

Immediately after the pasta is finished, the meat and the vegetable dishes are served, the traditional *secondi* plates. A light salad is served as the vegetable dish in light of the fact that a lot of food has already been consumed. The meat dish is slow-cooked pieces of beef *in bianco* (white) meaning cooked by themselves in olive oil and herbs or wine, and not in a tomato sauce. This is a common, simple and inexpensive Roman dish. The meat is the cheapest and toughest cuts and is stewed for a minimum of two hours until it is tender and falling apart. It is served with crusty white Italian bread.

The conversation resumes as the meat dish is eaten slowly. Because I have at my disposal two old communists, educated and articulate and now working as teachers, I never tire of quizzing Luciano's parents about Italian history, politics and society. I don't often get the opportunity to ask an older, wiser generation about these things. In addition, today I have the perspective of the proletariat greengrocer at my elbow, as well as the younger, overeducated but underemployed generation of Italians.

Political philosophy, as well as politics itself, is a common dinnertime or social conversation. It doesn't only centre on politicians or current politics, which most Italians are frustrated by and generally quick to want to finish speaking about, but on the philosophy of which type of governance is best to rule a country by: communism, socialism, fascism or a mixture. It is still being debated loud and long in Italy, and the level of knowledge of these philosophies by the average Italian always amazes me. The greengrocer will easily be on an equal footing with the lawyer or the musician in these kinds of dialogues.

A few of the guests need to move and have a cigarette break out on the balcony by now to digest and make room for dessert, so a small pause is conducted between the savoury and sweet dishes. But sooner than we need, Brighton is proudly bringing his contribution to the table. Tiramisu is such a common dessert that I would eat it more than weekly, and no-one in Italy ever seems to tire of it. Italians are not into experimenting or creating new dishes. All their art and creativity go into perfecting what is already thought up, and I have no problem with that. It means you are never going to get served a bad tiramisu, even if a Canadian makes it. It is also actually a very light dessert – the true Italian recipe at least – to eat on top of a heavy meal.

Coffee is immediately made after dessert, and chocolates and digestive liqueurs, such as Amaro and grappa, are served along with it. The mood at the table is languid. The scurrying to and from the kitchen by Luciano and his family has ceased. Some of the guests are smoking on the balcony but most are slumped at the table, engaged in quiet, one-on-one conversation or just in reverie of good food, wine and company. Now would be the time most families would go out for a walk in one of Rome's parks to recover from lunch and to get outside. Our dinner table conversations mosey along until it is almost 6pm and we all reluctantly agree to leave.

I feel like I have been at an amazing private restaurant where I had incredible food and wine, could relax on a couch with friends and a glass of Prosecco, was unhurried and leisurely, digested more than just food, built or solidified relationships and got to wear some of my glad rags. I forgive Italy once again for its lack of modernism and for having no convenience stores, glad to be forced to be truly Italian on a Sunday.

SUMMER

Chapter 11

The city under the sun

It is summer in Rome. There is no mistaking it. I leave the house early and feel the only coolness I will feel all day on my skin. In an hour or so, the heat will be overwhelming and it will be best not to be outside. For now it is calming, peaceful and tranquil, like I am walking through a forest of silk. The air is heavy with warmth, thick with sunshine, soft with summer. It entices me outside, into the open, from dark and closed-up dwellings. Romans are outside as much as possible in this first half of the day. They know that by 1pm they will need to be inside, away from the sun, managing the heat the best they can through little movement, a siesta and closing their apartments up so they are in pitch darkness.

The cool air of the evening is still lingering on the trees and flowers. Hibiscus and oleander in pink, purple and white are in flower everywhere. Bougainvillea comes in bright shades of fuchsia and is so profuse it seems as though giant purple tarantulas are poised in every garden. The lantana flower changes from its baby blue hue to neon blue. Magnolias as big as my head burst forth and a tree provides shade through soft pink petals in a symmetrical curve.

The pines look out of place in this heat, like tall shaggy dogs with too much winter fur. In spite of the searing sun, Rome retains its greenness and its foliage. The dark, icy green of the ivy and the laurel cast their presence everywhere and mute the brilliant sunlight. Seen through this kind of foliage the sunlight becomes softer, yellower, benign. As an antipodean that is used to brown barren landscapes, a sun that sucks all the life out of plants and trees that are mostly brown and grey, I find the summer landscape in Rome lush and inviting.

The city of Rome is made mostly out of stone, punctuated with water and the occasional tree. All of these elements make the heat bearable. Cold water gushes out of water fountains, is held in concrete pools and sluices over stone to cool the place down. It is enough to stand under a tree on a ground of stone and feel cold water run over your feet to be able to enjoy the Roman summer. Rome is built for heat. It has always had it and knows how to make the most of it.

Everyone and everything moves outside in the Roman summer. People sit on stairs and in chairs placed on the sidewalk outside their shops. Doors and windows are open to let in the cool air, to create breezes and to store up the freshness for the afternoon ahead. Every few doors a café awaits to pour out an icy, sweet homemade peach or lemon tea, a cold glass of water from the tap via the Roman aqueducts, or their magnificent coffee slid over ice and doused with cold milk.

The pavements are alive with people walking, talking, sitting, shopping, drinking and smoking. Even though this is the cool part of the day you can tell it is summer; everything is slower. Movements are languid, no-one hurries, people stay seated for longer in flopped-down positions as they sip their iced coffee or tea, not speaking or looking at anyone, recovering from sleepless nights and making way for the sweaty siesta ahead. People are outside more often and for longer in the summer because it is the nicest you feel all day, in the cool of the morning and the cool of the evening.

Passing time is a big activity in summer. Talking about nothing, doing nothing, just passing time until it gets cooler in October. And what lovely surroundings to pass time in. The trees that keep their greenness provide cool shade; just their colour being spread all around you provides a feeling of freshness. The cicadas sing their songs all day and there is nothing lovelier than lying on some grass under trees and flowers, to while away a summer afternoon.

It is an unproductive, and at times infuriating, season. Like quicksand, the more you rail against it, try to get ahead, accomplish what you normally would in a day, the quicker you sink and the worse you feels. It's necessary to give in to a Roman summer, to lie back and think of nothing, to give in to her soft, silky touch that allows for small bouts of unplanned activity and long bouts of inactivity. To contemplate the inside of hibiscus flowers, to listen to the sea, to digest cold vegetables and light mozzarellas, to lick ice-creams and to wait for the cool of night to ingest anything heavier. It's a time to lock up grand plans and lock down ideas of doing anything strenuous until the cooler months. It is a time to conserve your energy, to sit and wonder, to rest and ponder, to savour cool intermittent breezes that allow the brain synapses to function just long enough to remember to call the plumber.

In Rome, everything finishes in early June. Shops begin to shut up and everything, from shoe repairs to car mechanics, must be put on hold until September. All businesses begin advertising when they close so citizens can plan their schedules and not get caught out. From early June, every discussion about work that takes place is punctuated with the sentence, 'But now it is too late, we are talking about September for beginning this, right?' Things have improved from a few years ago, since the government legislated that a minimum amount of shops and services must remain open in each area.

When I first came to live in Rome seventeen years ago, everyone shut up shop for the whole of August, based on the assumption that no-one would be left in the city to need services. This meant that if you ran out of toilet paper you had to wait. It was also not convenient if you were birthing a baby, and if your car broke down you walked until September. You had to literally go in search of stores to buy food. Supermarkets were a thing of the future even fifteen years ago, and as most businesses closed for the whole of August you had to stock up on supplies in July if you were one of the unlucky ones not leaving the city.

Even today there is usually a mass exodus from the city on August 1. Holidaymakers are stuck for hours on Rome's highways, exiting the city. The airport is at a standstill and the city holds more tourists than Romans. Now Romans stagger their holidays more, which can begin from July 1 and continue until the end of August. Most people take a minimum of two weeks. It is tradition, however, to take the whole month and spend it either by the sea or in the mountains.

Many Romans have a second house, or at least the same one they rent each year, in their seaside or mountain locations. Romans can be divided into two categories of people: those that love *il mare* (the sea) and those that love *le montagne* (the mountains). As well as the usual conversations about food, the most common conversation you will have from June to October is about holidays. After asking what you had or will have for lunch or dinner, the second most common question is, 'Where are you going for your holidays?' The answer either results in an argument or a mutually-confirming discourse on which location is better for a holiday. It is as serious as football or politics.

The debate regarding holiday locations centres mainly on the relaxing and recuperating properties of each location. Those who need the sea are sun worshippers who require heat, not much clothing and the slowness of a seaside resort to unwind. This helps them ignore the chaos, queues, noise and the other million sun worshippers who are doing the same thing. Mountain lovers need nature, coolness and tranquillity to relax and recuperate. This enables them to eat as much as they would in the winter and not mind that they are more German than Italian in their holiday tastes.

Romans are great travellers, too. The airport is crammed from July until August with holidaymakers going all over Europe, North Africa, the Balkans and the USA. They most often take chartered flights and holiday packages due to the limitations of their language. No-one speaks Italian outside of Italy, and English as a second language in Italy is only barely beginning to catch on. Then there are their dietary requirements. As explained earlier, Italians are not as adventurous as culinary travellers.

Sitting in restaurants in other countries, I have often listened to long and painful explanations in broken English from patrons advising a waiter how to cook their pasta. Many bemused Greek and British chefs know by now that Italians are not kidding when they say they can't eat it otherwise. For this reason, a large proportion of Italians choose to go on holiday packages to resorts that cater specifically for Italians. I must admit, this has been an unforeseen advantage for me, in being able to speak Italian. The packages and resorts catering for Italians always have the best food, without fail.

Despite the staggering of holiday periods in recent times, in August the city still becomes deliciously quiet, parking is to be found everywhere and traffic is non-existent; a peacefulness descends. The city without its chaos and noise. The city with only its monuments, its parks, its river, its beautiful and graceful architecture. The city that can be enjoyed without fear of being run over by people or machines the minute you stop to look at something. A languid and slow city. But beware: do not try to do anything except be languid yourself in such a city. It is deserted for a reason. It is too hot to do anything except laze, graze and contemplate. Literally only mad dogs and the English are out in the midday sun.

In an effort to make the city more efficient and to keep it functioning throughout the summer, the Roman local council has enthusiastically supported those who choose to stay, or can't afford to leave, during August by turning it into a world-class outdoor entertainment complex. Major parks become outdoor venues for an exhausting program of dance, music, opera and film. The riverbank, deserted at all other times of the year, becomes festooned with temporary outdoor eateries, markets and Moroccan-style bars, complete with cushions and carpets to lounge on while watching the Tiber flow by.

Any night of the week you can find jazz concerts under the stars, sip a beer in an outdoor bar in the park overlooking the Coliseum, dance to live Latino Americano music at the dance village constructed on the Roman racecourse, drink Prosecco under ancient pines while watching a ballet, or listen to an opera amidst Roman ruins. The festivities culminate each summer in a free concert at the Circus Maximus, the same site where the ancient Romans came to watch concerts over 2000 years ago.

These modern-day concerts have included artists such as Elton John, Sting and Earth Wind and Fire, and are free. This has not stopped enterprising Romans selling tickets for them. Each year the newspapers are full of reports of unsuspecting tourists who have come to Rome to see the big-name concert, expensive tickets clutched in their hands, only to find that there is no-one to take their tickets, no entry points or fencing, and that no-one else has paid.

* * *

Today I have set off early on a mission. I plan to see an exhibition which, although is in residence all year, is only open to the public for six weeks out of every year. It is an international show and world-famous. It opened in the middle of May and is advertised as closing at the end of June. Today is the last day. The exhibition is the Rose Garden of Rome.

Tucked away on the side of the Aventine Hill, one of the original

Seven Hills of Rome, the gardens are in a small area opposite the Circus Maximus. Usually only opened for diplomatic, papal or royal visits, they can be gazed at through the wrought iron fence and enjoyed by Romans all year, at least from a distance. They host specimens from all over the world and some ancient species of rose that date back to Roman times and which are unique to the area. I love roses, and although I have seen the gardens from the outside I have never, in my whole seventeen years, been able to walk through them. It never appeared open to me. So today is my opportunity to finally see them.

I decide to walk there and enjoy the balmy morning and all that Rome's summer streets have to offer. There is no need to check the temperature or weather because from June onwards it is always the same temperature: very hot, humid and sunny. I savour the tenderness of the summer morning, its warmth, its light, the way it tickles my skin. I walk out of my suburb and cross into the old Roman Empire, marked by entering through the remains of the large gate that sits in the middle of a busy intersection. I am not walking for precision but for enjoyment, so I take the most scenic route possible as I duck behind the post office and into a large park.

It is almost deserted and it beckons me with its shady olive trees, water fountains, stone seats and greenness. I am enticed ever deeper into its green shady folds and almost lose my will to keep walking.

Europeans know how to do parks. They are sculptural and pebbled, and carved so that each part draws you further in. Like a clever maze, they always appear bigger than they are. They make you experience them slowly, bit by small bit. I begin to feel as though I am in fairyland and that I could wake up before having even reached the Rose Garden. Any other day and I may have given in, but I remember today is the last day of June and the last day I have until next year to see the roses.

As I wander closer to the cool of the shaded fountain I notice it is still, bright green and very dirty. It is a metaphor for Rome. From a distance it all looks terribly enticing and perfect but up close you notice the rubbish, the neglect, the decrepit air, all hurriedly tidied over.

I walk out of the park and cross over the road, before ducking down another dark and green street which I know will lead to my destination. I climb the Aventine Hill. Most people expect the Seven Hills to be either a monstrous myth or seven gigantic snow-capped peaks ringing the city. Given that Rome was the centre of the known civilised world for nearly 2000 years, you might expect a large sprawling city, on par with Cairo, London or Mexico City. Rome was a large city for its day, very large, but not by today's standards; you can walk around the ancient city limits in a couple of hours.

The Seven Hills, therefore, did ring the city but were quite low, benign hills. They weren't very good real estate options, as they were mostly a little far from town. This is all except the Palatine Hill, where all the best families lived; those that ruled, or intended to, lived there.

The Aventine Hill lies behind the Palatine and in front of the Circus Maximus. The Palatine Hill has been kept in its original form and still houses the ruins of Rome's best families' houses. But the Aventine Hill has taken over its role of being prime real estate and is covered by a variety of monasteries, churches, parks, embassies, hotels and expensive apartments. It is packed with beautiful old apartment buildings, and gardens with views over the river of Rome and beyond.

I am near my destination. The Rose Garden is opposite the Circus Maximus, about halfway down the hill towards the river and the beautiful medieval church of San Cosimato, which holds La Bocca della Verità, The Mouth of Truth. Legend has it that if you put your hand into the mouth of this stone face and tell a lie, your hand will be bitten off. Made famous by Audrey Hepburn and Gregory Peck in *Roman Holiday*, this church always has a queue outside of it, not of earnest prayer-seeking Christians, but of tourists wanting to have their snap with their hand inside the mouth of the statue.

As I have never actually been to the Rose Garden before I am not quite sure of their entrance, but I follow my nose and head towards what I think is the back of them, picking my way through medieval ruins and more parks. I am so excited that I am having a chance to do this. It was by accident that I read an article in a magazine last weekend about the gardens and noticed they were open.

I reach them and gaze with contentment past the iron bars into the flowered hillside beyond, imagining being among all those fragrant fronds. Then my eyes reach the sign on the iron bars.

The council of Rome, as it commonly does, has a contradictory view to the rest of the Western world on how many days June has. In spite of advertising that the gardens are open for the whole month of June, it has decided that the month ends on the 28th, not on the 30th. I am thwarted and somehow not very surprised. In Rome, with all things one must ebb and flow, not take anything for granted and agree that days of the month, like other numbers, are subjective and open to interpretation.

I am not too disheartened though, as I walk along the shaded pine avenue and view the roses on the hillside from the outside, as I always have. Next year I will try on June 15, just to be safe.

I decide not to let the morning go to waste and visit my favourite Roman space, the Orange Garden. It is tiny and entered into from arches set into medieval brick walls, part of the Monastery of Santa Sabina. Once inside you are taken back to a more tranquil time, when lovers reclined under sweet, dark-leafed orange trees set on bright grass. Small stones crunch underfoot as a vista more luscious than summer fruit greets you.

Miles overhead swing the ancient pines, providing a canopy for the whole park. Not an inch of sunlight can get in. You can see across the river to the distant Janiculum Hill. Bright orange specks of fruit are scattered on the ground and on the laden trees. They provide stark relief to the private and dark interior of the orange groves. Set around the garden are stone benches, neatly arrayed along the well-trimmed paths and grassy areas. Medieval bricks make up the stairs and the lookout from which the whole of Rome is set out below. In the distance the blue dome of the Vatican, the high walls of the Coliseum, the statues of the winged Venus, lesser domes and the low, murky river of Rome intertwine to show the stones and edifices of Rome at their best.

It is a quiet park, given to contemplation, relaxation and lovers. The signs to not lie on the grass are ignored, as couples and individuals stretch out in full recline with books or each other. Once through the small arches, it draws you on towards the edge of the lookout and the magnificent view over Rome. It is difficult to remember walking. Somehow your limbs remember to move while you are taking in the sights on either side, sighing and longing to take shelter under the shadowy grove. You are propelled to the end to see the view and then back again to meander through the grove to find a place under the orange trees. It is another fairy paradise where you could while away the entire day.

A small open-air stage is set up in this garden for the summer, where free nightly concerts of Rome's most popular folk songs are performed. After a suitable amount of time gazing at the tall pines overhead from a horizontal position on a stone bench, I reluctantly gather myself together to leave. But I cannot leave the Aventine Hill without paying homage to its other beauties, no matter how many times I've seen them before.

I stop in at the Santa Sabina church. It dates back to the fifth century AD, making it an early Christian or Byzantine-style church.

It is beautiful for its simplicity; a large space, lots of marble columns, light and bright. It, like most of Rome's churches, was built on top of a Roman temple, making it a place of continual worship for nearly 3000 years. All those prayers. I add mine as well.

Just a small walk from the church is the Sovereign Military Hospitaller, Order of St John of Jerusalem of Rhodes and of Malta. It is commonly known as the headquarters of the Knights of Malta; part religious order, part non-State sovereign entity, part charitable hospital and organisation, part legend, it was a movement founded during the crusades in Jerusalem. The headquarters are housed behind a high, thick stone fence that spans a couple of hundred metres. There are some huge wooden double doors, with a plaque next to them so you know what the building is. These doors have a very special and quite famous keyhole.

Many years ago, while still a young backpacker, I heard a legend. It was one of those legends, usually concerning a location, that gets passed on from one backpacker to another across the trails of Europe, until its true location or description is hidden but its status has magnified a hundredfold. I heard of a keyhole somewhere in Rome where, if you looked through it, you could see the Vatican. And it wasn't the keyhole of a building anywhere near the Vatican. I told this story one Sunday morning, also many years ago, to my ex-backpacker flatmate, Eilish, and her houseguest. Eilish listened with rapture and claimed that she too had heard the story of the 'Vatican keyhole' in Rome. The visitor laughed her head off at us and jeered rudely.

My flatmate and I were jeered at all day from the time we left our apartment, all during our bus ride to the Aventine Hill and all through our walk in the Orange Garden. Our visitor would not leave it alone, until we saw some people bending over at a gigantic doorway to look at a keyhole. Then the jeering turned to taunts.

'Look, look, there are some people looking through a keyhole. Maybe that is the keyhole you are looking for, ha, ha, ha!' the visitor said.

Although Eilish and I had pored over our guidebooks all that morning, we had been unable to find any references to a keyhole. The internet had not yet been invented. But as avid legend-followers we had not pooh-poohed the idea, just acknowledged that we didn't have the faintest clue how to find it. So imagine our surprise when, during our 'Plan B' walk around the Aventine Hill, we found a group of people bent over, looking through the keyhole of a large door set into huge stone walls on top of a hill.

'Hey, maybe you'll see the Vatican if you look through that keyhole,' our visitor taunted.

It beckoned us. If others were looking through it then there surely must be something to look at.

There were armed military police on guard near the large door, swinging their semi-automatic machine guns around as they drew on their cigarettes. They were obviously unperturbed by people getting so close to the door and looking through the keyhole. It signified that it was a habitual event.

Eilish and I felt the magic at the same time. It was one of the reasons we were friends. We had never met before agreeing to share an apartment together, both having stopped backpacking at the same time and desiring to linger over the love of our lives, the city of Rome. Eilish is Irish, of strict Catholic background with IRA sympathies, and an engineer by training. I was Australian with no clue about 'the troubles' in Ireland, a Protestant, a collector of the most garish and grotesque Catholic icons I could find, an anthropologist by training. We did not envisage getting along. But our backpacking, journeying, adventurous natures bonded us immediately. Once she understood that I was not a religious maniac but had a penchant for religious memorabilia – I blamed it on my anthropologist rather than my kitsch tendencies – and I understood that being a strict Catholic did not preclude her from drinking as much Guinness as was humanly possible at every opportunity, then it was all smooth sailing.

We ran together towards the keyhole, with our visitor's taunts dying on her lips. Could it be possible that we would see the Vatican if we looked through this keyhole? Even we were half-joking as we bent over to look through it. Eilish went first and stood back up, mute, and with an expression I found hard to decipher. I immediately followed and understood why. A sound that was a mixture of a huge laugh, overwhelming joy, a scream and an expletive wanted to come out of my mouth, and it rendered me mute. I literally couldn't speak. 'Struck dumb' I think is the correct expression. Our visitor was demanding an explanation by this stage and bent down herself out of frustration at neither of us being able to answer her.

'Well, fuck me!' was all she said.

Eilish and I were rolling around the tarmacked car park, in full view of the machine gun-wielding guards, unable to control ourselves. How had we done it? How had we stumbled across the very thing we had given up searching for? It confirmed its legend status in our eyes.

Our glee contained several facets. We were laughing with the joy of how divine our backpacking gods were that day for showing our loud-mouthed, doubting visitor how wrong she could be. We were laughing with the joy of how wonderful we felt life still was at thirty-two, when you could believe in legends and have them come true. We were brimming with the glee of how life really is at times magical.

You *could* see the Vatican from the keyhole. Behind the huge wall was a beautiful garden belonging to the whimsical Knights of Malta. The owner had sculptured the garden so that a row of roof-high hedges formed a corridor down which the eye was led. At the end of that corridor, across the river, was the dome of the Vatican. The hedges filtered out all light and distractions, making the Vatican seem closer and just at the other side of the keyhole. It was a brilliant piece of tromp l'oeil and a satisfying end to a journey taken in faith.

* * *

I stop and pay homage to magic once again, by looking through the keyhole as part of my meanderings on the Aventine Hill. Yes, the Vatican is still there, just behind the keyhole. But now it is lunchtime and time to head home. I walk down the shady dark green hill and find myself deposited onto a busy, noisy, tram-lined street in full sunlight to wait for the bus with other heat-stricken commuters. This is the bus that comes only every forty minutes but comes in pairs to make up for the fact that one of them is twenty minutes late.

As the precious Roman lunch hour grinds on and every other numbered bus had passed twice, I begin having pasta fantasies and remember I'm standing only a few paces away from Volpetti, one of Rome's most famous speciality food shops, that has a small cafeteria attached. I felt myself being convinced. I am a good convincer of myself, especially when I am able to remind myself that if I stop off at Volpetti for lunch I will actually be closer to the next bus stop and so have the choice of two buses to catch home.

Five minutes' walk later and I slide into air-conditioned comfort, along with about twenty other eaters, to sample the wares of the Volpetti chefs. There are all manner of pastries filled with mozzarella, ham and spinach, two or three varieties of pasta and rice salad, roasted meats, dishes of vegetables glistening and crisp or battered and stuffed, fresh seafood and breads. I choose a dish of *pasta calabresi*, which can mean different things but generally, and in this case, means shell-like pasta shapes coated with tuna, cherry tomatoes, black olives, fresh parsley, olive oil and garlic. Cool and filling, I wolf it down and follow it with chilli and room temperature *cicoria*, another speciality from the south of Italy. At this point I am sated but unwilling to move.

The little place is cool and quiet, filled with only a few other diners who have taken refuge to eat and rest. Outside, the midday sun beats down on the asphalt. No-one is on the street. I know that ten minutes' walk will be all I can manage before the sun bites my skin and addles my brain.

The cafeteria is closing. If you think waiting for a bus at lunchtime in the sun is difficult, waiting for one during the siesta hours is long, tortuous and guaranteed to require considerable recovery time.

Then I remember a dark, shady piazza not far from the cafeteria. It is also next to a *gelateria*. I lunge out into the siesta-time sun, stepping quickly and hugging the shade wherever possible. I walk along deserted streets and I have the pavement to myself. No cars, no people, nothing open at 3pm on a summer afternoon. I reflect upon the fact that if I die right now it would be some hours before anyone found me. This is in a city where by 7.30pm you would have to regularly step off the pavement to let people pass by, risk being run over or honked at by the hundreds of cars that will be speeding along the street. It does not lack a population. It does, however, have a strict social routine that is dependent on the weather and tradition rather than trade and business. It is one of Italy's best qualities.

There are three people in the huge piazza, which covers several blocks. Two of them are asleep under trees on stone benches and one is reading a newspaper. The gigantic children's playground is empty, as are all the seats around the centre of the round piazza, which will host groups of up to ten people each come evening. The *gelateria* is open, however. The service I receive is surly and disinterested, barely mustering up the enthusiasm to scoop my ice-cream into a cup. This is punishment for coming in at 3pm when all decent people are resting, or at least not bothering shop owners who have chosen to stay open.

I choose the flavours of *zablioni* and *pinoli*, best described as eggnog and pinenut. They are medicinal. If you can imagine eating eggnog or pinenut as ice-cream, this is it. It cools me and lifts me at the same time. I want to sing the Italian national anthem as, once again, I get why this country is so fixated on its daily gelato. Maybe it's why they defy all economic and social diagnostics, why they were able to change mid-war to the winning side, why they are so good at football and what sustains them when their government regularly collapses. Ice-cream this good is probably the cure-all for everything, and I can understand how if you have access to this every day then nothing else can really go very wrong.

Cool on the inside, calm and quiet on the outside, I think of nothing in the leafy shade, alone in the large piazza. I wait out the afternoon siesta as I know, contrary to the timetables, the buses will be taking one too. It is over too quickly and I hear the unmistakeable noise of shop fronts opening up their metal shutters, the squeal of bus brakes and the noise of small children coming to play. In an hour the piazza will be teeming, the woman in the ice-cream shop will be run off her feet and I will be sharing this park bench with at least five old women who will squash me in, blow smoke in my face and shout to each other across me. Although it has been hot, I am happy to pay that price in order to have had a few quiet hours to myself in the city. I get on the now-punctual bus and head for home to take my late siesta and recount my day.

Chapter 12

Does it count as exercise if it finishes in a café?

Is it really a jog if it ends with a *cappuccino*? This is the question I ask myself this morning. Personally, I think it's perfectly acceptable to run along with a one euro coin bouncing around in my shoe so I can buy a *cappuccino* at the end of it. In my mind, it's actually very Italian. You should never get so sweaty that you cannot walk into a *bar*, order a coffee and sip it quietly without drawing much attention to yourself. I realise I have become truly Italianised in my attitude to exercise; Italians always seem to be able to combine exercise with something else, mostly while looking good.

When I first arrived in Rome seventeen years ago, I had an Australian attitude to exercise – you did it regularly and as a matter of course, like eating or sleeping. You generally had fun, made a fool of yourself and really didn't worry that much what you looked like, as long as your heart rate was up and your muscles were being used. Imagine my surprise when I went to my first ever Italian gym and saw women putting on make-up and blowdrying their hair *before* the exercise class. I soon realised that aerobics Italian-style wasn't really for me.

I decided to try swimming, another favourite of mine. I went to the pool at the bottom of my street, and was marched firmly out the door and told not to come back unless I had:

a.   a doctor's certificate saying I was fit to swim (that necessitated me registering as a citizen and asking the council to find me a doctor, a process that generally takes six to twelve months, if you are eligible, which I was not)

b.   special shoes that would not be worn anywhere else except by the poolside (they had someone checking if you wore the same shoes to the poolside as you had coming in the door)

c.   a bathing cap, goggles and racing swimmers

d.   swore never to use shampoo, a razor or bath foam under the showers

e.   didn't mind paying the equivalent of a dinner out every time you used the pool

f.   gave them a down payment which was on top of the charge to actually use the pool and which was non-refundable, called 'a subscription'

In spite of this I was undeterred, partly because I was desperate. As an alternative to aerobics I had started running – my least favourite form of exercise. It was so unusual to see a woman jogging in the street that I had gotten stopped twice by people asking if I was okay and what I was running away from. Add to that the dog poo every two metres and the groups of people on the sidewalk that never moved but just watched me and blew cigarette smoke into my face as I tried to run by, and the pool seemed like a pretty good option.

My flatmate Eilish had discovered a doctor that would see us 'under the counter'; that is, we didn't have to be on his registered client list. He wouldn't ask us for our 'papers' and we in turn would pay him whatever he wanted, which he wouldn't declare. In the end it was only about AUD$20.

I faked the special shoes, bought the racing swimmers and my flatmate and I shared the cap and goggles. I also had a shower when I got home after swimming rather than at the pool and I put aside a part of my income every month so I could go swimming every week.

I must say though, it was a glorious experience. It was a huge pool and pristinely kept. I was in the company of budding Olympic swimmers and well-behaved rich kids, the only other people who could afford or be bothered to jump through all the hoops. Every time I as much as looked like I was going to stop, an attendant was there wanting to know if I was okay, if I needed my cramping foot rubbed, if I needed my towel brought over. Eventually, I moved house and so had to think of other ways to keep fit.

* * *

These days in Rome, exercise is a bit more common and not only for those with money or Olympic prowess. It is still looked down upon by most older Italians as a brilliant waste of time and money – they say to work hard like they had to, then you will keep your weight down. I must admit, in my neighbourhood of manual labourers and low-income earners, you hardly ever see anyone having to actually exercise to keep off kilos. However, gyms, pools, joggers and exercisers are a much more common and appreciated sight. Exercise is also much more understood as a thing foreigners do now, so these days when I go running I get less looks than I once did. This may also be because my runs end in a *cappuccino* rather than a sweaty mess like they did fifteen years ago and therefore there is less to look at, or more, depending on which way you look at it.

I start by stretching and warming up in our communal garden, which generally gets all the elderly patrons who occupy the garden seats all morning up and craning their necks to watch me. They are unabashed in their staring, even when I wave and make 'what are you looking at' gestures. Sometimes they come and ask me what I am doing and then start a conversation with me while I am trying to warm up. This occurs particularly with one elderly woman who has dementia and asks me every time she sees me if I will show her some exercises for her leg.

After warming up under the shady green trees I leave the gates of our apartment block and begin. I walk fast or leisurely, depending on how I am feeling, or sometimes break immediately into a run through the beautiful walled gardens of the public housing that makes up the centre of my suburb. I move past carefully tended flower gardens, bushes, palm trees, flowerpots and fragrant trees of jasmine and magnolia. I am alone and in heaven. There are no cars, no dogs and no people – it is too early in the day for them to be sitting around, except for the very elderly. I climb through gates hidden by wisteria, wend my way around shady paths, scale stairs in secret alleys and revel in the quiet tranquillity of it all.

Today it is hot, the beginning of the warm summer when such 'jogs' will become out of the question. But also I am not feeling so great, so I don't push myself. I burst out at the top of the hill from under some stone archways, into the piazza where again all the old men that are taking their perennial coffee turn to stare at me as one. I continue on to the park and dive again into shady coolness. As I crunch my way over small stones set along a path with young olive trees I hear a woman yelling.

'Excuse me but what kind of cleaning do you call that?' she yells. 'You've been pushing that broom around for two hours, back and forth, back and forth, on the same spot without picking up a thing. The park is in a disgusting mess, the children's playground in particular. I go to work so my taxes pay your wages, and what work are you doing for me or for my children?'

I want to go over and hug the woman. I often come to this park to exercise in the mornings. I stop and use the seats to lie down and do stomach crunches on. This is because there is so much rubbish and dog poo on the grass that I can barely walk on it, let alone use it to exercise on. I noticed the last time I was here that there was a council cleaner with a broom made of twigs – they still use them here – and that for the entire time I was in the park he swept back and forth on the same spot. I actually watched for a while, as I found it hard to believe that someone could do something so incompetently for so long.

So I was a bit relieved to find that someone who had been there a lot longer than I usually was had finally snapped and asked why he was doing this, two steps away from her and her children who were using the playground.

'Children can pick up any one of the hundreds of bits of rubbish in this park and in this area and put it in their mouths while you stand there watching and sweeping the same spot for two hours,' the woman said.

The voices escalated and got more and more insulting. The woman was incensed and losing control. All around the perimeter of the park bystanders had stopped and were listening, me included. He was rude and insulting. *What kind of a man yells at a mother with little children?* I wondered.

I see this situation from time to time in Rome. In fact, you can tell the general social climate and level of satisfaction with the political system on the basis of how often you see this. I am seeing it more and more, and so is my husband. Shortly after I witnessed this incident there were riots on the streets of the historical centre of Rome, cars set on fire and shops destroyed. What is particularly interesting about these confrontations is how it immediately captures so many bystanders who become like an audience at the Coliseum watching with bloodlust, not doing anything to get involved, but seeming to be partaking in some communal releasing of tension. The mother with young children is speaking on behalf of all of them. She is speaking on behalf of all dispossessed citizens who, on a daily basis, watch with futility their old and crumbling State mechanism, once set up to protect the weak and now mostly sheltering the lazy and protecting the cunning.

Many Italians I speak to these days are so infuriated with the way they have less social services, infrastructure and communal services than any other European country they see around them, apart from Greece, and not to mention the Anglo-Saxon countries that are held in awe for how they 'work'. 'Everything works there, nothing works here' is a constant complaint I hear. It is echoed from the queues in banks to the Law Courts, from engineers, teachers and IT professionals. The response from the State to this dissatisfaction is similar to the one I got when I once complained to a ticket inspector. I was about to get fined for not having a ticket on the train going to the airport. I had been to every single ticket machine in the station and none of them were working, and I was complaining that nothing works in Italy. 'Don't come here then,' was the response as he wrote out the fine.

This is the case for the Italian State. Italians have no option but to use it and depend on it, and generally they feel that is their right. They are not fooled by slogans such as 'it is your right to work whenever you want to, make up your own pension fund, and individually achieve'. Those are duties firmly in the hands of the State and the fact that it doesn't do them is not cause for changing it, but cause for getting infuriated with it for not doing its job.

When I tell my Italian relatives that in Australia, and in many other countries, you can be given two weeks' notice to leave a job they are horrified. 'What kind of barbaric country would allow that to happen?' they ask me. 'Just toss someone out on the street without work?' They always feel terribly sorry for me that, as a consultant, I sometimes have work contracts of only two weeks. It doesn't matter how many times I explain to them that it is the nature of my work, they are always hoping that one day I will get a job that will be permanent.

The thing that they can't conceive of with the two weeks' notice for dismissal is that it is relatively easy to get another job, that we have a fluid market where people are chopping and changing not only job but career. We also have unemployment benefits that are not based on how long you have worked for, as in Italy, and that until recently did not cut out after a certain time period. The problem with Italy is that it has the worst of both worlds. It doesn't have any aspects that promote or allow you to think and perform as an individual economically, but neither does it have a functioning State that steps in to help you.

This is why Italians stand in quiet support when one of its citizens rallies against the injustice of poor or non-existent social and client services, against which they feel powerless to change except when it is being acted out so brazenly before their very eyes. It is one of the reasons I think Italians are so patient in traffic. They are used to waiting for their State to move, what's sitting in a traffic jam for a few hours? There are none of the usual recourses for action that there would be in other democratic countries.

This makes them one of the most patient, creative and positive cultures I have ever come across. It underpins the 'might as well have a coffee and a chat/rest/cigarette' mentality that pervades everything and, of course, the 'Rome wasn't built in a day' maxim.

Below are just a few examples of what I have personally experienced as a customer dependent on Italian State services. Get any group of people together in a room in Italy – Italians or foreigners – and you will get a similar collection of stories:

a.   Being asked for my phone number from a bank teller (for his personal use) as a condition of getting my paycheque cashed.

b.   My bank giving me a chequebook that was connected

to someone else's bank account and giving this person a chequebook with my bank account attached to it. The bank not picking up on it until both customers brought it to their attention. The bank then forgot to fix it and had to be asked again.

c.   Waiting for forty minutes in a queue to see a bank teller and then when it is my turn having them tell me they are exhausted and need a coffee break, closing the teller window and leaving me standing to wait until they return.

d.   Ordering a credit card through my bank, it taking so long that they order me another one, them giving me the original which was actually in their possession the whole time but which had by now been cancelled. Using the credit card in a shop and having them call the police and cut the card up, as they are instructed to do when they receive a cancelled card. Having the bank manager say to me, 'What do you want me to do about it?'

e.   Sending three identical amounts of money from Australia to my bank account in Italy at the same time. My bank in Italy losing one of them and telling me I have to call another number in Milan to find it. Them giving me the wrong number. My bank in Australia finding it in my Italian bank, at great personal and financial cost to myself.

f.   Finding out that the most common way of getting a job in a bank is to buy one. Relatives generally get together to offer a proposal to the bank manager and then all the employees get a cut. This way, when you enter you get a cut of the proposal money of the next person who is recruited and so are less likely to whistle-blow (this practice is slowly dying out but explains a lot of the above).

g. Being given a book that is soaking wet at the post office after having ordered it from Amazon in the USA. When I complained that it was wet I was told I had to call another number and that it was nothing to do with the post office, that it had probably gotten wet in America two weeks ago.

h. Unless I send parcels by registered post (which costs a lot more) they arrive without the gifts that were in them, every time.

i. My graduation photos arriving from Australia being sent to my work address even though the address on the package was my home address (does someone at the post office know where I work?).

k. Being given a fiscal (tax file number) code without a work permit or visa. Being denied a work permit or visa. Being employed, paying tax, having a legal work contract with a State affiliate without ever having a work permit or visa.

l. Being told at the immigration office when I was applying for my residency based on marriage, that as my husband had faxed the copy of his Identity Card from Geneva (where he was working that week), it was not valid as he was not in the country and they had no proof he actually lived in Italy (even though they had a copy of his Italian State-issued Identity Card stating that he did). Being accused of coming to Italy for the purposes of prostitution and fabricating a husband by the immigration officials.

m. Being told a completely different thing one week later when I went back to the immigration office with my husband.

n. My local bus coming once every forty minutes instead of every twenty, and two of them usually arriving at the same time.

o.   Regularly having to guide bus drivers on the route through my suburb.

p.   Having my dentist tell me that it is quite common to buy a dentistry degree, having this backed up by several Italian friends. This is why I always went to the dentist back in Australia.

q.   Being offered two 'jobs' at a State institution: a very glamorous one that involved travel and sleeping with my boss, and another that required me to actually work and be responsible for the terms of my contract. Finding out that the other girls employed in this institution had mostly taken the first option and that this was common practice.

Italy is a long way off from a meritocracy. What started out as a brilliant social contract with its people to make sure that everyone was taken care of and given the means to provide an income for their families has become a system that operates on doing what you can get away with. It is highly frustrating for the majority that want to be rewarded and recognised based on what they contribute. It is also not possible for these two ways to operate together.

When my husband first came to Australia, I gave him a tour of all our beautiful beaches and ocean spots. He took in the beautifully manicured grass areas that the beaches backed on to, the fencing, the rubbish bins, the picnic areas and barbecues, and he asked, 'Who pays for all that?'

'All what?' I asked, not seeing anything myself except what I considered to be 'Australia'.

'You know, the barbecues, the plants, the tan bark and the little stones that make up the borders,' my husband said.

It was quite a lot when you looked at it.

'We do I suppose, through our taxes,' I said. 'The government gives our taxes to the States and Territories and they give them to the councils and the councils do this on our behalf.'

He turned slowly, stared at me incredulously and said, 'The government does this?' And then, 'The government actually gives you your taxes back in social services?'

Up until that point I had never, ever felt sorry for Italians, believing them to be among the most blessed races on the earth. But I could see the frustration in his eyes and wondered how he would ever be as patient again now he had seen what happens when taxes don't get siphoned into family businesses and bribes.

On that same trip, we stopped at one particularly lovely lookout post on the Great Ocean Road, a spectacular set of beaches and uninterrupted coastline. We looked down at yet another wide expanse of pristine sand and water, devoid of humans as far as the eye could see, and he asked, 'How do the police keep the people off this beach? I can't see any fencing and yet there isn't anyone down there.'

At that moment, I knew the boy whose backyard had been a metre of concrete suspended five floors up a building really had been scarred by it. I knew he needed rescuing and that Australia was the place where his inner-city soul would be let loose.

I couldn't answer the question because I couldn't believe it. It was yet another example of my 'social anthropology is the answer to the universe' belief, that culture is the software of the mind. It is the filter through which we understand all 'truth'. Meaning that if you can understand a group of people's shared beliefs and collective assumptions then you can pretty much work out how they are going to react in any given situation.

In Italy, all the beaches are owned by the State. They are rented out to businesspeople who set up fences and umbrellas, and charge others to come and sit on them. This is unless they are near sewerage drains, then it is usually free to sit on them and they are called 'free beaches'. In both cases, there are always many more people than there is adequate beach space. So not for one minute could my darling conceive that a beach might actually be 'free'; free for its citizens to use at any time, or that there might be more beach space than there are citizens.

I took his hand and led him gently down the path and onto the first free beach he had ever been to not connected with a sewerage system or under a freeway, and the first beach he had ever been to where he was alone. He stood and stood, and looked and looked for ages, the software of his mind slowing changing, new neural pathways being forged that showed other possibilities. And he liked it. He liked it a lot.

* * *

At the park in Rome, I restrain myself from joining in the communal discourse. Slowly the sound of shouting dulls, as the distance between me and the standoff between the Italian State and the enraged citizen grows. The woman looks like she is holding her own pretty well. It is difficult to rage against a nameless, faceless State bureaucracy, though the dispossessed citizen is usually spectacularly graceful at going for the jugular. It's because they know they are right.

I head for home and arrive back fresh and relaxed after my exercise.

'How was your *cappuccino*?' my husband asks me when I walk in the door.

Chapter 13

How to recognise and take advantage of
a money laundering enterprise

At the end of my street is a small circular piazza, at the intersection of five streets. On each of the angles there are historically interesting buildings, and businesses that are conducted within them. There is a chemist, a jewellery store that sells high-quality jewellery for the lowest prices in Italy, a restaurant that comes and goes, and what my husband and I call 'the dodgy *bar*'. It is down some steps, set lower than street level and set in a small paved area with a few trees. The entrance is back from the street and therefore hard to see into.

Most Italian *bars* are thronged with people day and night. We rarely see anyone come and go from this *bar* and there doesn't look like there is much in there to eat or buy. However, it is open every day and every evening most days of the year. Normally having a café at the end of your street would mean that it is the one you go to for your daily coffee. But my husband and I have never been game. It is more than mysterious that this *bar* is generally empty; it is wrong.

During my stay in Italy I have seen my fair share of dodgy businesses: hotels which are always open and ridiculously cheap, though they are located in gorgeous spots on gorgeous islands; shops that have nothing in them; *bars* that attract no custom and yet employ a dozen waitstaff; work contracts that are given and salary paid when you are not expected to do anything or even show up. At first it was a mystery to me that I mostly enjoyed and took advantage of, thinking to myself how 'un-business like' Italians were, not caring about making a profit, not smart enough to do market research. Then I realised that the only market research required in some instances was how to set up a business that wouldn't make any money, so that the money you *are* making can be registered against it.

I don't ask any questions when I see the price of the jewellery in the store at the end of our street or when the restaurant at the end of the street appears and disappears. Or why, whenever I or any of my friends have tried to go to it, we are told that it is reservation only but we are never allowed to reserve a place. When my husband and I went one night and were told we needed to reserve in advance we asked how to make a reservation, for a phone number or something (there were no identifying names on the outside of the building), the waiter just turned on his heel, walked away from us and never returned. We stood there for some time, hopeful and expectant, before my husband suggested we just go.

My girlfriend actually managed to get the number and was told she had to book five days in advance, unheard of in this neighbourhood and in most of Rome. She then called five days in advance.

'There's a woman on the phone wanting to make a booking,' she heard, 'what do I say to her?'

'Tell her she can't,' was the response.

* * *

I am quite perturbed one morning when another girlfriend and her husband, both foreign and just moved to the area, announce they have been to the *bar* at the end of our street for a coffee. In fact, I am in awe of her.

'You mean you just walked in there?' I ask. I suppose the fact that they are two innocent foreigners protected them.

'Yes, there is nothing in there,' my friend says, 'no sandwiches, no *cornetti*, no drinks, nothing. But we got a coffee from the old lady that works there. She's eighty-four and her mother is one-hundred-and-two. She has lived and worked there for fifty-two years. I got the whole family history.'

I have to go. If the two newcomers to the neighbourhood can do it, so can I. I announce to my husband that we're going to take our regular Saturday morning restorative breakfast and coffee at 'the dodgy *bar*' this weekend.

'Do we have to?' is his response.

'Don't worry, we are taking Katrin and David with us for protection. They've been and it's alright.' He is as incredulous as I am.

'What possessed them to go?' he asks.

'It was Easter Sunday and the only thing open,' I say.

'Well, if they can do it we can,' is his heroic response, reminding me of one of the many reasons I married him.

Many weekends pass, however, before we can quite give up the idea of forgoing our regular *bar*, where we know the coffee is fantastic, the pastries are guaranteed and where we can relax in the company of others doing exactly the same thing. But finally the day arrives, a Saturday where we don't have much else on and so can afford to take on a new experience that might damage us forever. Unfortunately, we are woken by a pigeon at 5.30am who has taken to using the balcony outside our bedroom window as his love nest.

He is a Casanova and coo-coos for two-and-a-half hours in spite of us banging on the window, and at one stage me throwing rocks at him with my eyes half-shut, which means the rocks just ricochet off the walls of the apartment block and probably wakes everybody else up. We are bleary-eyed and in bad humour when we meet David and Katrin at 10am at the bottom of our street, just under their new apartment opposite 'the dodgy *bar*'. We are longing for our usual *bar*, *cornetti* and coffee, and my husband is threatening to bring his own. But we have committed ourselves, and Katrin and David are even bringing along their houseguests from London.

We enter and are peered up at by the smallest, oldest wizened woman I have ever seen. She barely comes up to my shoulders and is frail and grey, with a long length of hair running down her back. Her face is lined and she has the bluest cornflower blue eyes, alert and sparkly. Oh, and no teeth. She gapes up at the six of us foreign giants entering her *bar* and for a second we hold our collective breaths, her included. Will she ask us to leave? Will she just ignore us, as has been our experience before? Why do I feel embarrassed and like we are somehow menacing her? It's probably more foreigners than she has seen in her life, definitely more strangers at one time than she is used to.

She lets out her breath, gives us a wide, confident toothless smile in which her eyes are included and asks, 'Whose family are you from?' We all smile back.

'No, you don't know our families. We live across the road and these are our houseguests.'

'Ahh, okay then,' she says. 'Well, you know I was just asking because I have lived here for fifty-two years, I'm eighty-four and my mother is one-hundred-and-two, so I know most people. I just didn't want to forget in case I had met you before.' Her answer is lucid and sprightly.

'Could we have some coffees?' Katrin ventures.

'Of course, no problems,' she says. 'I can easily do you some coffees. What would you like?'

We give our orders for *cappuccini* and short blacks and watch with trepidation as she slowly puts out six cups and saucers.

There is nothing else in the shop except the counter with the coffee machine on it. There is some milk in the fridge and a packet or two of breakfast biscuits for sale, which I suggest we buy in lieu of *cornetti*. Outside, under a few trees there is a table and some chairs set up on the concrete paving stones. It looks luxurious and quiet, a treat in this area. Half of us go outside to sit under the shade, including me as I am having trouble watching the slow and painstaking method of making coffee. The woman can barely reach the machine and it is like watching a five-year old try to make dinner. Thirty minutes later, Katrin and her houseguest come out with what was almost our order. It took her so long to froth the milk that the short blacks are cold but we are all relieved to get something, especially my husband and I after our early morning with the pigeon. We sit back and relax, fuelled by our coffees and breakfast biscuits, enjoying the ambience.

'We did it!' I exclaim to my husband. We had coffee in 'the dodgy *bar*'; we crossed the threshold, and instead of finding a couple of blokes in tight white t-shirts playing cards, we have found a little old lady, a shady spot and potentially a place to come for a summer evening beer. I am quite excited. Even so, we drop in to our usual *bar* for another fortifying coffee before heading off to the rest of our Saturday.

* * *

That evening we have a date for dinner. A very sought-after and important date. It is with Antonello and Petra, at their house. Antonello is a criminal court judge and lawyer, as well as an incredible cook. He is tall and large, smokes excessively and when he talks about food uses expressions such as 'it will make you want to turn the lights out' or 'it will extinguish all the lights'. All of his holidays centre on the meals he eats, of which he manages to fit in around eight a day. He has been a friend of my husband's since they were young students and comes from Taranto, the same town as him.

He was my chauffeur on our wedding day on account of the fact he owned a green Alfa Romeo Spider, which I wanted to be driven to my wedding in. As we were coming up to the last intersection before turning into the street that would lead to the ceremony, he announced this by giving me one last chance to back out.

'This is it Bronté,' he had said. 'I need to turn right at these next lights to take you to get married to Alfredo, but if you want I can just keep driving you straight ahead and that will be okay too, no questions asked. So one last time, are you sure you want to do this?'

To my great surprise he was serious, not out of any impropriety but as a friend wanting to check that I wasn't being pressured into this marriage and that I really did want to do it. It was a dangerous ploy, not because I didn't want to marry my husband but because I was so nervous about the ceremony that it really didn't help to give me an out at that stage.

Antonello once made me another dangerous offer that was hard to say no to, and could also have changed my life irrevocably for the worse if I had accepted. My husband and I were driving down to Taranto with him to see our families. Antonello, who always took an exceptionally high interest in all my foreign girlfriends, asked me about one of them who was just recently left by her husband. She was alone without any support in a foreign country where she didn't speak the language, didn't work or have family, with their two small children. Her husband ran off with a woman literally half his age.

As I was updating Antonello on these events, he leaned back from the front seat to look me in the eye and said quietly, 'Do you want the name of someone who could take care of him? I could find you someone who would do it for around three thousand euros.'

Wild thoughts of passing the hat around to a few other girlfriends who would gladly put in for it flashed through my head. At the same time I was weighing up the pros and cons, and vaguely wondering if I should be worried that Antonello had made such an offer. In the background, my husband was laughing loudly in a way that makes you realise they are trying to make light of a situation so you think it's a joke. I never refused a dinner invitation from Antonello after that.

This hasn't been difficult to do. As a lawyer and judge, Antonello travels a great deal. He delights in bringing back specialities that are usually too much for even him to finish off alone, so he has to invite friends. He will call up and announce that he has just been to X and bought an incredible Y, so we must come over and help him eat it. Usually my husband doesn't pay enough attention to know what it is we are actually going to eat, he just says yes, and we are never disappointed, even if we never quite understand what it is we have eaten. This time it is a typical dish from Ferrara, a beautiful medieval stone town to the north-east of Rome. The dish is called *la salama* and is a combination of minced and dried meats encased in a sausage wrapping and boiled in a saucepan of water for about eight hours. It looks like shavings of dried meat when it reaches the plate and is served over lashings of potato puree.

The serving is small and there doesn't appear to be much meat on the plates, but at the first bite I know why. It is salty and tangy and needs a lot of mashed potato with each mouthful to balance the flavour. And what flavour it is! Soon we are all sweating and fanning ourselves on this unusually hot Roman night. It is a heavy dish and one that encourages you to keep on eating it way past your capacity to do so. We wash it down with a light Lambrusco that is slightly sweet and bubbly. Just as we are letting our groaning stomachs out, the second course arrives: a smoked provolone cheese, huge and white, looking like an overgrown mozzarella dipped in dirt – the outside is brown – plus a big bowl of little mozzarellas.

Antonello explains that these are procured from a little town just out of Taranto, where they are famous for their mozzarellas. He is the only person I know who would, after driving seven hours to get to Taranto from Rome, take a forty-minute detour to pick up some cheese. But I am so glad he has. The smoked provolone has a taste I have never experienced before and it sates a part of me I never knew existed – it does 'extinguish the lights' for me. It is sweet, savoury and tangy at the same time. I need to check it against the taste of the baby mozzarellas again and again to be sure, but I am pretty convinced by the end of my third slice that this is really, really good. Now that I can't move, there is nothing to be done except to sip the cold white wine that comes from the very north of Italy.

That is, until dessert.

'I just have a little thing,' Petra says.

I know not to trust her. She brings out a homemade fruit flan, chunky and with only slightly sweet pastry, fresh pineapple, cherries and melon, supported by a layer of what the Italians call *crema della pasticceria*, 'pastry chef's cream'. It is akin to custard but much, much lighter, creamier and sweeter. It is accompanied by melon vodka, which I decline until I smell it and then capitulate.

During our dinner conversation I have picked up a tip or two, as I always do, on how Italians manage the dilemmas regarding their State services.

I am particularly intrigued with Sergio's story of the bank. Sergio is a childhood friend of my husband's and a university friend of Antonello's. When none of them want their wives to understand what they are saying, the three of them switch into dialect, the Tarantino dialect. Mirella, Sergio's wife and a Roman, is starting to get the gist of it though, so it won't be long before we have cracked it.

There was a lot of discussion in dialect a few years ago. Each of us got married within a three-year period, one after the other. I take the credit, as I gave Alfredo an ultimatum to move in with me or move on. The three men shared an apartment together and I could see it going on forever. It must have been in the air, as around that time both Sergio and Antonello got similar requests. They decided that if one of them left, the household would break up anyway so they might as well obey their better halves. It started a slew of weddings with ours, as the youngest couple in terms of time together, as the last.

Weddings mean bachelor parties, in Italy. And bachelor parties mean visiting a strip joint, a fact that neither of the two Italian wives wanted to know about, hence the discussions in dialect. I, on the other hand, could not imagine three more unlikely candidates at a strip club, so I wanted to know everything about it. As I imagined, it was a ritual that was as tired as the clubs that perpetuate them, and the three of them enjoyed the dinner together afterwards much more than the young Slavic girls gyrating in front of them. At least, that's what my husband told me.

Sergio is an economist and works for an employer association, and his wife manages a branch of an international retail business. They have been going to the same bank for many years. Like most in Rome, is it always full to the brim of people; crowds, queues, pushing and lots of waiting. Most banks have a number system. Actually, in Rome most post offices, pharmacies, delicatessens, ice-cream parlours and bread shops have a number system.

Italians are not very good at queuing. They don't stand in line like the British; they all stand next to each other in a big messy heap, vying for first place. In order to avoid the inevitable arguments, and possible generational revenge-killings, most stores use a number system. You take a number when you arrive and wait for it to show up on a screen behind the counter. This also means you can chat and look around or go out for a coffee while you are waiting, and means that the staff can take their time, chat, look around and go out for a coffee, as they are not pressured by queues of pushing.

Usually, queues are long and there are many numbers ahead of the one you first procure from the ticket machine. Waiting times of forty minutes or longer in a bank are fairly average, unless you know the security guard. All banks in Italy have a security entrance where you can only enter one at a time, through a metal-detecting machine and after close observation by a security guard who carries a gun. This is to stop the proliferation of armed holdups that occurred daily before such measures were taken and was the only disadvantage of having a bank job. Sergio told us that, as he has been going to that same branch for so many years, he has gotten to know the security guard. At various times throughout the day, the security guard will himself select tickets from the number machine and have them ready for 'preferred' customers. That way, you can enter the bank with a number that is only a few digits away from being called, instead of the eighty or ninety it usually is.

Antonello told me of a similar system at the post office. He said the trick is to look on top of the ticket machine, as people often take a number, see how far away it is and give up, leaving their ticket there. If you are lucky, you can often get a number which is only two or three away from being called. This also explained to me the mystery of why so many numbers are called out and no-one claims them. It's like bingo sometimes; the number is shown on the screen, there is a small wait while everyone holds their breath, no-one appears, we all breathe a sigh of relief as it brings our turn closer. Sometimes, five numbers can go past before someone will yell 'bingo' and hold their ticket up while they breathlessly rush to the counter. Well, they don't yell 'bingo' exactly.

I remember the first time I went into a bank in Italy. It was to cash a paycheque. Before then, I had used only ATMs for my Australian account or received cash payments for any work I did.

I approached the big glass bubble at the entrance to the bank and pushed the button to open it. Nothing happened. I did it again. At that point I could see something moving out of the corner of my eye. It was the security guard behind some heavy glass, gesticulating and pointing at something on me. I looked down and couldn't see what was wrong about my person that didn't allow me in. He started gesticulating even more wildly. What was very disconcerting was that he was gesticulating with his handgun, at me. I thought for a moment, and in the end put my hands up in the air. It was the only response I could think of and I didn't want him to get any more annoyed. At this point he rolled his eyes, put his gun away and came out of his glass cage. With a look that said 'it's people like you that give foreign blonde girls a bad name', he took the bag off my shoulder, took it towards one of the many lockers at the entrance of the bank, locked it in and gave me the key.

Again, my defence is social anthropology. Entering a bank had never before meant that I had to denude myself of any containers. My behavioural experience did not cover a country where bank holdups were a daily activity, not since Ned Kelly anyway.

After locking my bag up and pushing a button, I stood in the glass chamber for half a minute as it sealed me in properly before opening up to let me enter the bank. Thoughts of, *I hope there isn't a fire and I hope I remember which locker my bag is in*, completely unsettled my first banking experience and made me one of the first people in Italy to sign up for internet banking.

* * *

Since conquering 'the dodgy *bar*', which still retains its name, I feel completely at ease in visiting it by myself as part of my morning exercise routine. I stop in first thing on Monday morning after my 'run'.

The proprietor is asleep in her chair in the middle of the room.

There is no-one else around. Maybe I'm not so comfortable, I decide, as I am half tempted to back slowly out, just in case she is dead. Before I can think too much about it, I hear myself say '*Buongiorno!*' loudly. No response. I start to back out, then try once more: '*Buongiorno!*' The cornflowers open and her whole face comes alive. There is no grogginess or dazed expression, but an instant consciousness that belies her eighty-odd years.

'Are you the one whose mother is from Bolseno?' she asks me.

'No, that's not me,' I reply. 'I was here on Saturday with a group of friends. I live here.'

'Well, it's just that I have been here for fifty years and I know so many people so I wondered if I knew you as well. I'm eighty-four and my mother is one-hundred-and-two."

'I was one of the people here on Saturday and I live here,' I repeat.

'I know, I know, I remember you were here on Saturday,' she says. 'What can I get you?'

I ask for a *cappuccino* and wait as she prepares it. It is still painful to watch and I have to get the milk from the fridge myself, but in the end she hands me over a pretty good flat white. I sip in silence on the patio at the front of the *bar*, proud that I have conquered my fears regarding it and enjoying the fact that it is a silent place to take a coffee, a rarity in these parts.

I take the one euro coin out of my running shoe and go in to pay.

'It's 1.20,' she says.

It's the most expensive coffee in the whole suburb. I am mortified that I don't have enough. I offer to bring the rest later and explain again that I live around the corner.

'That's okay,' she tells me, 'but there isn't any need to bring it back straight away. That would be tiring, even though you are young. You can bring it back when you are next passing.'

She adds that it wouldn't be tiring for her, even though she is eighty.

The next day at the end of my exercise, I decide to give myself a more conventional *cappuccino* reward and head to another *bar*. As I am walking past the entrance to 'the dodgy *bar*', three tall men in suits and a woman come striding out. I feel silly that it has been such a big deal for me to go in, as it obviously isn't for others. They are carrying official documents and I am curious as to what they are doing, so I decide the logical thing to do is follow them.

I should explain at this point that it is rather easy to follow someone in Italy. Mostly, you are always following someone anyway. The sidewalks are narrow or non-existent and are always crowded. So it is not too difficult or obvious that I am doing it, when suddenly the woman stops in front of me, turns around, and an inch from my nose in a desperate voice says, 'Do you know where the closest *bar* is?'

I answer directly and politely, explaining that I too am going to the one I point out directions for. But I am intrigued.

'Didn't you just go into a *bar*?' I ask innocently.

'Yes, and we couldn't get out of there fast enough,' answers one of the suits. 'Can that old woman really make coffee, do you think?'

Chapter 14

My perfect Italian weekend

My perfect Italian weekend begins on Friday night. We are invited to our neighbour's for homemade pizza. Francesca and Rita are coming too, driving up from their new home in Anzio. Silvio and Loretta live just one floor down from us. Their son Massimo grew up with Rita, so they have known each other all their lives. Silvio was the man who cleared the leaves from the drain on the apartment block roof and stopped the flooding in our apartment the night we met Francesca and Rita. He also saved us another time, when our key got stuck in the lock and we couldn't enter the apartment, leaving us and our guests from Australia stranded. As he was recently retired as a handyman he said he enjoyed the regular challenge.

Silvio grew up in one of the beautiful old houses built by the Roman council as public housing. They were nine people in a two-room, semidetached house a few minutes' walk from where we all live now. He is a jovial, grey-bearded man who is kind and talkative. His wife is younger and still works cleaning houses for private customers. She is sprightly, with red hair and a kind, earnest face, like Silvio's.

The apartments in our current block are large, even by modern Roman standards, with plenty of balcony space. Silvio recounts to us his wonder when he first moved into one of those with his wife. He couldn't believe the amount of space. They had one child, in the Italian post-war tradition, and have never been tempted to alter that number. I completely understand why. His only son is about to begin his apprenticeship, Silvio is newly retired and is fixing up a Harley Davidson motorbike piece by piece in a garage he has hired a few streets away. He says his life has never been better. So good, in fact, that he has taken up smoking again.

Massimo has just returned from Ireland and a three-month stint learning English, while trying his luck in the job market over there. He dropped out of university here in Rome, an engineering degree, much to the disappointment of his parents.

'Speak to him in English,' Silvio pleads with me, 'so at least I can see where all my hard-earned money went.'

Massimo wants to be a carpenter and has found an apprenticeship. He is tall, with long, wavy red hair like his mother, and with dark Italian eyes. I can imagine him being a big hit with the women in Ireland. He confirms this with a wry smile when I tease him, in English so his parents don't understand. Massimo is kind, mature and gets on well with his parents, telling his dad to stop dominating the conversation, leaning over his mother's chair to hug her – he has been home for only a few days – and making the coffee for everyone at the end of the meal. He neither smokes nor drinks.

We enter their flat at 8pm. I am usually rather tired on a Friday night and so am relieved that I can go out and have company, firstly while wearing more or less my pyjamas, secondly it only taking me two seconds to get there and get home again.

The table is already laden with pizzas. There are about fifteen different types; we are eight people in total. Loretta is just tending the last of them as she admonishes us to sit down and begin eating. Smoking and drinking wine has been happening for about an hour. It is the first time I have been invited inside to eat with anyone from our apartment block, besides Francesca and Rita, and it is a big honour and, as usual, an eye-opening experience.

During dinner conversation I realise more and more that our apartment block is like a warren or beehive, consisting of people who have known each other more or less their whole lives and who are connected by the fact that they have lived next door to each other, on top of each other, or under each other for more years than I have been alive. It is one big seething family, complete with disputes, sex and other scandals, broken alliances, friendships since childhood, jokes, dependencies, history and everybody knowing everybody else's business. I realise I have been living in ignorance all these years, smugly thinking that I am an island, living just in the same vicinity as these people but not being known by them.

I hear how Silvio and his wife had to bribe the couple downstairs to be allowed to stay in this flat, as it was to be given to someone else by the administrator of the apartment block. The respectable old lady and her mother who I see go out each day in their hats together, to shop and walk the neighbourhood, were the ones who coolly accepted a huge bribe to not call the police on Silvio and his wife. Silvio jokes that Massimo slept in his pram by the door for the first few years of his life, as they had to be ready to leave at a moment's notice in case she ever changed her mind.

I listen to them make fun of the elderly man who is almost deaf and blind – and who I will later learn was tortured by the Nazis – as although he lives alone, twice a day can be seen walking along the street with his shopping trolley.

'What is in that shopping trolley? I want to know,' says Silvio. 'He must have enough food in his apartment to last for years. If there is ever a disaster and we can't get out to get food, I know where I'm going to go to get my supplies.'

They move on to another neighbour, Marianna, the one Alfredo and I call 'customs', who is described as having a heart of gold. She has a little dog that she takes for a walk twice a day and never lets out of her sight. We all know the dog's name because she calls it every two minutes. It went missing last Saturday and she was distraught, calling her over and over again until the whole apartment block knew she was missing. She was found later, safe and sound, after having found a spot under the building that was cool, dark and quiet. We all knowingly look at one another and Silvio voices what we all feel.

'I am sure the dog wasn't lost,' he says. 'She probably just wanted to have a few hours of peace away from Marianna.'

We all roar with laughter, our full bellies reverberating with the pizza, wine and tiramisu ice-cream we have just eaten.

Loretta had made an enormous amount of pizza with a variety of toppings. They all had a light and thin crust, some crunchy, some soft, depending on the amount of yeast she had put in them or the amount of time in the oven. She had some staple Roman-style toppings, such as potato with mozzarella and sausage, or tomato paste with mozzarella and eggplant, as well as some of her own making. There was one with almonds, radicchio and mozzarella, and one with asparagus, mushroom and mozzarella. There were the cold pizzas of tuna, fresh mozzarella, and tomato, and there was salami, *rughetta* and fresh tomato. There was also the soft hot pizza of roasted capsicum and melted mozzarella. Every time Loretta sat down, it seemed there was another ping from the oven, and yet another pizza appeared.

Italians love their pizza. Friday night pizza and beer is a staple and I am excited I am getting the home-cooked version, complete with storytelling by Silvio, smoking at the dinner table and a chance to see an Italian family in action. Being invited to someone's house is usually reserved just for family and close friends, and I feel privileged we have broken through the barrier. It is mostly because of our friendship with Francesca and Rita, who were considered social royalty in our apartment block due to Patricia's pedigree of having arrived here when she was four years old. Any friends of theirs have an immediate acceptance and entrée into the whole apartment block.

I can ask Francesca anything about any of the apartments in our block. What they look like, where their washing machines are (no Italian apartments actually have laundries, and washing machines are usually in kitchens or bathrooms) and if they have a handheld shower or one attached to the wall. She will know, just as she knows the precise date of who moved in and when, what their parents did and what their children are doing now.

Tonight I learn from Loretta the story of the woman who owns 'the dodgy *bar*'. She has a daughter, a bit younger than me, who was beautiful and who was intended to help her mother in the *bar* and would by now be running it. About a decade ago, something started to go wrong with her. Her personality changed, her looks changed and some kind of undiagnosed mental illness took her over. She now sits most days in a catatonic state, grossly overweight and hideous to look at, at the back of the *bar*. No-one knows what is wrong or how to fix it. Hence her mother, at eighty, is still running the café.

We discuss the works going on in Francesca's old apartment. They seem to be taking forever. I feel sorry for the new owner, who I have seen a few times waiting for the lift. He was already going to find it hard to fit in after having kicked Francesca and Rita out (it was not exactly him, as he just bought the apartment from their landlord, but this was a mere technicality in the face of great emotion), let alone disrupting all the inhabitants of the apartment block for months due to the noise and dirt of the building works. Gianni had met him in the lift some months ago and had harangued him all the way to the fifth floor.

'What are you doing up there, building the Coliseum?' Gianni had said to him.

Loretta has her feet up on the couch as soon as she has served the ice-cream, slippers on, cigarette in hand and apron still tied on. As I sit in familial comfort with my neighbours, I realise how privileged I am. Loretta is paying me a compliment by not treating me as a guest and not keeping everything formal, like a member of her family. I wonder yet again what it must be like living in what I now realise is actually more like a dormitory or fraternity house, living so closely with the same people for so many years. I imagine it provides a sense of continuity and safety that I have never had in my life.

With this incredible freedom I have courtesy of my education, lack of family ties, statelessness and twenty-first century outlook, comes a loss of the other. Being held in place by lack of opportunity, jobs and education, a close family, strong traditions and cultural identity provides everyone here with a place, a sense of being known and a clearly defined role in life. These intangibles are what help most Italians I know to weather incredible storms, defeats and uncertainties and still come up smiling a *dolce vita* smile. Maybe that's what the Mona Lisa was smiling about after all.

* * *

On the Saturday of my perfect Italian weekend I go shopping! I have, of course, finished The Changeover, *Il Cambiamento*, and so now must do 'the shop', stocking up on items for this years' summer and spring seasons.

Shopping in Rome is presumed to be, by most people, one of life's better experiences. I have never found it so. In fact, it is only when I literally have nothing to wear that I finally hit the shops. I usually have to psych myself up for at least a week beforehand, then reward and bribe myself with promises of treats, and of not having to do it again for ages. Afterwards, I often need to lie down in a dark room and have my husband hold me.

In Australia, shopping is a fairly independent and relatively private thing. Not so in Rome. In most shops here you are greeted the minute you walk in the door and then followed about by someone who is attached to your shoulder. As a foreigner, they are used to us rummaging around on our own, but after you are asked if there is anything they can help you with and you say no, they continue to shadow you and watch your every move, while at the same time eying your size and comparing it to whatever you are looking at. Often I will get, 'Would you like to look at that in your size, *signora*?' as a big, bold hint that I have no idea what I am doing if I think the garment I am holding is going to fit me.

The usual shopping experience for an Italian is to be greeted at the door by someone who asks you what you are looking for, and who then proceeds to show you all the garments they have which equal that description in your size. It is not so usual to browse unaided, although this is more commonly accepted than it was when I first arrived in Rome. Many years ago, if you touched the merchandise you bought it. Some shops still operate that way, not because they are expensive garments but because they are boutiques run the old-fashioned way. If you help yourself in these shops you will be followed along huffily by a shop assistant, who folds everything and puts it back the minute you have finished looking at it. Still, things have moved along from the day I went to buy my first bra in Italy and the shop assistant, a woman, simply cupped my breasts in her hands without saying anything, felt them for a few minutes, and then turned on her heel to get me what they had in my cup size.

An Italian's relationship with their clothing is important, and therefore everything must fit and look perfect.

'See how it bunches over the shoulders? This is not right for you, *signora*,' I get told in relation to a shirt that looks like every shirt I have worn all my life.

It was not until I came to Italy that I realised certain cuts are for women with busts, such as myself, and certain cuts are not. There is a distinct lack of judgement in this. The comments are not about thinness or fitting into the clothes, they are about you as an individual and finding what make, style and designer will match you. This is, I am sure, someone else's idea of heaven. For me, it is all too up close and personal, and I don't want a stranger knowing more about why my butt looks good in a skirt than I do.

I have to know what I am looking for, fend off shop assistants when I don't want them, stop myself squirming with embarrassment when I do need them, have the courage to say I don't want something even when I have tried it on, look at my body a zillion times in a myriad of mirrors, make split-second decisions so that the entire shop is not pulled apart on my behalf, and not mind that my size is usually reserved for a very overweight, elderly *signora*. As an Anglo-Saxon I am by definition bigger, taller and rounder than most Italian women, who can be described as 'bird-like' and for whom the word cellulite is a strange Anglo-Saxon word, probably meaning a low-calorie mobile phone.

All this is particularly important today, as I have the worst summer item of all on my shopping list – bikinis. One may be tempted to ask why I am even bothering with the torture of buying bikinis at this stage in life – post-husband, post-thirty – however, I feel that if I ever succumbed to buying a one-piece, that would be the end of any effort on my part to keep trim for summer knowing that I could hide it, as I do all winter long. As well as that, a vast number of elderly Italian *singore* wear bikinis, and while I am under sixty I reserve the right to wear one. Over the years I have been exposed to a life-changing amount of sagging brown stomachs, childbirth scars and stretch marks, paraded up and down the beach in front of me. I've seen floppy brown skin that clings to the bellybutton in a parody of what it once was, leathery textures and ample bulges. Italian women don't seem to think that being perfect is the only way to be beautiful and I celebrate that for all it is worth, which means buying a bikini instead of the one-piece I know all my Anglo-Saxon peers are by now wearing.

I am greeted upon entering the store and, as I know what I need, I let go and allow the assistant to offer me a huge selection of bikinis. To their credit, I often find that Italian shop assistants can choose well for me. When I am in a relaxed mood I sometimes allow this, and am amazed at the stunning clothes I walk out with that I would not have chosen for myself. It is this loss of control though, this pushing to new frontiers, that I often find stressful. 'Just let me buy the same thing I bought last year,' I want to say. I am, however, often complimented on my 'fashion sense' by my other foreigner friends, and when I tell them it is because I allowed a shop assistant to essentially dress me, they look at me in awe.

The shop assistant, *la commessa*, chooses a colour and style of bikini that is so not me. Until I try it on, that is, and then it is the new me. I buy four more pairs that I choose myself out of the hundreds she shows me, but it is this first pair, the one she picked off the rack immediately without any input from me, that becomes my favourite and causes my husband to ogle me every time I wear it.

As much as I complain, I do find it useful that when I need to replace my wardrobe, it is a fairly efficient process. I walk around the shop with my assistant attached to my shoulder, I point out what I want and then retire to the changing room. I can stay there for hours while the garments are brought to me, all in my size. If they don't fit then alternative sizes or styles are brought to me, without me ever having to get dressed and exit the changing room. Hems are taken up temporarily, sleeves are pinned, matching blouses and tops are brought for all my suits and trousers, and coffee offered. In short, I am truly served.

The shop assistants at the one or two shops I go to regularly always wave me off like best friends they see once a year. When I turn up the next year they know the drill: this woman has nothing left in her wardrobe and she needs the lot. Put the coffee on.

Although the bikini shopping experience goes remarkably well, the subsequent one does not. It is a new dress shop I have not been to before. I try on five dresses I have admired in the window for some time now. Not one of them fits me or would look any good even if they did fit me. Worst of all is that it is lunchtime and no-one else is in the shop, so I have not one, but three assistants fussing and adjusting and exclaiming over me.

I arrive home, sweating and concentrating on exhaling.

'How did it go?' my husband asks me.

'I need to go into the bedroom and for you to hold me,' I reply, dumping shopping bags and not even stopping for our customary kiss. He knows it is bad.

I collapse on the bed on my stomach in the position of a teenager having a tantrum. He collapses on top of me. The weight of his body on my back, pushing me down into the mattress, seems to squash all the bad feelings out of me and I giggle.

'There,' he says, gently pulling me over and pushing a pillow under my head. 'It can't be that bad. What happened?'

I begin to explain and he starts laughing, which he immediately reigns in and counters with male logic about bad mirrors, unconditional love and the importance of self-acceptance until I tell him to stop. He prescribes a long bath, a siesta and takeaway Chinese, which he offers to go and get.

* * *

On Sunday morning I go for a run. It is really just an excuse to smell the flowers, though. I am accompanied almost the entire way by a heady perfume of jasmine, lavender, magnolia and rose. I breathe deeply and languidly, wondering at my good fortune to have found a place to live in where I can exercise in perfumed corridors.

Spring has finished and the flora is giving itself over to full-bodied summer. The heavy, heady scents are attesting to the fact that the sun is becoming stronger each day, beating down on the blossoms and causing their fragrance to pulsate in protest. They will not be able to keep this up much longer. Soon they will wither and dry out on their vines, leaving only the hardy green foliage to survive the summer sun.

In the morning air the blossoms are lying fully-flowered and sprawled open, laid bare in the sunshine, like whores after a hard night's work. They are still luscious, but tired, having lost their freshness. I pass a fence full-blown with jasmine, doubling the fence in width. The vine undulates outwards and causes me to change my gait so I avoid running into it. Right next to it is an early summer version of another flower that is round and bright, deep red. I feel like I have run into a bowl of strawberries and cream and it stops me in my tracks. Even flowers remind me of food in this country.

I run to the park and marvel at the stone walls lined with deep purple bougainvillea. I trace the round path laced with bushes of lavender as high as I am, and can't resist taking a few stalks to tuck into my cleavage. I run to the top of a small path that I know will lead me to some foundations of a Roman building, two kilometres outside of the ancient walls of Rome. Even in the suburbs we have our own Roman ruins. I pace back down the path a different way and am assaulted by magnolia. It is the cleverest flower I know because it grows underneath the leaf, so it is only by looking up that you can see it. It is therefore dedicated entirely to the user, those who are underneath the tree enjoying its prolific shade.

I continue up the shady paths to the top of the park and exit, pausing a few moments in the shade of a large fig which I am monitoring weekly for signs of its luscious fruit, which I will put in my tucker bag and run off with in the Australian tradition. I continue on along the quiet road laced with orange and red blossoms, the colours of the Roman football team. In this neighbourhood, where team emblems and murals of the faces of the footballers are painted on the walls of houses, I am quite sure the choice of blossom is premeditated.

I reach another small piazza, with a flowing fountain and bathing pigeons. On one side I have a view over the whole suburb, and the other contains a large ancient building complete with a loggia and fake medieval turrets. In the shade of huge pines and with the tinkle of the fountain, I lie down on a marble bench and do some exercises and stretching. Large cornices and tops of marble columns litter the ground around me, as do beer cans, cigarette butts, rubbish and dog poo – a typical inner-city Roman scene. It is peaceful and tranquil, though. Not a soul is around so I have the cool breeze, the sound of the fountain, the tall trees waving above me and the open space to share with only the pigeons.

Crossing back through the piazza, I enter into a small arched tunnel which forms part of the neo-medieval building. To one side is a popular traditional Roman restaurant. In the cool of the morning, an elderly man is shelling peas in the shade, preparing for lunch. *How timeless*, I think.

'What the fuck are you doing in there? Have you fucked everything up again?' the elderly man says in ancient Roman dialect, not the words I expected out of his mouth. A young man comes running out, pleading excuses and carrying something in his hands.

I am stopped in my tracks yet again by some huge pink flowers that look like upside down horns. Tumbling down the side of a fence, the flowers are yellow on the inside and as long as my forearm. How can I keep up a level of cardio when there is so much to look at? I stop to admire them and am tooted at for getting in the way of a car attempting to pull out.

* * *

Later that evening, my husband and I go for a walk and dinner in the centre of Rome, the ancient and medieval part of the city where you can wander down streets which have not changed their aspect since the 1600s. The large cobblestones are uneven and have ankle-turning gaps in them. Even so, it is hard to keep my eyes on the ground when above me there are wooden eaves, painted medieval decorations on the outside of walls, picturesque columns and window frames, and glimpses into upstairs apartments and their frescoed ceilings or raftered roofs.

I love this part of town. Its streets were made for carriages and can barely accommodate a car. There are no sidewalks and often the corners of buildings are scraped off from years of carriage wheels shaving off their sharp corners. The houses are joined together and form a snaking corridor of stone, broken only by glimpses into central stone-covered courtyards where the main doors are left ajar. Traditionally, these buildings were for one or two families. Fortress-like, there are few openings onto the street except for a large, usually double, door to let in carriages, and now cars. The short, covered driveways open out into large courtyards, which the buildings open onto with a proliferation of doors, windows, staircases and balconies. This was the private world of medieval and Renaissance Rome. The streets were usually full of sewerage, stagnant mosquito-breeding water and food scraps. To avoid the smell and the disease, the buildings did not open onto the streets but onto these large private courtyards, complete with fountains and shady nooks.

We are on our way to a well-known restaurant that has been here for decades. It sits on one of the only piazzas in this quarter, and spills out into the small space of the piazza, whose walls are covered in painted frescoes.

We reach the piazza and I linger around a large plastic bowl almost big enough to be a small swimming pool, at hip height and filled with ice and champagne bottles. The glasses are casually slung around the sides and I am tempted to pour myself one as I wait, confident that they are for those who are waiting to hear if they have a table, as well as those who are actually waiting for a table. We are not in luck and I am not surprised. Even though the restaurant can seat hundreds, it is very popular and Sunday evening is as favoured for eating out to Romans as Saturday night is.

We head to a simpler establishment, also set up outside, but unfortunately on the type of cobbled piazza that is used as a car park and around which a small electric bus has to navigate every twenty minutes. We are residents and so are careful not to choose the table on the outer edge of the set, and we are entertained all evening by the couples who sit there and are faced with the front of a bus, a hair's-breadth from their spaghetti plate, every twenty minutes. Most shriek with laughter but then can be seen nervously pulling their seats in a little and hurriedly finishing their dishes before the next twenty minutes are up.

Even though this establishment is not in the guidebooks and is situated on the edge of a car park, the food is excellent, the service professional and, like many good Roman restaurants, you can order off the menu. We order grilled calamari and it comes soft and salty, laced with warm olive oil, its mild seafood flavour excellently balanced with that of the hot grill it has been cooked on. We sip a glass of cold white wine and watch the air get bluer and then tinged with mauve, a sign that even warmer evenings are coming. We sip in quiet, dark, peaceful silence in the centre of a medieval neighbourhood, and I am sure that I have had the perfect Italian weekend.

Chapter 15

Il primo bagno, the first swim of the season

Il primo bagno is a big thing in Italy. Everyone looks forward to it. Some lucky Italians can do it in April or May; some have to wait until July or even August. Romans can do it from June onwards. But Italians have rules about this, too, and most of them can't do it until after June 21.

Il primo bagno is the first time you bathe in the sea for that year and heralds the beginning of summer. It is looked forward to and hailed when it first occurs. It can, of course, occur as soon as the weather is warm enough which, depending on where you are in Italy, can be as early as April. However, it isn't as simple as that. One year I went to a seaside town in the south of Italy on a hot early June day. Spread out before me was the most gorgeous aqua blue water I had seen in a long time, lapping against a pristine and empty beach.

'Why isn't there anyone on the beach?' I asked my host.

He looked at me incredulously and said, 'We don't swim in early June!'

It was explained to me that summer begins on June 21. Incidentally, all the seasons start in Italy on the twenty-first day of the month, not at the beginning like in Britain or Australia, or anywhere else actually. It was explained to me that no matter what the temperature, folk only go swimming after that date, and therefore only in summer. Swimming is a summertime activity and to do it at other times is seen as risky. You may catch a cold and die or be seen as someone who does not take social traditions seriously, much like a foreigner. Spring is not the season for swimming; it's the season for walking and being in the countryside. In the same way that food cannot be eaten all year round, neither can activities be done. No-one would think of having a *pappardelle al cinghiale* in summer or eating a *caprese* salad in winter. It would be like eating pancakes with maple syrup for dinner or carrot soup for breakfast. It's just not done and would turn your stomach to even think about it.

So it is with much excitement that my husband and I set off for the day of our *primo bagno*, safe in the knowledge that it is July 5. But first we must stop at our local *bar* for our regular Saturday morning breakfast of coffee and *cornetti*.

It is crowded and chaotic, and that is just on the street outside. Most *bars* in Italy don't have anywhere to sit. Coffee and breakfast, or lunch, is taken standing up at the counter. However, many of them in the summer manage to put a few chairs and tables outside on the sidewalk to take your food out to. It is rare for a local *bar* to have table service. Our *bar* is like a meeting point of extended families in Garbatella, where mostly everyone is related anyway. People sit for hours – the elderly, babies, children, young couples – some smoking, drinking coffee, shouting and talking, hailing friends and relatives as they come along the street. For me, deep in my Saturday morning reverie of just coming out of a heavy work week, I find it stimulating and grating at the same time.

It jolts me out of my weekday mentality of heavy analysis and solving the problems of the world in the United Nations agencies in which I consult. It reminds me that I live in Italy, not a no-man's-land of every nation, where English and French are mostly spoken. And it reminds me that new babies, chores, illnesses and what people will have for lunch is really the stuff of life. These are the topics of conversation I hear shouted around me. And I do mean shouted. Sometimes my husband and I don't bother speaking, as it's just too hard to be heard above the din. We sip, bite, dip and revive slowly, letting the coffee run through our veins and our pastries full of custard or jam – or on really bad days, chocolate – tingle our tastebuds and bring us slowly back to life.

It is a point of pride for every Italian *barista* to know their clientele and how they prefer their coffee. This way, customers can just turn up, stand at the bar and the *barista* will place in front of them their particular type of coffee without a word having to pass between them. I am odd, not only because I am foreign and choose to live here when most of them would beg, borrow or steal to be allowed to live in Australia, but also because, unlike most Italians, I haven't chosen my type of coffee at birth and never deviated. Some days I feel like a *cappuccino*, some days I feel like an *Americano* (a long black macchiato with a little bit of cold milk on the side), some days I feel like a *cappuccino scouro* (with not much milk) and some days just a *spremuta* (freshly squeezed orange juice). It is a source of continual annoyance that they have to ask me my order every time, but I can't help it. I'm from 'the New World', as they put it, and I change with the wind.

I have been having a *cappuccino scouro* for some weeks now as it's getting too hot to have all that milk, so the *barista* tentatively suggests this as he sees me standing at the *bar*. He smiles when I nod. Ahh, he has it right today.

Today we are heading for Sperlonga. For our *primo bagno* we had to choose a special place, a place worthy of the first dip of the season. Sperlonga is a seaside holiday town about two-and-a-half hours out of Rome heading south. It has an ancient walled town on its cliff top, which is completely white and reminiscent of the walls in cities that the Moors built in Spain. It is beautiful, and sits above some clear blue water and a sandy coastline that runs for several kilometres. You don't have to go quite this far to find nice beaches, but the further south of Rome you go, the better they get. This one has the added advantage of having natural freshwater springs that bubble up from the seabed, sending ice-cold drafts up your legs as you are swimming. At the bottom of the cliffs, the springs are held in small concrete pools that were once used for washing clothes by the townsfolk. The pools are freezing and hard to immerse yourself in, but lovely as a quick dip.

In Roman times, the Spartans – Roman slaves turned revolutionaries – built a town here, and the Emperor Tiberius had his summer palace here, along with other Roman nobility. In the 1500s, the town was ransacked and destroyed by Redbeard, the dreaded pirate. A tower dating back to Roman times also stands on the promontory. Its origins date back further though, as it was originally part of a chain of coastal lookouts intended to spot raiding Saracens, the Arabic version of pirates. The danger from these ancient Arab raiders is evident in the city build, requiring so much protection that it sits miles above on the cliff and is only entered by a small archway that can be easily sealed off.

As the modern city of Sperlonga no longer fears marauding pirate raids, the shoreline is full of *stabilamenti*, privately-run beach clubs which you pay to enter. For fifteen euro you get the use of an umbrella, two sunlounges, toilets, changing sheds and the opportunity to pay for hot or cold showers. They all have their own *bars* as well. The beach is cheek by jowl with sunbeds and umbrellas. Along the main strip, hotels and restaurants spill out onto the sidewalks and holidaymaker's throng back and forth.

The old part of town is accessed by a steep path set into the cliff. About halfway up you enter through an archway, and from there staircases take you up and around into the town, along five different pathways. Most of the staircases are roofed over with stone, keeping them dark and cool, and making them into tunnels. Every few paces, small doors open out and crevices reveal further passages that lead to other doors and houses. It is like a town built for hobbits, with small wooden doors and geranium-filled windows. These features poke out of the walls as you wend and wind up the small staircases that are steep and never-ending. High stone whitewashed walls surround you on either side as you climb, festooned with balconies and washing, and peering eyes that calmly consider the wheezing, panting tourists that make the climb every evening.

You can spend hours darting up stairways, tunnels and passageways, to wonder at how many shapes a house can come in, and how a living space can be carved out of the rock and moulded around the natural shape of a cliff. There are many small piazzas crammed with bougainvillea, and restaurants that proclaim themselves simply by a few chairs and tables under some shade in front of a stone entrance that waiters run in and out of.

Artisans sell their wares from tiny stone shops, anything from handmade leather bags to hand-embroidered dresses and beachwear. Tourist shops sell trinkets, some serious artists sell their paintings, and everywhere there is ice-cream and food to be had. No views though. This is a serious walled town. The whole point of building the wall was so that there was no access to the town, and there are therefore no windows to look out from. From the moment you enter under the arch halfway up the cliff, the sea is no longer visible until you walk out of the town on the other side of the central piazza, where there is now a large car park and bus stop, but where there was once just the other side of a steep mountain.

From the central piazza, locals and tourists alike gaze down at the sea and the sand from the top of the sheer cliff. The water is a lovely green colour – clean, clear and shallow. You could swim for kilometres in a straight line here.

* * *

As soon as we are driving out of Rome I start thinking about *mozzarella di bufala*. This cheese may look the same as a normal mozzarella, but it's made from buffalo milk rather than cow's milk. *Mozzarella di bufala* should always be eaten as fresh as possible, as it quickly loses its taste and texture. A fresh one has a soft springy texture, like you are biting into a cream puff, except it springs softly back, ready for you to take the next bite. It is surprising that the taste is so delicate – unique and hard to describe. It isn't a sweet taste, but it's creamy and filling. Suffice to say that I hear goat bells on distant rocky cliffs in the Greek Islands whenever I taste a really good *mozzarella di bufala*. It's one of the first things you should taste when you come to Italy – and you may end up staying here seventeen years if you do.

Sperlonga is famous for its local production of *mozzarella di bufala*. Shortly before you reach the town on the motorway, advertisements for this cheese begin. I only have to look at parched fields with big rolls of wheat standing in them, the typical countryside that surrounds Sperlonga, to feel my mouth watering. For five days a week I live in a concrete city where I can't see the horizon or feel the earth under my feet, and where the only animals are dogs, cats and mosquitos. It is such a treat to see a field, and it tells me loud and clear that I am out of Rome. I can see for miles and miles. I can see green mountains and baked brown fields, so I know that I am:

a.   not at work

b.   out of Rome

c.   it is therefore the weekend

A Roman summer, like a Roman winter or spring, has its own menu. There are foods that are only eaten and available in the summer and I look forward to them each year, as I do to each season's goodies. The advantage of living in a country where food is only eaten seasonally is that there is always something to look forward to. You greet each season and its menu like a long-lost friend. You know that you will be able to briefly enjoy its company and personality, and that it will soon move on, often before you tire of it, and leave in its place another long-lost friend.

Whether you are ready or not, there is continual change. The change of seasons forces sometimes drastic changes in habits, activities, work, sleep, clothing, food and lifestyle on everyone. The changes force you to participate differently, push you forward whether you are well or sick, happy or sad, and they provide a continuance to life that supports faith and hope in it. It also binds the country together; no matter what else is happening to you, you are eating the same food at the same time as everyone else, preparing for the same rituals, sharing in them and their aftermath. You are all engaging in the same activities at the same time, and it fosters community and closeness.

Maybe this is one of the reasons Italians seem to have no trouble striking up conversations with perfect strangers; there are a myriad of topics they have in common. They are all experiencing the same weather (a big favourite for conversation), they are all going to the beach on the weekends, they are all getting ready for the festival of *Ferragosto* or recovering from *Pasqua*, and they are eating strawberries or fish or mozzarella at the same time, often on the same day.

In August and July, sleep becomes a big topic of conversation. As it gets hotter and hotter, sleep becomes less and less possible. Many Italians seem to give up on it completely, preferring to spend their evenings outside in the piazzas smoking, drinking coffee and talking about how hot it is. This also makes it difficult for those who are attempting to sleep, as the necessary open windows can't screen out any of the local noise. People are up and around a lot later in the day, work changes pace and slows down, everyone is tired and everyone talks about it. I'm usually so tired in August that I give up my *straniera* (foreigner) habit of not talking to strangers and just join in, mostly because I am so sleep-deprived that I am generally babbling away anyway, and others seem to join in and answer me. I'm usually in such a stupor by mid-August that I can barely remember where I am, let alone whether I know the person I am speaking to or not.

The area around Sperlonga was once a big farming area and still retains some of its rural characteristics. There are tractors in fields, greenhouses chock-full of tomatoes, as well as fallow fields that lie on either side of the road. There are large cliffs in the distance that rise straight up from a flat plain, and small canals filled with pleasure boats. Sperlonga and other hilltop seaside towns come after this, along the coast from Rome to Naples. There is a holiday feel about this place and many people come here for the weekend or whole months during the summer. Although it is still a functioning town in the winter, the population quadruples in the summer months, as all the holiday apartments are rented out or occupied by their owners

Today it isn't very crowded, so we can set up our umbrella close to the water. One thing I find incredible about Italian beach culture is that it is common practice on a 'free beach' to set up an umbrella, then go away and leave it as long as you want, effectively reserving your place on the sand. Spots close to the water are usually filled with closed umbrellas that are there all day from early morning, and not used until the evening when many Italians choose to swim. At least we have more space around us than those next door at the *stabilamenti*, the beach clubs, who are packed together like rolls of plasticine in a box, one sunlounge after another with barely room to swing their legs off the side without bumping their neighbour.

The water is icy cold and clean, and we swim to our heart's content before delving into our mozzarella and tomato *panini*, followed by fresh apricots. And then it is the precious Italian siesta hour, which is taken even at the beach. It is the best time to take a nap. From 2pm onwards, all the children are pulled under the shade of the umbrellas and little sand beds are made for them with towels and pillows. Parents snuggle up next to their young ones, teenagers sleep on their backs under the sun, the elderly nod off in shaded chairs and all is quiet on the beach. It is a marvellous time. The shouts, music and noise of balls being kicked are all stopped and you hear only the waves, as all around you the inhabitants of the beach fall asleep. It's like a scene out of *Sleeping Beauty*, as one by one they lie down and nod off. As usual I am out of kilter with the rest of society, and I enjoy with astonished amusement the silence and the sound of the waves, and manage my frustration that I won't feel sleepy until they all wake up, and then I will need earplugs to doze off.

Too soon it is time to pack up and head off for the other part of our summer ritual: an evening of fresh seafood, sightseeing in the old town and ice-cream. As it takes several hours to get here, we make it worth our while by staying as late into the evening as possible, pretending that we too are some of the many tourists that are staying here all week instead of returning to a hot flat this evening in the centre of Rome. Our *primo bagno* has been delicious, relaxing and uneventful in terms of sharks, jellyfish, seaweed or any other hazards that are present outside of the Mediterranean Sea. We are refreshed and relaxed, though we need a shower.

Some *stabiliamenti* allow you to use their pay showers even if you haven't paid an entrance fee. Others insist that only their customers can have the privilege of paying for a shower, and in that case you have to pretend that you have actually been one of their customers and lying on a sunlounge all day. In either case the showers are usually only cold water, are in the open, usually queued for and you cannot use soap or shampoo. So perhaps the term 'shower' is a bit misleading. It's more like a public hose down, where you have to pretend that no sea water could have gotten anywhere behind your bathers and you really only need to rinse your hair. But it's better than nothing.

We change at the car, which is parked in a quiet and out-of-the-way parking lot. In Australia it's quite normal to see people changing into their bathers next to their car, taking off wetsuits and putting on dry clothes. You use the car door, a towel or the car boot as protection from the public, though the public don't generally crane their necks to see. Doing the same thing here is considered akin to a naked floorshow, and whole carloads of families slow down to watch, while parents hide their children's eyes and then call the police.

The only way you can get away with it is if you are foreign, and having been a backpacker helps, as you can never quite transition back. After many years, my husband has realised that I will never stop doing it so has resigned himself to joining in. He always sits down in the car, however, and as a consequence spends the rest of the evening adjusting himself, as his underpants never quite go on the same way as when he is standing up. No matter how many times I offer to hold a towel up, he never takes up the offer to put his underpants on in the open. It is seen as un-Italian.

We meander slowly back to the town as the sun is setting, hair wet on our backs, fresh dry clothing on and our skin aglow, ready to enjoy the delights of an Italian seaside town at night. We have reserved a table at a restaurant on the beach, one of the only ones actually facing out over the sea. Most of them are on the inside of the town or up in the old town on the hill. This is one of our favourites, as you can watch the sun set and the moon rise while drinking cold Pino Grigio and tucking into some lightly battered calamari and prawns, or *fritto misto*. It is an example of a dish you can only ever find on the menu in summer.

The sky turns pink, then mauve and then a deep purple as the moon rises just over the white-walled town on the cliff. Andrea Boccelli is playing, and my husband and I look at each other in sweet sated satisfaction, and in anticipation of the meal ahead.

Our summer meal includes *alici marinate* and a prawn cocktail for *antipasto*. *Alici marinate* are marinated anchovies, so tangy they are like sucking on a lemon. But they are divine and mostly a summer dish. Of course, the exception for all seafood is New Year's Eve and Christmas Eve, where seafood feasts are traditional.

My husband has *spaghetti alle vongole,* another seasonal special, where the tiny crustaceans are drowned in garlic and oil and then added to the spaghetti. Afterwards, we wander out into the warm summer air and move slowly through the crowds that flock the sidewalk.

It is 9.30pm. Everyone is out walking, talking, eating, smoking or playing. The playgrounds are full of children, the restaurants are full of people, the sidewalks are full of queues of people waiting to get into the restaurants, and the *bars* are doing a roaring trade. Traffic is honking and jammed-up, as the traffic police desperately try to get it moving along a street built for carriages and a population tenth its current size.

We soon leave the chaos behind as we start to ascend the gentle curves of the path up into the cliff. Soon wide stairs appear, and there is a break at the top just before going into the town, so we can stop and look over the sea. It is a magnificent view all along the coastline and the last view of the sea you have before entering into the ancient walled-in city. Under the archway all you can see are stairs, leading off as far as the eye can see.

I can immediately see how this would have been daunting for an invading army. By the time you figured out which way to go, the townspeople would have filled up their vats of boiling oil and grabbed their bows and arrows, and you would have been dead before you got to the fourth stair. Everywhere is upwards, everything is on top of you.

We choose the more meandering-looking set of stairs. Even though we have been here almost every year for seventeen years, we still never manage to remember exactly how to get up to the town centre. We do know that whatever set of stairs we choose, they will all lead us there.

We ignore the tantalising views of small white staircases going up into the heavens that appear every now and again through gaps in the walls. One thing I do remember on my first few trips here is being enticed by them, like Ulysses and the Sirens. They looked so quaint and irresistible, and benign. They looked like they lead somewhere, to another universe maybe. But they twist and turn, taking you higher and higher, always promising that just around the next corner you will have a view, or it will flatten out, or you will come to an opening. Onwards and upwards I once went, wheezing, sweating and panting, with my thigh muscles screaming until I could no longer hear or see. And then the stairs spilt me out suddenly onto a large public piazza full of people eating ice-cream, relaxing and laughing. They all turned to look at me, it seemed, as I staggered around and tried to mop up the sweat and catch my breath in full public view. Another time, I found myself deposited into a tiny quiet piazza the size of a handkerchief, almost on top of three old ladies in black who were embroidering and giving me incredulous stares for having barged into their courtyard. I have learnt that it is best to stick to the wide, benign, meandering, perhaps not so interesting but much safer, sets of stairs.

We walk slowly up the wide and low staircase. It is covered so it's like walking through a tunnel. Doors and windows face out onto this tunnel. We continue past and notice small shops built into the stone. It is hot, so their owners are outside sitting on chairs. The shops get more prolific the closer we get to the main piazza, and there it suddenly is. The main piazza is filled with low tables and lit candles, cushioned seats with groups huddled around them and couples relaxing and looking at the passing show of promenading people. We take our seats at the edge of the piazza to have the best view of the passing people. This is our ice-cream stop.

These kinds of *bars* are everywhere in Italy. They exist mainly outdoors. If you go inside, it's like looking behind the podium at the Wizard of Oz. Behind all the comfy cushions and candlelight is a tiny neon-lit cavern full of refrigerators. The *bar* exists outside and in its menu only.

This menu promises all kinds of splendiferous ice-cream creations, just what I am looking for. I order a *coppa mista con panna*, a cup of mixed flavours of ice-cream covered with cream. Italians quite often have cream on top of their ice-cream. My *coppa mista* comes with chocolate topping, wafers, lashings of cream and a sparkly papered stick. It is divine. My husband is already complaining about the price and the standard of the ice-cream. It costs four times what it would cost in our local ice-cream shop, where the ice-cream is about one hundred times better.

'But we wouldn't get a stick with sparkly paper on it,' I counter.

He's right though. The standard of ice-cream is less than ideal and way overpriced. But here it's not only the ice-cream you pay for. It's the experience of sitting in a lovely piazza in the middle of an ancient, protected, cliff-top town on a balmy summer evening. It's the experience of watching and being watched, and of being able to sit down, eat your ice-cream and relax in candlelit splendour. All of this is worth it once in a while. I tell my husband it's really his underpants that are bothering him and he should untwist them for both of our sakes.

We speed on home through the night and get back very late and very tired, but very pleased with our *primo bagno*. Another long, hot summer is ahead of us.

Chapter 16

Summer loving

My parents-in-law, Renato and Checchina, are celebrating their sixtieth wedding anniversary and have asked us to celebrate with them at a small family dinner. My mother-in-law never asks for anything, is embarrassed by gifts and usually declines our invites to dinner or to come and holiday with us in Rome. Therefore, her request for us to share a celebratory dinner for her wedding anniversary is a great opportunity to give something back to a wonderful couple. I wonder what that must feel like, having been with someone much longer than you have been on your own or with your family. I wonder if you even feel like two people, or just one, after so many years.

I think of my parents-in-law as my reward for having been the daughter of my own parents. Aged eleven, when my parents divorced, I had to quickly become an adult and I missed out on a lot of being looked after. This is something that Checchina and Renato specialise in and I enjoy it immensely, even if I am now forty-three. I don't actually have much choice. Checchina, in her late seventies, once arm-wrestled me to the ground because I tried to take a plate back to the kitchen after finishing eating. I have never tried it again. She has also told me that her name is not *grazie*, thank you, so could I please stop saying it.

I am in heaven whenever we visit for the weekend. They live in Taranto, a small city at the very bottom of Italy in the province of Puglia. It sits halfway along the Bay of Taranto, the curvy instep shape that makes Italy look like a boot. It is flanked by Calabria and is 500 kilometres south of Rome. We used to visit much more regularly, but now we make the drive mostly for special occasions: Easter, Christmas, summer holidays and the odd weekend in between. The eight-hour drive, at least three of it in slow-moving traffic, makes it very difficult to muster up the enthusiasm after a long week at work.

The drive down this time is uneventful, if you are not a novice, that is. If it was the first time you had done it you would notice several accidents along the way, complete with smashed-up cars, ambulances and miles of queues as one lane of the *autostrada* (the freeway) gets blocked off. You would also notice the amount of cars that seem to have no working indicators, the drivers who are unable to drive within the lines of the lanes who often turn three lanes into four, who are frequently speaking on their mobile phones, smoking or combing their hair while looking in the rear view mirror, or doing all three activities at the same time.

Huge trucks slam along with only a metre behind each other and cars try to race them, causing others to hurriedly brake. You often see the same cars further along, in one of the aforementioned accidents. But if you can manage to take your eyes off the road and your foot off your imaginary brake, the scenery is often breathtaking. After the one-and-a-half hours of factories that line the road between Rome and Naples, you come to a huge mountain which sits just behind the turn-off to Naples, where many of the more distracted drivers also turn off.

After this, you head inland and south, between green rolling hills coated with huge wind turbines, curvy roads, bridges across gigantic chasms and tunnels. Once you are through the high and rolling landscape of Campo Basso, you come out briefly in Basilicata and then Puglia. There the terrain becomes very dry, full of earth, rocks and olive trees. It is flat and barren-looking. As you come closer to Taranto you start to see *trulli*, round stone houses, some of which date back to before the year zero. Though many of them are from only a couple of centuries ago, the style of house has been used as dwellings from pre-historic times.

Our trip is punctuated by the usual quick lunch stop at roadside 'fast food' places. Packed to the gills with other families travelling south for the weekend, or truck drivers passing through, it is nevertheless one of the treats of the weekend.

Italy does everything to do with food well. Even their truck stops offer fresh *mozzarella di bufala* and *prosciutto* on soft white Italian bread, thinly sliced salami with sheep's cheese on crusty rolls, freshly squeezed orange juice and stupendous coffee. This is fast food in Italy; standing up at a counter eating a crusty white roll packed with fresh tomatoes, basil and mozzarella cheese. This is opposed to sitting down and taking your time over a homemade pasta or meat dish, which is the other eating option at this truck stop. Or you could have a freshly made, handmade pizza with tangy tomato paste and melted *mozzarella di bufala*.

Travelling by car for eight hours also permits usually forbidden delights, like potato chips, cola and chocolate. Somehow, getting in the car to visit my parents-in-law always seems like the beginning of a holiday and a time to celebrate. And perhaps I just need to prepare my stomach for the onslaught of food I know will be coming from the moment I step in the door.

We finally reach Taranto at night via a bridge that opens up for battleships to go through into the sheltered natural harbour that houses Italy's navy. It was also used for the battleships of all the civilisations that have ever lived here over the past thousands of years – the Greeks, the Saracens, the Venetians and those who lived here before that. It features a medieval castle, built as a lookout to protect the city.

Taranto reminds me of Melbourne, in that it is situated on a large bay with a major port at one end. The remains of a huge Greek temple just to the left of the medieval castle, however, makes this city differ a little from Melbourne.

Even though it is nearly midnight when we finally reach our destination, my husband slows down, winds down his windows and recites poetry in local dialect as we drive over the drawbridge, past the castle. It is this first glimpse of his city that he loves so much, and he gulps in large lungfuls of sea air which he savours like a sailor coming home. He slowly drives through the ancient part of the city, the one that has been there for over two-and-a-half thousand years, with the sea on his right. He arrives in the central business district, with the Fascist-era architecture mixed in with the Baroque-era churches and the much uglier apartment blocks of early last century. He rejoices in every sight and sound.

Before I was familiar with the city, I thought Taranto was huge. It took us nearly half an hour to get to his house from the edge of the city centre. Slowly I realised that he drives in circles, purposely, so he can check it out. Like a dog leaving his scent, he parades up and down its length and breadth before finally turning home. It actually only takes five minutes to get to his parents' house from the edge of town.

His father is waiting on the balcony for us. Five storeys up and nearly blind with cataracts, he keeps watch for several hours when he knows his son is driving home.

Alfredo toots his horn and waves his arms out of the car for his father to see. His father, alerted by the horn rather than anything else, does a double-arm wave back in the direction of the horn. He straightens up, smiles and goes inside to tell his wife that we are here. She has been telling him for the past three hours that we are not even in the province yet, let alone ready for him to see us driving up the street. He doesn't care and has kept watch anyway.

As we drive up to my husband's apartment block, it is easy to recognise. There is an abandoned block of land next to it, so it has never been joined on one side by another building. This means you can see the entire side wall of the apartment block. These walls are supporting walls and are therefore completely blank. This is what makes it easy to remember Alfredo's block – it is the only one with a very small, square hole cut into it, five storeys up. In one of our earliest visits, Alfredo drew my attention to this.

'See that small, square hole in the wall that is otherwise sheer?' he said. 'It's my bedroom window.'

'How come you got one and nobody else did?' I asked.

'This exterior wall is a supporting wall,' he answered. 'Therefore, no building permission could be gotten to have a window.'

'So how did you get one?' I repeated.

'My mother got it for me,' he said.

Renato and Checchina moved into their one-bedroom apartment in 1960. Before that they had lived with relatives, sharing their bedroom with their other young son. They waited to have another child until after they had their own place. Taranto, like all of Italy, was a poor and famished place for almost twenty years after the end of World War II. Their new apartment, like many Italian apartments and like all the other apartments in their block, had only one main bedroom, a kitchen, bathroom and sitting room. At the end of the corridor was a tiny, narrow, windowless room used for storage or for a single bed for a child. Other children could sleep in the sitting room that was converted each day back into a family room.

Alfredo's older brother had already started his compulsory military service by the time Alfredo was big enough to need his own bed and so Alfredo got the small room off the corridor as his bedroom, and the family could preserve the sitting room. But Checchina didn't want her son to sleep in a bedroom without a window, so she just hired someone to cut a hole in the supporting wall to make a window.

Whenever we drive up and I see that tiny, high-up window, I am reminded of Alfredo's mother's love for him and her willingness to defy the law, and the safety of all the residents in the apartment block, for the comfort of her son. I am reminded of her determination, of the fact that it is and has always been her who runs the family, that she is quirky, unpredictable and lives life through her heart and not her head. She reminds me a lot of a woman like that in my own family. They would have been great friends.

* * *

We always have the same routine upon arrival. First we drive slowly through the old town, along the harbour, and marvel at the city and the magnificent water after so many hours of dry land. Then when we get to the apartment we drive around the block for about fifteen minutes, waiting for someone to leave so we can park, all the time waving madly up at Alfredo's dad, who has been on the top-floor balcony for the past hour waiting to spot us. There is no lift so every day, twice a day, Checchina and Renato climb ten flights of stairs with all of their groceries and their water. I wheeze up it on a Friday night when we arrive, and try not to have to do it again until Sunday when we leave.

We huff and puff up the stairs to be hugged continuously by Alfredo's mum, while his dad starts crying and then also hugs us while his mother tells him off for being so ridiculous, trying unsuccessfully to get him to 'buck up'. While unpacking, Alfredo's mum does the interrogation, one at a time, trying to get us each to inform on the other. To me she says:

'Is Alfredo really working?'

'Is everything really okay with his business?'

'Does he know he has to pay tax?'

'Why is he working nights? Can't he get anything during the day?' (Alfredo fixes large IT systems, such as those that run the electricity grid for Rome or the airport, and they have to be shut down before he can work on them. No matter how many times we have explained this to Checchina, she still thinks there is something dodgy about it)

'Is he eating enough?'

'Are you really okay?' (she means financially)

He gets:

'But why does she have to work/study so much?'

'Is she really okay after the miscarriage?'

'Is she really not missing Australia too much?'

'Why does she have to travel so much? Can't she get work in Italy?'

'Is she eating enough?'

All of this from a woman whose interaction with post-industrial life has been sporadic and is now almost non-existent, and who has only frugal means to live on. In the recent past she supported her other son, his wife and their two children for over five years on Renato's pension. She would do the same for us. Alfredo's dad still gives him ten euro every time we leave; his mother gives us fifty.

After settling in, we get our own back by interrogating them both at once about their health, checking they are taking their medication and have been to the doctor when required. Alfredo then checks that all the electricity, gas and water is working properly. The weekend before our wedding we arrived to the overpowering smell of gas coming from the apartment, which I took as a sign that we would all definitely die. Gas leaks and explosions are common in Italy, where many houses still operate from gas bottles. The elderly in particular are vulnerable, as they are not easily able to access repair workmen. Also, if they are of the war generation they are generally used to hardship and making do, so they leave things. On that particular weekend, we quickly used our contacts inside the State gas department to get someone over straight away. They had been living like that for a week.

After the mutual interrogation session we have dinner. It is always the same. Horsemeat cutlets, deep fried, with a green salad. It is delicious, although it did take me five years to try it. Horsemeat is a staple in many parts of Italy. It is very low in fat and very high in iron and I always feel boosted after eating it. We eat it with Alfredo's mother hovering around us and his father constantly offering us morale-boosting red wine. They go to bed incredibly early and will get up around 5am, a hangover from forty years of Alfredo's father working in the munitions factory at the navy depot.

We retire to the lounge room, which is our room and has a *divano-letto*, a fold-out bed. It has white walls, cold tiles and white lace curtains at the French doors, which open onto the balcony. The walls are covered in oil paintings by Alfredo's great-uncle who was a well-known local artist, and the furniture is dark polished wood. The house oozes peace and family love, and I sleep soundly. Until 5am, when I hear Renato shouting to his wife to make the coffee. He calls her Checchi for short. It goes like this:

'Checchi! … Checchiiiiiii! … Checchi! … CHEEECCHIIIIIIIII!' Renato shouts.

Checchina shouts back, 'EEEEEEH?' (meaning 'what' in local dialect).

'Is the coffee ready?!' Renato shouts.

'YES!' Checchina shouts back.

It's the same every morning at 5am. Used to living alone in their house, the couple can never remember to speak quietly.

I fall back to sleep as they both go into the kitchen, where they spend almost their entire day. I sleep soundly again until later, when the neighbours get up. The wall behind our bed is the adjoining wall to their lounge room and kitchen. In order to create a proper bedroom for their daughter they sacrificed their kitchen, which is now in one corner of their lounge room and right behind my head. It is only big enough for one person, and I can hear everything, from the gas faucets to their conversations. When Alfredo and I go for our customary 'greet the neighbours doorknock' later, we have to forget the intimate details of the conversations we overheard this morning.

We spend the morning relaxing and recovering from the drive the day before. We walk along the ocean frontage boulevard lined with trees. We meander in the pedestrian shopping strip and admire the magnificent clothes and the people wearing them. I am continually stared at. This is not a tourist spot, and pale foreigners stand out dramatically amidst the dark-skinned and dark-eyed people of the very south of Italy. It is friendly staring, curious and welcoming, but it is unabashed and after a while I get sick of feeling like I am an alien that has just landed. I gently suggest to Alfredo that it is time to go home and enjoy the siesta.

That evening we are all ready for the big celebration. The day has been full of preparation: what my father-in-law will wear, how we are going to get there, who is to be picked up first and by whom. There is a succession of relatives to be picked up on the way to the restaurant and, as not everyone has a car, a great deal of organisation, planning, arguing and changing of plans at the last minute has been going on for most of the afternoon.

Even though it had all been agreed by the end of the siesta time, nothing goes to plan. Alfredo's brother, Giuseppe, arrives half an hour earlier and without Aunty Lina, Checchina's sister who he was supposed to pick up. Checchina gets upset and starts yelling at her son. Renato is relieved. He has been ready for over an hour and pacing up and down the hallway outside our bedroom door behind which we have been hiding until the very last minute.

Finally we are all on our way, everyone is dressed and looks respectable, elderly people are packed into the cars, everyone is picked up and we are in convoy to the little town where the wedding anniversary meal will be eaten. Martina Franca is about an hour northeast from Taranto, deep in the Puglia countryside and on top of a hill. It is constructed completely from marble and stone and is accessible to pedestrians only. Its main piazza houses beautiful long paths of white marble, flanked either side by smart shops and *bars* made completely from stone. The entrance to the town is through a large arch, which opens onto a paved area with benches and flowerbeds. Alfredo drops me, his parents and Aunty Lina off at the edge of the town and goes to find a parking spot.

Lina and Checchina are like one person. As sisters, they both look alike and are only two years apart. They are both of average height and of quite slim builds for women in their eighties. They both have dark wiry hair without much grey. Lina comes weekly to cut or set Checchina's hair. They see or talk to each other every day. Lina was married to Renzo, a huge and handsome *Carabiniere* who died a few years ago. She is still not used to sleeping on her own, so Checchina's granddaughter Francesca goes to Lina's house every evening to sleep. Lina has two children and two grandchildren.

I can hear them speaking about me as they shuffle along, heads bent together, looking like twins. At first when I follow them, I am struck again by how much I missed out on in life not having a sister. It is something I have always wanted, and now even as an adult I am jealous of those women I know who have them. You can see the ether flowing between them. Renato looks on, following. He is joined to Checchina, but also separate and outside of this sisterly relationship. You can see that he accepts his place.

I overtake them and start to lead the way, anxious to find somewhere to sit down. It is stiflingly hot. We are walking in the shade of the buildings, which tower over the small paths below. The paths are only wide enough for pedestrians and keep the street below in constant shade. Even so, we are all sweating. As I walk in front, the women's observations of me grow more intense.

'She really is a good person, your daughter-in-law,' says Lina. 'You are very lucky. She is a genuinely nice person.'

I wince and try not to hear, not sure whether I am supposed to or not. The games and rules of daughters- and mothers-in-law are complex and ancient in Italy, and I try to stay wide of them.

Even so, Lina tackles me the minute we find a bench at the central piazza.

'Do you know that you are very lucky having a mother-in-law like Checchina?' she says.

I reply that I know and am grateful, because I really am. This is the point at which Checchina dives in. Facing me full-on, head tilted up at me, eyes needy and searching, she assaults me like a small dog wanting a pat on the head.

'Really, really? Is there nothing that I do that annoys you? Am I really okay as a mother-in-law?' she says.

I am taken aback at the directness of her question, her expressed need, and the fact that she is one of the sweetest, humblest, funniest people I have ever met and yet has doubts about her acceptability to me.

I remember the day I first met her, ten years ago. It was a group date, so if we didn't like each other we could dilute each other with the other company. Not that I would have been able to, as it was a group date of all of her friends and relatives. Alfredo took me to where they were all spending the summer together in the countryside near Taranto. It was Renzo's place, an almond and olive grove with three *trulli* houses on it. *Trulli* are traditional houses made entirely of stone; round, small and sometimes as ancient as the hills they were built on. We went for lunch and sat inside a cool stone house at a long wooden table, while I was fed incessantly. One dish from every woman that was present, and then the after-dinner liqueur they had made themselves with the almonds. I was completely finished after the first two dishes, but had to continue on. In the end, the fact that women in their eighties could eat and drink more than me was hugely in my favour. I may be the sophisticated career-girl foreigner who had travelled the world on her own, and who came from a country where most of Italy had gone to after the war, but I could not hold my food or my liqueur in any way deemed acceptable. I was a lightweight. They could all go and pick olives and harvest almonds after such a meal. I was taken groaning to the car.

As I said goodbye to Checchina that day, she gave me a shy smile. We looked into each other's eyes and found harmony there, and love, and sadness that we have found each other so late in life. We both knew that whatever time we had left together would not be enough. I never told my husband that in spite of his Italian good looks and southern European charm, it was his parents that had clinched the deal for me.

* * *

I hug the frail, short little body to me and say that no, there is nothing she does that annoys me and I can't imagine either of them offending anyone. At which point Lina hangs her head.

'No you are wrong,' Lina says. 'I am not a very good mother-in-law. Checchina is good at it but I am terrible.'

'What is it you do that is so terrible? What could either of you possibly do that would offend people?' I demand.

They both look down, shuffle their feet and have on masks of true shame. I am surprised and wait for the worse. Lina tells me that she has alienated her daughter and her son-in-law. Her explanation is long and complicated and given in dialect, so I don't follow it exactly. It has to do with her not being able to keep her mouth shut or her personality in check when it is required. I look again at both of them and wonder what other stresses you must need in life for the badgering of either of these two to get to you.

We finally all rendezvous at the stone bench in the piazza in beautiful Martina Franca. Parking has been found by all, and we begin to meander into the town as a group. Alfredo and I had our wedding reception here, and most family celebrations over the years have been held in this small, unique town, at a variety of restaurants and hotels. It is a big favourite in the region as a place to visit, especially in the summer as it is so much cooler than the surrounding towns. Its height and the cold marble help to keep temperatures down.

We walk through the town, taking part in what is known as *La Passegiata*, the daily slow evening walk that Italians take part in to be noticed and to notice others. Teenagers do it in gangs, and it is the major method of meeting those of the opposite sex. It is also an opportunity to look at the picturesque buildings and eye-catching shops while chatting and catching up with family members.

This is a common family combination for my husband's family and the smallest number of people that would be gathered together for a family event, signifying that it is an intimate and casual celebration. There is Renato, Checchina, Lina, Alfredo, Alfredo's much older brother Giuseppe and his wife Clo, their grown-up children Antonio and Francesca, and myself. Antonio and Francesca are both in their thirties, single and jobless, as is the whole family. This is a common scenario in the south of Italy, and a state they have all lived in for more than fifteen years. They live in a house given to them by Clo's family, in what has become a poor and dangerous part of town. They have only one apartment on top of them, in which the family of an ex-Mafia member lives. He is in protective custody somewhere in the north of Italy for giving evidence against the Mafia, of which he was a part of in Taranto. The entrance to the apartment block has a security camera and is watched over by the *Carabinieri*. Even so, it has been blown up twice in the past ten years, as the Mafia tries to intimidate, and even harm, the family of the Mafioso-turned-informant. Naturally, Giuseppe and Clo would love to move, but they cannot afford to rent anywhere and there is no possibility that anyone would want to buy their apartment.

In spite of their living conditions and having survived off Renato's pension for many years before getting a small pension of their own, they are a kind, happy and close-knit family. They spend most days together, and for four unemployed adults have developed a camaraderie and support for each other that is nice to watch. They love practical jokes and teasing each other, and are good company. Francesca and Antonio both left school at fifteen and neither have studied or worked much since. Antonio has become certified in driving heavy equipment and vehicles, and gets occasional work every couple of years. His wages are spent on mobile phones and jewellery for himself, perfume and trinkets for his sister, mother and grandmother, and petrol so his father can drive their car. The opportunity to eat out for them is a real treat and one they can only do if Checchina pays for it.

Everyone is in a good mood. Alfredo has organised a cake with 'Congratulations Checchina and Renato' written on it, and the feast begins. We are in a restaurant, organised by Checchina, on the edge of town overlooking the cliffs and fields below. The sun is setting and we are at a large family table. Dish after dish after dish is brought out and passed around in quick succession. There are lightly grilled capsicums which are full of flavour, little mozzarella balls wrapped in fried *prosciutto*, four different types of molluscs, most of which I don't recognise, calamari, cold squid in olive oil and three different types of mussels grown locally and for which Taranto is famous. The mussels are *gratinate*, lightly coated with breadcrumbs, garlic, pecorino cheese and parsley, then grilled. There are also fresh mussels and mussels stewed with cheese, bowls of olives, plates of salami and *prosciutto*, baked mushrooms, tomatoes stuffed with rice, mortadella, nuts and mountains of bread, breadsticks and crackers, along with carafes of wine and water.

We sate ourselves for what seems like a few minutes before the waiter comes back to 'take our order'.

'What do they mean?' I ask my husband. 'Didn't we just eat our meal?'

'That was the entrée, the *antipasto*,' he explains, gently holding my arm as he knows I am about to have a foreigners' freak-out about how I can't possibly eat any more and yet am expected to.

Checchina is looking at me knowingly and shrugs as the rest of her family quickly order a huge bowl of pasta each. She and I, and Lina, decline. We all know there is still the meat dish to come.

While we are waiting, Alfredo asks his mum and dad to recount the story of how they met and fell in love. Amidst much hilarity and teasing, Renato takes up the challenge to tell the story his way. Through a mouth lacking almost any teeth, in strong dialect and using a memory that comes and goes about everyday things, he begins to recount.

They had met when they were very young. Renato was eighteen, Checchina was thirteen. He had seen her come into his apartment building several times, as she came each week to sew for a woman who lived there. She was paid for this work, and she would do it along with her sister and mother. Girls, and many boys, didn't go to school past primary school in southern Italy in the 1940s. Renato had watched her come and go several times before he plucked up enough courage to approach her. She had spotted him also. One day, as she entered the large door to the entrance of the apartment block, Renato was already standing there with a delicately wrapped bundle of sugared almonds as a gift for her and to pronounce his intention of claiming her for his own.

Renato had been working for two years by that stage at the munitions factory of the Italian navy. He would spend a total of forty years there, and support Checchina and their two sons on this wage. Once married, Checchina never worked outside the home.

'The one that wears the pants is responsible for earning the money!' Renato always says.

However, for the entire forty years of his working life he handed his pay packet over to Checchina every week and accepted an allowance from her. This arrangement still works with his pension, which is how Checchina manages to give us fifty euro notes for petrol whenever we visit them and why Renato gives us ten.

In spite of his regular and quite good employment, both Checchina's mother and father hated Renato initially and refused to allow him to court their daughter. From what I can understand, almost every story of romance in the south of Italy begins this way. Its seems mandatory for your parents-in-law to disapprove. The courtship in southern Italy seems to be more about wooing the parents-in-law than the prospective lover. Giuseppe and Clo had to run away together to get permission to be a couple. At their age, spending a few days alone together meant they then had to be allowed to get married.

Eventually Renato's persistence, as well as his affable character, I imagine, won Checchina's parents over. But Renato had turned eighteen and was required to do his mandatory national service in the Italian Army. Usually this was a two-year stint of discipline and hijinks, but one year into Renato's military service, Italy joined Germany in war. Renato fought on the side of the Germans, as Mussolini went to war with Hitler against the Allies. He was fighting in the north of Italy four years later, when Italy changed sides and surrendered to the Allies. He noticed that something was not right that day. The Italian troops did not seem to be functioning as normal; there was a sense of restlessness, menace and impending chaos in the air. He noticed that many of the Italian officers were missing and the Germans with whom he was fighting seemed unsure what to do.

When it became known that he was in danger from the men who he had been fighting next to all these years, he and a fellow soldier from Taranto took off. They spent two months travelling by foot, from one end of Italy to the other, in order to get home. They had to walk by night and through the countryside rather than on the roads. They navigated their way south using the aqueducts built by the Romans 2000 years earlier to bring water from the north of Italy to the centre and the south. Renato and his companion were still in uniform and therefore immediately recognisable by the Germans as soldiers, but also by the Italian resistance movement who would have shot them on sight. They slept in barns and out in the open, drinking water from creeks and aqueducts. Every few days when they needed food, they would knock on the door of a farmhouse and the women of these houses would always provide them with a meal. When he made the journey, Renato was twenty-one years old

I initially thought I had misunderstood this story, as it seemed unlikely, until I read more about the history of that time and realised that thousands of Italian soldiers were making their way back through Italy from Europe and the north of the country. It was a nightly occurrence for many households to have fugitive soldiers begging for food as they made their way back home. I imagine that each household hoped someone was doing the same for their own returning men.

When Renato finally arrived in Taranto two months later, no-one had heard from him for over a year or knew where he was or if he was still alive. He went to see his mother first, then Checchina immediately afterwards. Checchina was coming back from doing some shopping for her mother and when she saw him on the street coming towards her she dropped her shopping bags, which emptied all over the sidewalk. She ran into Renato's arms.

'The rest,' as Renato's says, 'you all mostly know.'

Although I have been moved by this story, as are others around the table, I am perturbed by Aunty Lina and can no longer ignore her. Neither can Clo or Francesca. At the end of each course, which by now has included a meat dish, a vegetable dish and the anniversary cake, I have noticed her surreptitiously requesting the remaining food to be sent down her end of the table. To my surprise she has not been eating it, but spiriting it away into a variety of plastic bags she has brought with her. She is trying to do it so no-one notices, but in the end it becomes very obvious. Clo and Francesca start passing her down the cutlery, bread baskets and salt and pepper shakers in an attempt to jolly her out of her hoarding behaviour, but it doesn't dampen her enthusiasm or embarrass her in the slightest.

She begins telling me her version of the events around the time of Renato and Checchina's romance. She recounts that their father was a carpenter and worked in a factory or a studio. His weekly wage was the same as the rent they paid for their house, so each month they had to make a choice whether to buy food or pay rent. Sometimes the women of the household got paid for sewing, and then they could do both. I begin to have sympathy for Lina, for why she can't let food go to waste, and am reminded of Renato and Checchina's reluctance to use the air-conditioner unless one of them is about to pass out, as well as their insistence on turning the heating off as soon as possible.

We all roll back through the town later that evening, sated and with spirits lifted. We have had a meal to end all meals. As we drop Lina off at her apartment, around the corner from Renato and Checchina's, she fishes out a plastic bag.

'Here is something to put in your *panini* tomorrow, Renato,' she says.

Chapter 17

August! *Agosto!*

It is August and I'm babbling, as predicted. Although it happens every year, the heat still takes me by surprise and I continue on as if nothing has changed, until it finally forces me to curtail my routines and expectations. I reluctantly modify my daily schedule and work goals, until they are whittled back to:

get up

eat

do something for a very brief period of time

eat

sleep

get up

eat

walk around briefly

eat

sleep

I am aware that other cultures have incredibly hot temperatures and yet still function as business centres, where the heat is not an excuse for being late or for not working at all. However, in most of these other climes air-conditioning is a big factor, and life is primarily spent inside air-conditioned offices, cars, shops, restaurants and public transport.

This kind of air-conditioning has never caught on in a big way in Rome for several reasons. Household air-conditioners only appeared in the shops in the late 1990s. Being a new product, they were prohibitively expensive. The price is what stops many Romans still, but there is also a strong belief in its unhealthy, and downright dangerous, qualities.

Most people believe air-conditioning causes ill health. It is related to the ancient Roman fear of fever. One of the things you will hear when you come to live here is how absolutely imperative it is to blowdry your hair and to never ever leave it wet for any period of time. You must not, under any circumstances aside from a death wish, venture out of the bathroom with wet hair, let alone outside. There is a belief that being cold or wet on any part of the body at any time of the year, including the middle of summer, will lead to a fever and probably death. It is one of the reasons children are towel dried as soon as they come out of the sea, especially their hair, and then encouraged to go out in the sun and run around to get warm again. It is also one of the reasons people will stare at you in the street if you have wet hair, or even approach you and tell you to go home quickly and get your hair dry.

Once again, my social anthropology hackles are raised and I have deduced, after much historical research, that this is because there have always been marshes and a large population of mosquitoes in Rome. The Romans fled the city each August due to the fear of diseases, precipitated by fever and carried by mosquitoes. Mussolini once drained many of the marshy areas around Rome, and much of Rome is sprayed for mosquitoes each year, which just about keeps it in check. But flu and other diseases ran rife throughout Rome for centuries due to poor sanitation and close living conditions.

Even today, fever is common and treated very seriously. If you are diagnosed as having a *febre* (fever), under no circumstances will you be expected to come to work or do anything. It is quite common to have discussions about what temperature your fever got to and subtle competitiveness among fever suffers abounds. I don't think I ever had a fever until I lived in Rome, but sure enough within a few years I too was developing them. A thermometer is not something I ever imagined owning, yet one was procured so I could measure my *febre* and duly report:

Me: Sorry, I can't come in today as I have fever.

Work: What number do you have?

Me: Forty-two.

Work: *Madonna*! Stay at home and in bed. Make sure you rest and don't do anything.

The fear of fever, though not usually deadly these days, is still part of everyday conversation, and one of the biggest perpetrators is not the humble mosquito but the air-conditioner. To give Romans credit, it is quite devastating to go from an air-conditioned office to the fierce heat of the Roman outdoors. If everywhere was air-conditioned, then the chopping and changing of temperatures would not be so much of a problem. But most of Rome moves outdoors in summer, based on centuries of habit. The tradition of opening everything up in summer to catch the breeze is at odds with keeping everything closed to conserve the coolness.

Do not be fooled when speaking with Romans, who will tell you their public transport is air-conditioned, as are most of their shops and restaurants. They are, but when every window of a bus or shop is open while the air-conditioning is on, then what the rest of the world understands as 'air-conditioned' does not really equate. I make a habit of asking traders and bus drivers why the air-conditioning is on while all the windows are open and when it is apparent that everyone is sweltering. The answer is always the same: they get complaints. Customers and commuters – mostly the elderly who are closer to the visions of death by fever – prefer to be bathed in sweat than have the air-conditioning noticeably on. Bus drivers also can't smoke if the windows are closed.

Conversations about how bad air-conditioning is for health, as well as complaints of colds and muscle aches caused from air-conditioning, serves to keep us all well and truly in the age of the ancient Romans. I can't say I mind it too much. It is rather nice feeling the change in seasons, being affected by the heat and essentially ruled by it. There is a sense of community, like we are all in this together, and you can talk to anyone in the street about it at any time. '*Che caldo*, hot isn't it?' is the conversation-opener for the entire summer.

I whittle down my daily routine and give in to the long, hot heat of summer, crazed and amused by it at the same time. My *cappuccino* runs have become slower and now end with an iced coffee. The hot air and wind makes any movement a struggle. I walk so slowly I feel as though I am swimming through the heat. I wonder if I should still wear trainers and sportswear if I am dawdling along rather than running or even walking. Instead, I force my way along my regular route of gardens and flowers to get to the top of the hill, where I collapse on a stone bench under a tree and try to do sit-ups.

One morning after pushing myself up a hill, I burst from one of the large walled-in garden areas and out onto the street. Hot and sweaty, barely able to see, I almost collide with a group of elderly men lolling in the shade against the fence. Crisp white linen shirts and long shorts, they are all tanned and smoking cigarettes. With an average age of about eighty, they look like a street gang that has stayed too long together.

'*Buongiorno!*' they exclaim as one, grinning widely. They move to make room for me and look me up and down like I am a gift from the *Madonna* on this hot morning.

I continue my run. I am refreshed every few metres by one of Rome's most intriguing and undervalued characteristics: free, cold, drinkable water that comes gushing out of stone fountains. These are not the type of fountains that come with statues; these are utilitarian fountains, solely for the purpose of bringing free, clean water to all residents. They have been here since Roman times and the water still flows into the city from the aqueducts that the Romans built.

These fountains look like fire hydrants – cylindrical concrete posts coming up out of the ground. Water flows from a small pipe at right angles to the post and spills into the drain below, twenty-four hours a day. What many don't notice is the small hole drilled into the pipe of every fountain. If you put your hand over the end of the pipe it forces the water back up and out of the smaller hole. This makes a thin stream of water gush into the air, in a small arc just perfect for drinking from. It is the ancient Roman version of our modern water bubblers.

The water is freezing cold and I drink it, then use it to douse my face, arms and legs. It is cooling and refreshing. Others come to use the fountain as I have. In the evenings there are always water fights among teenagers, but even then no hair is wet and it is called off immediately if that is the case.

I languidly do my sit-ups while an octogenarian reads his paper on the stone bench next to me. He doesn't even turn his head. As a foreigner, anything we do will be, by definition, strange. The word for foreigner literally means 'stranger'. I often hear conversations that include phrases like 'that is something only foreigners would do', or 'for foreigners it is alright to do that sort of thing, but not for an Italian', or 'well that's because you are a foreigner'. For Romans, there are only two sorts of people: Italians and foreigners, and anyone from outside of Rome is halfway between the Italian and foreign label.

Foreigners living in Rome can be placed in the category of either Embassy staff or those who work at one of the three large United Nations agencies based in Rome. It is not an open or enticing job market, and there are limited openings and little need for non-Italian professionals or workers. It is common for me to be approached by people with, 'So you work at the UN then?' as a way of opening conversation. This question will only be asked if they notice I can speak Italian, otherwise it is assumed I am a tourist. Non-Italians living in Rome out of choice, other than for work, had not been a part of Italian society until very recently.

To describe foreigners that look Anglo-Saxon, the word *l'inglese* (English people) is often used. It refers to anyone who speaks English, or someone who is definitely not Italian. It is common for me to go to a restaurant and before I let the waiter know what name the booking is under, for him to say, 'The English people are already here,' and lead me to the only table full of foreigners. Sometimes this works, but occasionally I am meeting Italians and instead get taken to a group of people I have never seen before who are usually quite surprised that an unannounced stranger will be joining them for dinner, according to the waiter.

Last week I went with a group of friends to one of the outdoor cinemas set up in our neighbourhood for the summer. One of our group was late and, as we wanted to claim seats, we went inside without her. I explained to the ticket collector on the way in that we had one extra ticket because we were waiting for a friend, and we would return to give her the ticket once we had claimed our seats. He nodded and waved us in. Ten minutes later, she appeared inside.

'Oh no!' I exclaimed 'Did you buy a ticket?'

She said that she hadn't. She was waiting at the gate and the ticket collector asked if she was with the English group, and then waved her in.

The fact that none of us are actually English, and are instead French Canadian, Australian, Icelandic, Norwegian and German, is something we all take in our stride now. We are foreigners, we speak English together, so we are therefore *l'inglese*, the English people. It is a subtly nicer tag than *stranieri*, foreigners.

* * *

I make my way down the hill again to the *bar*, where I have my iced coffee. It is a different *bar* to where I go on Saturday mornings and work mornings. It is much closer to home, requiring only two minutes rather than five minutes to walk to it. Unlike my Saturday morning *bar*, it has no chairs and tables and is quite utilitarian. There is rarely any food available, and is used primarily as a place to stop and stand at the counter and drink something, on the way to somewhere else. But it makes a good iced coffee.

An Italian iced coffee doesn't actually have any ice in it, although you can ask for it. It is usually black coffee made with an espresso machine, heavily sugared and poured into a large bottle that is kept very cold. When you order one it is poured into a long, heavy glass and topped up with cold milk. It is delicious, fresh, sweet and exactly what is needed to combat the energy-sapping properties of the heat.

As this is a *bar* that I have started frequenting only in the past few months, I am a stranger and am not treated with the warmth that I am treated with at my regular *bar*. It takes time because they have to get to know me. They have to find out how committed I am going to be to coming here and they have to get to know my coffee order. I am a foreigner, wearing sports clothing and no make-up, and I am a woman on my own; I could order anything.

Gradually, as I appear twice a week and order the same thing, the *buongiorno* starts to get warmer. I often read the free daily newspaper while I am sipping. One day there is a word I don't understand, and I figure it is about time I had a conversation with someone here. I ask the general population in the *bar* what the word *fiacca* means and explain that I have read it as part of my daily horoscope as a description for what kind of an evening I can expect. I get laughs. It means tired, weary or listless.

The woman who serves me tells me that with that forecast it is better to plan an early night and nothing else. The woman next to me starts asking what my star sign is. She has studied astrology and, together with the *barista* who knows nothing about it, we have a passionate conversation.

I am in. The next time I go, the elderly gentleman at the cash register peers down at me and greets me with, '*Come stai?* How are you?' I know I have crossed the border from foreigner to resident.

I love the role, purpose and routine of the Italian *bar*. Even though I have lived here for seventeen years, I still get excited at the thought of going to the *bar* for breakfast or for a coffee. I never tire of the fact that I can walk into any Italian *bar* at any time of day, from early morning to late at night, and without fuss or ceremony or waiting receive an amazing coffee, with or without food. I can stand for as long as I like, talk to my companion, sip, admire the contents of the *bar* or listen to the conversations going on around me. Some bars are very swish, offer exotic chocolates, wines and jams, have floor-length tablecloths, and shiny brass and mirrors everywhere. Others, like the one closest to me, have a fridge of milk and ice-creams, a row of liquors and chewing gum, with free newspapers at the counter. Most are in between.

The role of the Italian *bar* is hard to play down. It is somewhere between community centre, old folks home, leisure centre, playgroup, eatery, checkpoint, information booth and general sanity provider. It is a pivotal link between members of a community that live within 100 metres of it and yet whose daily routines must include it at many junctures. This includes when they begin their day, are returning from errands, rising after the siesta, coming back from work and waiting to go out. Friends, neighbours and families meet there. New babies are shown off there; others are minded there by their grandparents while their parents do the shopping. Passers-by are hailed and forced to explain where they are going and what they are doing.

They often know each other by name, the customer and the *barista*. It is comforting and warming to walk into a *bar*, have someone greet you by name and then, without placing your order, have it set down in front of you. None of this is artifice to get your business – you have to earn your place over many years. Only then do you secure your place at the *bar*, after demonstrating you are loyal.

I love this morning ritual. I stop for a *cappuccino* three days a week on the way to the train station when I go to the office. It is early for me to be up, and my nerves are usually jangled and I have not spoken to anyone yet. I enter into the noise and hubbub of a *bar* at full capacity. '*Buongiorno!*' I shout, to make my presence known and because it is polite. Sometimes the *barista* hears me and sometimes they don't. Whichever of the customers who hears me looks around and makes eye contact while eating or drinking. I don't actually know any of them, but a general *buongiorno* is often met by an acknowledgement.

There is a lot of noise; the smashing of crockery, shouting and laughing. Eventually, the *barista* sees me. They check my order. '*Cappuccino scuro?*' I am asked, to check if it is my usual order that I want. A place is made for me with a saucer and I move up to take my turn. My coffee is put down and now it is my turn to place my elbows on the counter and savour it. I am facing the *barista*, who continues to work and talk to the others, but doesn't make eye contact with us to allow each punter to enjoy their morning coffee in peace. I am standing next to the woman who develops my photos, the guy who serves me fish at the supermarket and my hairdresser. We sip in total silence, elbow to elbow, staring into space, slowly waking up to the day. In the midst of a crowd, each of us is alone for a few minutes in a private breakfast ritual.

I finish and place my cup down. I pay and shout, '*Grazie!*' and then '*Buongiorno!*' to indicate I am leaving. Sometimes I get a response and sometimes not. It is okay, as I will be back tomorrow for the same ritual. Sometimes, for months on end, the *barista* will see me at midday in a sloppy tracksuit with bed hair, and then one day they will see me at 7.30am in a suit and high heels, made-up and coiffed. They have never once changed the way they serve me, or asked me a question about my dubious and changing lifestyle. Whatever I want to do with my life is my business. Theirs is to help me to keep it going and they do a wonderful job.

* * *

I know it is August, not just because I am babbling from lack of sleep and from the heat, but because slowly, bit by bit my neighbourhood is shutting down around me. My fresh pasta maker has a sign on his door that wishes everyone happy holidays and that he will see us all in mid-September. This is the last week I will be able to get my iced coffee at the *bar* around the corner until he opens again at the end of August. My favourite shoes remain heel-less and my dry-cleaning is piled up at the front door. Both will wait the whole month out.

The third-most important conversation you will have in Rome in summer, after food and vacations, is about when a shop is closing. This is important, as you don't want to be stuck without your morning coffee or any fruit and vegetables. You have to ask and to time when to start changing *bars* so you can guarantee that at least someone will serve you a coffee in August. So far, my husband and I are okay with our Saturday morning *bar* and our fruit and vegetable shop, as both of the owners will go on holiday in late August, at the same time as us.

My suburb is getting quieter, as more people pack up and go away. Friends and neighbours salute us; they invite us to their holiday homes and wave at us as they back out of the driveway, laden down with a month's worth of suitcases.

Those who don't leave wreak havoc. The other reason I know it is August, aside from babbling and having nowhere to shop, is because those who are on holidays from work, school or university and who don't leave on holidays take theirs in their apartments. This is much to the chagrin of those who are not on holidays and who must get up for work.

It is the first week of August and, like clockwork, on Monday evening singing, music, dancing and laughter is ringing out from three of the five apartments opposite us. The other two are boarded up, with their occupants away. Lucky them.

It continues until after midnight most evenings, and until midday you can hear a pin drop. Due to the heat, it is necessary to sleep with all the windows open for the sake of a slight breeze or temperature drop. As it is August I can't shout out of my window for them to shut up as I normally might, so I grin and bear it. At least it is soft, romantic Italian crooning.

I remember my routine for the next day and remind myself that everything is okay. All I really have to do tomorrow is get up, eat, do something briefly, eat, sleep, eat, walk around briefly, eat and then try to sleep.

Chapter 18

Life is a cabaret, my Roman friend

This weekend is the Garbatella cultural festival. The suburb of Garbatella where I live is loved by all Romans, but especially by its inhabitants, and it is being honoured for its uniqueness by a festival. The festival celebrates the humble working-class and socialistic roots of its original inhabitants, the architectural contributions made by the design of this suburb and the fact that some of Italy's best actors, writers and artists grew up here.

This little area, which started as an experiment in communal living and socialist principles by providing housing for the poor, is now famous for its restaurants, colourful inhabitants, and beautiful buildings and gardens, which are unlike any others in Rome. It is a secret and hidden place, difficult to see or access unless you already know about it or someone shows you.

Until a few years ago it was difficult to admit you grew up here, yet Mahatma Gandhi visited this tiny borough in 1920 to admire the kind of community care being provided for Rome's poorest citizens. It is difficult to access socially, to become really accepted here, and even after ten years of living here I am still assumed to be an American tourist passing through.

Tonight I am taking up an invitation to *festigare*, which literally means 'to festival' but actually means 'to party'. This will be as a fully-fledged and longstanding member of the local community.

Garbatella is situated uniquely for staging anything from theatre to music to dance. It has a number of built-in architectural features, which create natural stages, amphitheatres and performance venues. The first place we stop at is a tiny piazza, where the fountain of Carlotta is situated. In a place where I often sit in the shade and listen to the water, there is a group of older women sitting under photographs of themselves as five-year olds in the local school when it first opened in 1930. There are artists exhibiting on the wide stone stairs which go slowly upwards from the little piazza, and halfway up are the props and background of a play to be put on later. We talk and exchange pleasantries with the exhibitors. Everything is so close that it's impossible to admire anything without the creator right next to you.

'Are you American?' is the first, and not unkind, question. I sigh and tell myself that it is enough that I at least know I have lived here for ten years now.

We continue up the hill towards the next stop. Halfway up the tiny street is a small space in front of a *bar*, where music and folk dancing is taking place. Off this small space are lower stairs leading up to a bigger space, with houses and gardens opening onto it. Live music and a large audience are slowly filling up the space. We meander to the next venue, which is actually the meeting of five small streets. This evening there is a full sound stage set up in it, with plastic chairs provided for the audience. A keg of beer is being kept cool under the running water of a street fountain. At the moment there is a wind band performing various marches. I recognise a colleague playing oboe just as I see another colleague in the crowd. She tells me that she has just seen two other colleagues in the modern dance performance in the garden.

When you get the chance to see colleagues in improvised modern dance exhibitions, I think you should take it. I zip off to see them. They are performing in one of the loveliest venues in Garbatella, inside one of the communal garden compounds. These are kept green and flowering by the residents, and small paths meander in and out of rockeries and kept lawns, which butt up against look-alike medieval stone cottages. All this is encased in low stone walls that fence in the allotments, as they are referred to here. There is a band screaming out anti-racist poetry to a heavy metal background. This is not them.

We go further into the green garden, around the corner of another house, and there they are. They are in flowing robes, with bare feet, undulating back and forward, rolling around on the ground and making movements that involve handling large pieces of tulle and pouring water through funnels. I can't wait to congratulate them on Monday morning.

There is a beauty to their performance which I can't help admiring. They are performing in a large, flat concrete area in the middle of the housing allotment, which is crisscrossed with wire and was designed as the communal clothes line. This means the dancers have to watch out for the wire, though it gives them a beautifully large and uninterrupted space to muse around in. This space is surrounded by a low cement wall, perfect for sitting on. Behind that, across a small path is another low wall and then a gently sloping piece of lawn. It could seat around five hundred people to watch anything going on in this space. But my crowd is hungry for the fairy floss and the bright lights on the other side of the allotment wall, so we have to go before I have had a chance to call to my colleagues and wave at them from the audience.

The street leading up to the main piazza is full of stalls and packed with people. We weave through the throng and make it to the large stone piazza, another natural stage with seating all around it. I have read an Italian author who described all Italians as actors and that if you saw them as the main actor in their own play then you could understand the gesticulations, the exaggerated miming and the staged conversations much better. All this comes to mind as I see almost every public space in my suburb able to be converted into theatres with the minimum of fuss and a few electric cables. The main piazza, although set up for a large band, features piped music and twelve women dressed in black performing Tai Chi. It is beautiful to watch, but our stomachs are rumbling and we have a dinner engagement just down the hill.

Katrin and David, our neighbours, have invited our mutual friends, some who live in Garbatella and some who don't, for dinner. Those of us who live here have waged a relentless campaign to get everyone else we know to come and live here. That way, we would never have to leave. One of my neighbours and I have discussed how we think it is a big trip now if we have to go ten minutes down the road to the centre of Rome for dinner.

We begin our communal dinner with what is, for most of us, our Rome family. They are friends we have worked with, socialised with, been on holidays with, lived with, fought with, helped, lent money to, grieved with and had lots of laughs with for over ten years now. Friends with whom we have celebrated career and relationship highs and lows, and with whom we have celebrated many marriages. Around the table we have two Italians, who are both partners of friends, one Canadian, one Norwegian, one Brit, one Icelander, one French Canadian, one Aussie, one German.

We begin our celebratory Garbatella festival dinner with fresh peach Bellinis, a combination of crushed, seasonal peaches, fresh mint and Prosecco. We drink them overlooking one of Garbatella's many piazzas from Katrin and David's balcony. This is the same piazza on which 'the dodgy *bar*' sits. This is a rather special piazza, as it contains the sculpture of the woman for which the suburb was named after. She overlooks this piazza, with her name written in stone underneath her, from one of the walls of the apartment blocks that surround the piazza.

We sit down to our not-quite-Roman, but rather internationally flavoured, feast. First we have poached pears, which are in season and prolific. They are filled with blue cheese and walnuts; definitely not an Italian recipe. Even so, they are delicious. A carrot and pear soup spiced with sesame seeds is next. It is accompanied by homemade wholemeal bread. A fresh spinach and feta salad follows, laced with marinated chickpeas in balsamic vinegar. Katrin and David have made rhubarb and custard ice-cream to finish. We are all suitably impressed. About half of these ingredients are not available in the Italian market so you have to make them or import them yourself.

Rome has Italian food – that's it. If you want to seek out the cuisine of other nationalities it is possible, but you have to really seek them out; they are not prolific and you will only find the food of those nationalities that actually live in Italy. Hence there are no Greek restaurants, for example, or Turkish, Lebanese, French, Russian, German, Spanish or Vietnamese. There are one or two Malaysian, Thai and Indian restaurants, and mostly you can't get in without a booking. If you come from a country that is used to a medley of international cuisine then it's hard to fathom. It is also hard to adjust to, so when we get together as friends we do each other a favour and cook non-Italian food. When Italians want to change flavours they go to a Sardinian restaurant, or one that specialises in the regional cooking of Tuscany, Abruzzo or Calabria. This for them is as different as they want to get.

Many of my Italian friends and neighbours have never tried any other cuisine but Italian and are adamant in their desire to never ever do so. For many Romans, Chinese food is hugely radical as a choice of cuisine. It is the reason that some Chinese restaurants have to serve bread or pizza along with the rest of their Chinese menu. I have been here so long that my palate has changed, too. I used to crave the food of other nationalities for about the first five years, and then slowly my palate forgot about other tastes and got used to the subtle differences in flavour of the same Italian dish made in different restaurants or by different people. Now give me a good *spaghetti alle vongole* or *Amatriciana* any day over a Thai curry, a French pate, a Turkish kebab, a Russian borsht, an Indian samosa, a Spanish paella or a Vietnamese noodle. There is one thing my palate refuses to give up though, and it is intensely annoying as there is no possibility of recreating it here or getting it anywhere outside of Australia. I have never stopped craving fish and chips. And don't tell me to go to Britain – cod and peas is not the same thing.

Even if you want to cook multicultural food here, you can't. The ingredients are not available. To get the roquefort cheese for the pears, Katrin went to Denmark, via the UK, as Denmark is a country that sells French cheeses. To get the wholemeal bread, the kind with grains and softness, she imported the flour from Norway, where she is from, and made it herself. It has only been within the past five years that ginger has been known here, due to the influx of Bangladeshi immigrants, and Katrin had to travel to the suburb where they live in order to get it for our soup. Feta cheese is also unusual, being Greek, and can be only occasionally procured. The rhubarb was tinned and bought in the UK. It also required a long and animated discussion with our Italian friends, who had never heard of it or seen it and needed to be convinced of its use. To them it was red celery, not something that should ever go near an ice-cream maker.

Italians are incredibly conservative in general regarding their food. It's not that they have been cut off and deprived from the rest of the world's food; it's that they don't want it. They consider their cuisine to be undeniably, indisputably and irrefutably the best. They have curiosity about other cuisines, and I am often asked about what food is typically served in Australia, but there is little desire and no interest in including other nationalities' culinary repertoires into their own, or in changing or adapting theirs with new ingredients.

Given the variety and seasonal nature of Italian cooking, it is easy to see how it doesn't get boring, as it hasn't for me even after seventeen years. When I ask Italians about what kind of food they think Australians eat, they roll their eyes and tell me that Australia is the 'New World' – it can't have a cuisine of its own yet. They imagine that our cuisine is primarily British, as is America's cuisine, and then they give me a pitying look. It is a well-established fact among Italians that the British have excelled in most things but their food.

Outside, the festival is heating up. The piazza below is filling up with cars, which is quite usual for a Saturday night in Garbatella. There are not enough car parks for the residents, let alone the influx of tourists who come every Saturday evening, and particularly tonight. Katrin is watching the piazza closely, then excitedly exclaims something and runs off to get her alarm clock. She comes back, sets it for ten minutes and tells us that there are now so many cars parked illegally in the piazza that the bus coming down the hill on its route will not be able to turn and get out of the piazza. We go back to enjoying our ice-cream.

Ten minutes later, Katrin comes back as the alarm goes off. Everybody goes out on the balcony to watch the bus. We don't quite believe that she is asking us to watch a bus not turn, or what that means exactly, or how she knows about it. But we do it anyway.

The bus lumbers down one of the streets in full view of Katrin's balcony, right on time as she predicted. It gets to the entrance of the piazza and can't turn into it, as the space left by all the illegally parked cars is only big enough to let a car through. In seconds, the piazza is full of people. All the passengers get out, as does the bus driver. Passers-by gather and there is a cacophony of car horns. Everyone comes out onto their balconies and the spectacle begins. The actors are in the centre of the piazza, the audience is either at ground level or on the balconies that ring the piazza. Katrin passes out more ice-cream.

The bus driver begins by wildly gesticulating and shouting Roman obscenities. All the passengers are on their mobile phones and there is a chorus supporting the bus driver, with gesticulations and lamentations in dialect. Horns draw more people into the piazza as patrons from nearby restaurants spill out to check whether it is their car or not. It is hoped that each person who comes running down the street is the owner of the car blocking the bus's turning path. Each time, the collective audience lets out their breath in disappointment – it is not the owner of the car. At the end of the first act, we are left wondering what the passengers and the bus driver will do.

Opening of the second act. Katrin passes out more ice-cream. By now the Italians are eating the 'red celery' with no qualms.

A group approaches the car. Together they do a dance around it; in, out, circling it, touching it tentatively and moving away. The audience starts participating.

'Move it, you pansies,' comes the shout from the balcony. 'Go on, you can do it. There are enough of you!'

A tentative attempt is made: '*Uno, due*, PUUUUUSH!'

My husband yells out, 'You have to bounce it first before you can move it.'

We all look at him as one. The other Italian on the balcony concurs.

'It's the only way,' he says. 'Otherwise the brakes will stop them.'

But wait! Someone else is running down the street, car keys in hand. We all hold our breath. Then even the runner himself looks disappointed as he realises that he owns the car next to the one that needs to be moved. He looks around at the crowd, shrugs up to the balconies, and gets in and drives away.

By now the mutterings are getting more serious. There is

nervousness and shuffling, even among the audience. Emotions are running high. We know it would be better now for the much-cursed driver to not show up at all. Another dance with the car begins, this time a more threatening, aggressive one. Together they begin to bounce the car. The more violently the better, it seems, both in order to move the car and to teach the driver a lesson. The spectacle is wearing thin.

They manage to substantially shift the car from the back wheels, sideways. The audience shouts approval and encouragement. They clap and hoot from the balconies. Passengers run quickly to get back on the bus and back into the cars stuck behind the bus. The bus driver extinguishes his cigarette and strolls over to take his leading role behind the wheel. Bystanders remain to guide the bus through the narrow strait. As it takes off again it is heralded by hundreds of onlookers, like a bridal couple taking off from their reception. The lights go down. The audience drifts away and everybody goes back inside, exhausted and happy.

Chapter 19

Positano

In spite of the millions of tourists that come each year to Positano, it remains a picturesque and relatively unspoilt place, where you can bathe for free in a jewelled sea, then wrap yourself in a sarong and tuck into lobster and cold Pinot Grigio two minutes later, complete with sandy feet, windblown hair and a stunning view over the bay. Its lack of road access means that there never seems to be too many people here at any one time. Also, it is not everyone's cup of tea, I guess, to have to climb up a million steps after lobster and Pinot Grigio. For me it is the perfect balance and I have been coming here regularly for over seventeen years, just to get my fix.

The views are beautiful and remind me a lot of Greece, my other favourite place. When I first arrived in Italy, Positano became my little slice of Greece outside of Greece. Most people make the comparison. The clear, deep water, the soaring white cliffs and the towns that spill down them are all similarities they share. As in Greece, there are always views in Positano, wherever you are.

The drive to Positano is along a high and winding road hugging the side of a cliff. The views are sweeping and of magnificent blue water, sheer grey cliffs, tiny white boats bobbing together, bright pink bougainvillea and fresh green vegetation. There is sky and sea as far as the eye can see until, between two cliffs, you glimpse a series of square white boxes that line the dramatic cleft in the rocks, and tumble down until they reach the small, black, sandy beach below.

It is impossible at first to imagine being able to get down there, let alone back up. As we huff and puff up and down the cliff all weekend, we are regularly overtaken by much older locals who are *running up* the stairs, some of them with shopping bags or suitcases balanced on their shoulders. You can always tell a local from a tourist by the speed they are travelling up and down the stairs, as well as the pitying looks on their faces as they pass you.

Positano is one of those many places in Italy that is far larger on the inside than it looks on the outside. Around and around you go, until you feel completely disorientated, like being put inside a bottle of water and shaken up so you don't know which way is up. It always seems you are just about to burst out onto the beach, when the road takes yet another turn and you find yourself deep in the underside of a lushly vegetated cliff, an alternative universe that has a proliferation of *bars*, clothing shops and views. Although it is only two or three kilometres from the cliff road at the top to Positano and the beach below, it can take you days to reach it.

* * *

On our first foray by foot, it takes us two hours to walk two kilometres downhill before we finally arrive at the beach. I am pushed out onto the sand at the bottom of the path, blinded by the sun after having spent a good half-hour in the shady alleyways lined with shops. I am carrying all kinds of new trinkets, including lemon candles, soaps, pottery, sandals and a huge pink beach bag that I have no recollection of buying. My husband sighs with exasperation, vows not to let me bring my credit card to the beach again. I blame the configuration of Positano – the shops come before the beach. It should be the other way around.

I suppose this is what makes Positano so special, in spite of its touristy image. It is a natural beauty, a spot which cannot be engineered

much. It is not possible to build a helipad, install a lift or make a road –
you must work to get here.

It is a great leveller. Everyone has to walk. Everyone has to climb the
steps. Everyone swims in the same sea. Families from the poorer areas
of Naples eat next to retired captains of international industry and their
coiffed and bejewelled wives. Everyone who comes to Positano has the
same experience; it does not change to accommodate different classes
of visitor. It has retained some of its fishing village characteristics.

I first came as a penniless backpacker. I arrived via two trains and a
bus from Rome, stayed in a small and cheap *pensione* and ate takeaway
pizza *margherita* by moonlight on the beach for dinner. Nowadays I
come by car, stay in a hotel that has a jacuzzi in my room and I eat
lobster at one of Positano's best and oldest restaurants.

As I have come often, there has been a gradation of experiences
between these two, as my status has changed from backpacker to income
earner. I always struggle to judge which experience has been the best.
The essential elements of Positano have always been there: the beach,
the sea, the feast of flowers and fashion, the early morning mists, the
moonlight making a path on the still water, the homemade ice-cream,
the *limoncello* liqueur, the bright pink bougainvillea, the friendly and
kind locals, the views from stomach-lurching heights and the dessert
known as *delizia al limone*, or lemon delicious, that even a backpacker
can afford. It is just me who has changed.

I have been responsible for a lot of 'firsts' in the life of my husband:
first time meeting a foreign girl, first time on a plane, first taste of non-
Italian food, first time to have a passport issued. I was also responsible
for his first trip to Positano, over a decade ago and not long after we first
met. I couldn't wait to show him, and I assured him that I knew how
to get there and would organise it all. I neglected to say we could not
actually get there by car and that we would have to walk down hundreds

of steps while carrying luggage.

It was a blustery Friday night and we had arrived well after sunset. As I was plummeting down the stairs in the dark, hoping that any minute now I would get my bearings and be able to tell my husband that I knew exactly where we were, it struck me as rather risky that I had not booked anything. Especially as it was now near to midnight and any hotels with vacancies would probably be shutting up. I could hear my husband, then boyfriend, Alfredo huffing and puffing behind me and hoped that in his first risky foray into trusting me with travel arrangements I would not completely delude him. I was planning on this being a long and exciting travel partnership.

I arrived at a stretch in the road that was familiar and recognised it as not too far from a cheaper *pensione* I had stayed in previously. I led the doubtful Alfredo to the dark door and buzzed on the bell two or three times. Eventually, a window opened above our heads and the proprietor, who I recognised, looked down at us.

'What do you want?' I considered it a bad sign that the head poking out of the window had to ask.

I piped up in my best Italian and explained to him that I had stayed there before, thereby denoting my respectability in spite of the current circumstances, and was it possible to have a room for two nights? He hesitated, and in that split second my husband pleaded, 'I know we haven't booked but if you don't give us a room we will be spending the night in my car.'

With a 'you are Italian and should know better than to travel like this' look to Alfredo, the proprietor unlocked the door.

The next morning I woke to find Alfredo at the balcony, speechless. The whole of Positano was laid out before us: the high peaks above filled with vegetation, the ceramic-tiled roofs and the sun glinting on the green sea. It was a beautiful sight. I did not have to sell anything for the rest of the trip. Whatever I suggested, Alfredo went with it and has ever since.

* * *

Once in Positano, you do not need your car. We have googled and GPSed our hotel, and realised there is a staircase that leads from the cliff road directly down to it. We manage to park right next to it. The staircase is long and zigzags downwards, getting cooler and darker as it wends further into the crevice between the two cliffs that make up Positano. Our hotel sneaks up on us. It requires yet another set of stairs to reach, but once inside there is a lift up to all the rooms and the common terrace areas. Like all buildings in Positano, it hugs the cliff and has to be built using the vertical rather than the horizontal space.

One of my favourite views in the world is looking up at the township of Positano from the sea, while floating on my back in the deep, salty water. I love lying there and looking up at the cliffs, at the domed, mosaic-covered church and the town that climbs up the hillside. I always know it is summer when I see that view.

The water is clean, cold and deep, and only a metre from the sand I can't touch the bottom. It is so salty that buoyancy is easy and I laze, tread water and float around, all the while looking up at the view. The soaring cliffs on either side make me feel as though I am at the bottom of a well. Metres underneath me I can see unruffled black sand for miles out into the Mediterranean. I swim languidly up and down the beach, entertained constantly by the beautiful cliff faces, bobbing boats and endless parade of fashionable people.

On the beach the sand is black and very, very hot. First-timers are easy to spot. They are the ones screeching in pain until they hit the water.

Positano will always be a town reliant on the sea. Its produce comes from the sea and before tourism, fishing was its main livelihood. Many of the smaller and quieter streets, particularly higher up the cliff, are inhabited by descendants of fisher folk. The brassy 'you are so lucky to be here' attitude of much of the Roman population is distinctly missing here.

The desire to look your best makes it hard to put on a swimsuit and then emerge back into the town, salt-encrusted and without make-up. But if you don't partake of the beach, you have missed the main point of Positano. The opportunity to swim in its cool jade sea and then come up off the sand into a vine-roofed café to eat a *caprese* salad, or try on exquisite linen clothing and leather sandals while being salt-encrusted and without make-up, this is what I love most about Positano.

* * *

We go to our favourite restaurant, which is right on the beach. Huge terracotta pots overflowing with geraniums frame the view of the sea, while the vines provide a cool, green interior.

We order our usual *caprese* salad of cold tomato slices, garnished with fresh basil and *mozzarella di bufala* from Naples. Naples, just an hour away, is the world centre for *mozzarella di bufala* and so it is one of the best I have ever tasted. It goes perfectly with the tangy tomato, sweet olive oil and fresh basil leaves. The bread is crusty and doughy on the inside. It is bread from the south of Italy, very different to the bread in Rome.

At the end of our meal we look at each other guiltily, as we know that we both want an ice-cream. In Positano, they make my favourite flavour: vanilla. Or at least it has become my favourite, simply because you can't get it in the rest of Italy. Even though Italians make ice-cream out of just about every other flavour in the world, including nut, watermelon and an Italian sweet biscuit for children called Plasmon, apparently making ice-cream from the vanilla bean has not occurred to anyone.

Not all outings in Positano are made while being salt-encrusted and without make-up. After a dip in our jacuzzi, a siesta and a long shower, we emerge coiffed, made-up and suitably fashionable.

Positano is famous for its shops selling flowing white linen dresses, blouses and loose trousers. They are often handmade, original, exquisitely crafted and do not blow the budget. The other extreme is wildly colourful dresses, blouses, hats, jewellery, bags, shoes and scarves. They are full of appliqué and busy designs. I used to always come away from Positano with an item of clothing I could never wear outside of here.

Pottery is the other big item for sale here, and everything from small bowls for olives to planters for mini trees can be purchased. The designs often replicate ancient utensils, such as olive oil bottles and terracotta containers for water. They are decorated by hand in a myriad of styles, from modern Tuscan landscapes to ancient Roman or pre-Roman decorative designs and symbols.

Positano, in fact the whole of the Amalfi coast, is famous for its lemons. Anything that a lemon can be made into is made here: lemon soap, liqueur, perfume, chocolate, ice-cream, dessert, pasta sauce and candles are just some of the lemon-based products for sale.

* * *

As we walk leisurely down the hill to our dinner engagement, we savour the fresh sea air and take in the sights. Many stairs later, we wander into our favourite restaurant for our favourite dish, which we dream about all year. We checked at lunchtime that all was in order for our booking and that we had a table close to the windows. The proprietor told us that we had a table booked for 8.30pm, but he wasn't sure which one it would be and it would depend on how early we got there.

'How is that in any way a booking?' I asked my husband. Alfredo assured me that it meant there were enough tables for everyone, but those who came a little before their booked time would get their pick.

So we arrive at 8.15pm and manage to get a good table. It is in the corner of the restaurant, which looks out over the small piazza of Positano and the beach. This restaurant is open on three sides, so rather than an actual window it is more like you are sitting at the edge of a terrace.

We go to this particular restaurant, to Positano in fact, for the *spaghetti alle vongole veraci*. It is *vongole veraci*, as opposed to simply *vongole*, because the clams are bigger, juicier and harder to come by. They have a subtle yet distinct flavour that permeates the plain spaghetti, especially when carried through it by olive oil and garlic. They taste like they have been buried deep in the seabed. They are salty and delicious, unlike anything else I have ever tasted. We also order oysters and *tartufi di mare* (sea truffles) that look similar to clams but are slightly smaller.

Then the moon rises, full and red. Italians start singing songs behind us in the restaurant about *La Luna Rossa* (The Red Moon). It casts a long, gleaming red path over the sea as it rises above the white pleasure boats moored in the bay.

Evening in Positano is playtime. There are a proliferation of bars and restaurants at the water's edge or close by. You can have a full five-course Italian seafood dinner, or linger over one glass of *limoncello*, enjoying the moonlight and ambience.

We leave our restaurant table and meander along the edge of the sand, following the path along to the very outer edge of Positano, where the bottom of the cliff meets the sea. This is the deepest part of the ocean and where tour boats arrive each day to take patrons to Capri, the Blue Grotto and other tantalising destinations. In the distance we can hear glasses clinking, cutlery clanking, and the sound of laughter and voices.

Later, as I huff and puff my way back up the road I notice some younger people making their way downhill, their nights just beginning. I look at the enormous heels they are wearing, the perfect hair, the tight clothing and artfully arranged scarves, and wonder if they realise how far down they have to walk, and if they are going to be able to get back up again.

* * *

The next day, before we say goodbye to Positano, there is one more ritual we must partake of. We begin our walk towards Positano's most famous *pasticceria* to sample the *delizia di limone.*

This time our way back will be easier, as the *pasticceria* is about halfway between the beach and our hotel. It is well-known for causing bottlenecks in human traffic along the path from the top of Positano to the beach. There is a large window at hip level, which is stocked full of chocolate-covered profiteroles oozing fresh cream, baba dripping with sweet rum juices, pastry casings with tiny wild strawberries and dark blueberries, as well as *delizia di limone.* All of these delectable sights suddenly appear as you round a corner and has the effect of literally stopping people in their tracks.

We know what we want to order and so do not need the menu. A *delizia di limone* is a small dome of the lightest sponge, filled with a light, cheesy lemon-flavoured cream and then covered with even more sweet, lemon-flavoured cream, almost like a custard. It is truly delicious and lemony, and is offered in every restaurant in Positano as the standard dessert. Eating it where it is made and in the shade of the cliffs just sets it off.

AUTUMN

Chapter 20

The changing of the guard

It's autumn. I can tell because of the light; it is muted and slanted. The sunshine is still there, sometimes with almost as much heat and bite as the summer. But the air is cooler and bluer. Autumn has also begun because everyone is back from holidays. Cars have been unloaded at the door of the apartment blocks, summer wardrobes have been taken to the drycleaners and accessories such as plastic pools on balconies put away. The temperature drops hesitantly, sometimes twenty degrees Celsius from one day to the next, then rockets back up to summer temperature again, kisses it one last goodbye (sometimes more than once) before it stays firmly down. One day in September I went to work in open-toed shoes and a summer suit. It rained in the afternoon and when I left it was fifteen degrees cooler and autumn.

The trees shed their leaves and they pile up in huge mounds of fallen rust colour, ready to be washed down the drains at the first rains and to trigger the annual flooding that occurs, where streets become rivers and piazzas become pools.

I gratefully bid goodbye to summer, longing for freshness and cool air on my cheeks, for the vitality the crisp, sun-filled air brings and the excuse to drink a daily hot chocolate. As with the other seasons, I greet it like a long-lost friend, savouring in advance the culinary delights it brings, and thoroughly sick of last season's wares. It is the same at the end of every season. I feel if I have to eat another *caprese* salad or peach again I will die. I have fed and feasted to my heart's content on the offerings of last season, and I am bored and restless. With no sign of steadfastness or commitment in my demeanour, I shun the end of this season's delights and revel in the next.

The light and the air of this season is blue and green, suffused constantly with sunlight that makes you feel you are moving in a cool green sea. The air is bracing and stimulating. It doesn't cradle you like the summer air does, it doesn't softly support your languid movements and encourage you to lie back and take it easy. It is a sergeant major; you are a new recruit.

It's not as severe as winter, but it will not let you idle. Now is the time to pick your life back up again after the summer. It is the time to start things again: classes, work, exercises, learning, doing. It is out of kilter in this way. Although it is a month in which everything dies in nature, it is also the month that everything comes back to life for humans, in Rome at least. It is the last-ditch effort to get things done before the end of the year. It is the opportunity to catch up from where things left off in June. It is the time to start new things; new adventures, new work, new hobbies, new learning. Slowly, slowly the wheels of Italy grind back into gear after the long summer break.

For some reason things seem to move incredibly fast in autumn. It is like this every year for me. I feel like I get back from my summer holidays, have five minutes and then it's Christmas. I suspect it's this business, this making up for lost time and wanting to get things done by the end of the year that is to blame. It is always a busy and hectic season. But as the days grow shorter, as the shop opening hours change and the air grows colder, many delights await.

The sun still kisses the trees most mornings and at lunchtime sun worshippers can be seen all over the city, staking out a place in the sunshine, faces upturned, eyes closed, finding spaces in parks, on benches and staircases. The sky becomes a turquoise blue, no longer faded by the sun, its colour deepened by the clear yellow rays. The air ricochets off trees and buildings, painting them in freshness, highlighting their colours and textures and revitalising everything.

Autumn is an invigorating season in Rome. It is a season that makes you want to sit up and take notice, to burn off those extra kilos from summer, to throw off the languid stillness, to pick up the pace, to get into action, to feel your body move and sweat from effort and work, rather than just from lying down.

More things can be done every day. Energy flows into you as it is not sapped by the sun, brought back in by a crisp, green, light nipping at your extremities with its cold bite. By early afternoon, the rays begin to slant and the sun loses its power. The chill comes quickly then.

The sun takes on the hue of the seasonal pear before becoming brilliantly and sweetly pumpkin orange just before disappearing each afternoon. Twilight begins at 4.30pm and by 5pm an inky blackness has set in. It is cold and still and makes me feel like tucking myself up in bed by 7.30pm, but not so the Romans. Their routine of hitting the streets from 5pm until 7pm is still alive and well. Shopping, talking, walking, smoking, taking a coffee, working and doing business all takes place as valiantly in the autumn darkness as it does when there is sunlight to accompany them. Sometimes more so.

The streets are lit up and crowded. People are wrapped up warmly and stand around in groups talking and smoking, as in any season. Roman apartments are not meant for socialising in and the twice-daily need for interaction and activity is necessary, whether or not it's cold and dark. Besides, there is always the hot chocolate to bolster you up.

It's hard to describe the complete delights of an Italian hot chocolate, especially if you have never experienced one before. I grew up with hot chocolate; at least, I thought I had. It was a sweet, milky-brown liquid that tasted vaguely of cocoa and warmed me up, while creating phlegm and irritating my stomach. Therefore, I did not know what the thing was that was served to me the first time I asked for a hot chocolate in Italy. I thought it was a language problem, until I spoke to my friends who had the same experiences, and then to Italians who didn't get what the problem was.

Hot chocolate in Italy is literally melted chocolate that is hot, served in a cup with a heap of whipped cream on top to cool it down, if you prefer. It is faintly bitter, thick, dark and aromatic, nourishing and soothing to the mind and body. It is served everywhere, in every *bar* throughout the land, in a teacup with a saucer. It takes a long time to drink and can only be sipped. It is generally not taken with anything to eat and is taken standing up at the bar, like coffee, or sitting down, alone or with company. It is a tradition, such as Christmas. You have hot chocolate, every day if you want, in the afternoon or evening when it is cold. It fortifies you, much like ice-cream does in the summer. It feels like you can do anything after an Italian hot chocolate.

Roasted chestnuts in open coal-fire pans rest on every street corner, the new red wine and fresh-pressed oil of this season's grape and olive harvest is released and called the *novelli* (the new ones). Beans, chickpeas and lentils come out in force to greet autumn eaters in hearty soups and accompanying roasted meats. Pears and persimmons in every shape, colour and flavour burst onto the scene.

If you have never tried a persimmon, it's like eating a huge soft tomato that tastes like strawberry puree, apricot jam and crushed pineapple all put together. It requires a bowl, a spoon and a long time to eat, and is among the most sumptuous fruits put on this earth.

Chewy salamis, thinly sliced salty lard, soft piquant cheeses and deep red wines are all faithful friends that come back to greet me in the autumn. Rich tomatoes, pastas with meat sauces, artichokes, pumpkins and leeks come out to renew their acquaintance with me. And my need to bake cakes and make soups and stews comes back after a year of hibernation.

My *cappuccino* runs also return. Throwing off the summer slouch, I gird up for the first run of the autumn. I quickly return home to do some further girding up as I realise that I haven't put enough clothes on. I spend some time in the cool garden, warming up under the even warmer gaze of one of the pensioners that is the self-appointed guardian of our garden, and who has to be told every time I see him that I live here and that is why I am in the communal (stress on this word) garden. I then head out into the street for the first of this season's runs, acquainting myself with flowers and bushes, trees and birds that have been tired and listless all summer. The park benches are wet with dew and the cold marble nearly freezes me whole as I try to use them to exercise on. Everyone is out walking dogs in the beautiful morning sunshine. I pad by the familiar parks and gardens, and revel in the sunny patches instead of trying to avoid them.

I eventually finish and reach my final destination – my *cappuccino* stop. I greet them with the usual '*Buongiorno*,' as if it has been a mere matter of days since they last saw me, rather than the actual time it has been. It is cold and late in the morning, so I take a *cornetto* as well as the *cappuccino*, and stand up to read the free daily paper. The *cornetto* is soft and buttery, slightly sweet on the outside, and the coffee is deep, bitter and hot. I exchange words with the policeman who is standing next to me sipping a freshly squeezed orange juice, with his gun strapped to his body.

I enter into my apartment building with Enzo, one of the most elderly residents. He is deaf, blind in one eye, and shuffles and wheezes along slowly. He lives alone, and every day greets and cheers everyone he meets as he goes about his twice-daily shopping ritual. The lift is broken (again) and I wonder how he will go about getting up all those stairs. He reminds me he is okay, as he lives on the first floor.

It is me that has five flights to climb. We share complaints about the current superintendent and how lazy and good-for-nothing she is. We are supposed to be getting new post boxes which have not yet arrived, he reminds me. He goes on to complain about why we are paying for the post boxes when it is a State service to provide them.

'Why did I fight a war for six years,' he asks me, 'if the State is slowly going to renege on all its promises? Where were the current politicians, most of whom are now millionaires, when I was getting my teeth pulled out by the SS?'

He sees the reaction on my face. We have only ever exchanged pleasantries about the weather, and I am a sucker for war stories. I find them deeply disturbing as well as intensely attracting, making me want to cry and take care of the storyteller for the rest of their lives.

'Yes,' he continues, 'they used the tools that they use to take off a horse's hoof to take out my teeth, one by one, to make me give them information. I did this for the State of Italy. What is it doing for me now except cutting back all my rights and privileges, while retaining its own?'

I have no answer except to stare at this small, short man in awe and deep respect. I can understand Italy's desire to pull itself out of a state of stasis by rejecting old ways of governing the populace, but maybe they should have waited until all the old soldiers died first.

Enzo collects himself.

'Anyway, we have gotten a bit off track, *signora*,' he says. 'Sorry for that. I wish you a very good lunch!'

He shuffles up the remaining stairs to his apartment, a smile on his face and a cheery greeting on his lips. I know for a fact that I would not have such bonhomie towards the world if all my teeth had once been pulled out with agricultural equipment. It makes me wonder what other stories abound in this apartment building, what other adventures have been had by people I live with and see every day. It makes me feel humbled and very, very foreign.

Chapter 21

A tale of two tailors and autumn in the city

I am at my tailor's on a Saturday morning – I love living in a country where everyone has a tailor – when I see her. I first see her from behind. I study her black velvet trousers, thin legs and tailored black velvet bomber jacket. She has long, blonde hair, perfectly conditioned and recently blowdried professionally. She collects her very modern flannel boot-cut trousers from the tailor, who also does dry-cleaning. Her voice is strong and glamorous, and she attracts the attention of the entire establishment.

I am longing to see her face. The shop assistants call her Luciana. She turns to leave and I get a glimpse. Perfectly made-up in a semi-theatrical manner, as many older Italian women are. Large eyes with lots of dark eye shadow and mascara, tinted eyebrows, paler lips, high cheekbones and a luminescent smile. I almost have to step back when she flashes it at me. Not because she knows me, but simply because I am there, looking at her. *Luce* means 'light' in Italian.

She is in her late sixties, at least, and I hope with all my heart that when the time comes I will look like that. She is a type of Italian woman that is prolific here. Their mental mindset must say, 'I am twenty-five,' as they look it, even on the farthest side of sixty. This is not to say they act as though they are twenty-five, or are in some way immature or unaccepting of their age. These women are usually not of the generation and often not of the means to invest in plastic surgery.

I often see these types of women in bathing suits and their muscles, if they have any, have all permanently retired and are on the pension.

Wrinkles and saggy skin abound. They wear it with aplomb. Their attitude truly says, 'Beauty is at *any* age, not just for the young and firm.'

I admire them so much, for not leaving behind the opportunity to dress elegantly yet comfortably, to be playful and feminine, to be made-up and have your hair done, at any age and on a Saturday morning, when all you are doing is picking up your dry-cleaning. I love that about Italy.

I often saw Luciana around my neighbourhood after that first time at the tailor's. She always looked the same; radiant and enjoying her life. I reflected on the lack of angst in Italian women I knew compared to my Anglo-Saxon friends, who all declared that life was over for them as women once they were fifty. It seemed to me that there was no age limit on beauty in Italy and no expectation that there would be. A woman is still a woman at whatever age, and capable of being beautiful in any shape, form or stage of life. And once they are really old, they still deserve deference because they were once beautiful young women.

At one of the local *bars* there is a group of women, easily in their eighties, who are usually seated around a table outside, smoking and drinking their coffees in the morning. I often say '*Buongiorno*,' and they greet me back as I take a table next to them when I have time for a leisurely morning *cappuccino*. There is no table service at this *bar* but when these women want a refill, or anything in fact, they yell from the street to the *barista* inside, a man in his thirties, and he comes *running* out with whatever they have asked for. After a few hours, usually just before lunchtime, they raise themselves up as one on their walking sticks, and smoke and make their way back home.

One day as I was walking in a piazza in the centre of Rome, I was passed by an elderly woman wearing the apron of a cook, striding out of a restaurant. Behind her was a young guy in his twenties, who was desperately yelling out to get her attention. His manner was all deference. I expected her to respond kindly, based on her age and her maternal-like apparel. 'What the fuck do you want?' she said to him when he finally caught up to her. Women constantly surprise me here.

* * *

I *love* living in a place where going to the tailor is part of everyday living, not just the domain of the rich and famous. Everyone here goes to the tailor to get garments taken up, in, out, down or completely changed in form, such as from trousers to a skirt. It is essential that your clothes fit properly here, and there is no excuse when every area has dozens of *sarte* (tailors and dressmakers) and it costs about five euro to make your pants fit properly. Of course, this doesn't include the whole getting clothes actually made for you part of the *sarte* trade. Many people get suits, shirts, dresses and formal eveningwear made up by the local tailor.

Getting clothes to fit you properly is part of the whole 'everyone is a unique individual and starring in their own show' part of the Italian culture. It is important to make the most of your individual shape, weight and height. This contributes to the idea that beauty is diverse and not just in one kind of form. Beauty is taking your own form and appreciating it, approving of it and dressing it the best you can.

I have two tailors, actually. One is Rosita, who owns the establishment I was in when I saw Luciana picking up her dry-cleaning. It's far too large to call a shop and includes dozens of women on sewing machines, as well as several fitting rooms. The place is always packed with customers but she deals with everyone quickly, personally and with a smile. She makes me stand on a wooden block in the middle of the shop, one of many people she is working on at the same time. She pins and smooths garments over me, talking nonstop and commenting bluntly, in the way Romans do, on whether my bottom is sticking out or if too much of my breasts are showing, patting me intimately and adjusting parts of my anatomy as if I were a mannequin, in order to make the clothes sit straight.

I imagine this is what it must be like having a mother and I quite enjoy it, this intimate treatment of me. As the seamstresses buzz and whir on their machines around me, manifesting the personal instructions Rosita is giving them, I feel as though I am part of a special club, all sharing secrets about our anatomies and helping each other to create confidence in ourselves. We acknowledge and downplay our shared but slightly different weaknesses. It is a secret world of women that I have never been in before.

The other tailor I have is Francesca, who used to live in the apartment next door. She worked from her lounge room, which was always full of customers and included a mannequin and loads of garments in different states of repair. I went there when I needed a quick adjustment. I used to ring the doorbell with the garment already on me and she pinned and tucked it, offering me a cigarette and something to drink as I stood on her small coffee table. Then I would change into a tracksuit and chat with the other customers, who were also often tenants from my building or local shopkeepers, before going back home next door.

Francesca does all her own work and can design, cut and sew a garment without a pattern. She makes all of her own clothes and those of many of her friends in the *palazzo*. Her own large, short and fiftyish figure is always femininely clad in dresses of her own design made to suit her shape and celebrate its form.

Could it be that the Italians know the antidote for everything? Loss of youthful beauty: think 'beauty is at any age'. Less-than-perfect physical shape: get a tailor. I love living here, and I love that it is now autumn.

Chapter 22

Is this an earthquake or
is the building just collapsing?

I like accordion music, so it's lucky that I live in Italy. It's a bit stereotypical, though, imagining that accordion music is always wafting through the streets of Italy. It hardly ever is, except when I go to *la macelleria*, the butchers. When there are no customers he can be found on the other side of the counter, sitting in front of his music stand, playing the accordion.

It was quite disconcerting the first time I came upon him. He stood up hurriedly, wiped his hands on his bloody apron and carved me off a *bella bistecca*, a beautiful steak, as though butchering and playing the accordian were two seamlessly linked activities. I liked going there better than *la frutteria*, the greengrocers. There a wizened old crone serves me and she screams at me if I touch the produce.

You are rarely allowed to touch or pick your own produce in greengrocer stores in Italy. This also extends to clothing, shoes and just about anything else you want to buy; the salesperson handles the merchandise, you don't. In the case of my *frutteria*, the produce is all selected by the wizened old crone and sometimes takes ages when the shop is full. Everyone has to have a chat at the end of each transaction and talk about what they will have for lunch. Popping in to buy a kilo of oranges can take half an hour. As well as this, the bent-over crone delights in making lewd comments about the fruit and vegetables I ask for.

In the Roman dialect, the same legitimate words used for fruit and vegetables are also common slang for male genitalia and homosexuality, while others sound exactly like the word used for female genitalia. *Piselli* (peas) is the slang for male genitalia, *finnochio* (fennel) describes a male who is gay, and *fica* which is so close to *fico* (fig) is slang for a vagina.

I adore figs. I am always so worried about asking for 'a kilo of vaginas' in front of a shop full of customers that I can never remember the word I am absolutely *not* to say. Stammering and blushing, I eventually get so confused that I just point and ask for a kilo of 'those'. The crone loves asking me, in front of a shop of customers, if I will be having any *piselli* this evening. Winking, she wheezily joins in laughing at me with all the other customers. At the end of a hard day, a visit to the *frutteria* could just about send me over the edge. I always came away sweating, and once or twice, crying.

La farmacia, or the chemist, is bliss though. In Italy they have cut out the middle-man – the doctor. You can buy just about any drug you want over the counter. If you can diagnose yourself as having an upper respiratory tract infection or gastroenteritis, you just explain that to the pharmacist and they give you an appropriate antibiotic. The more you pay, the stronger medication you get. If you can't diagnose yourself, you just explain to the pharmacist what is wrong (even over the phone) and he or she will prescribe something for you. Ventolin inhalers and steroid dilators are given out over the counter, too. I know this, as I am an asthmatic. I used to pretend I was an English tourist on holiday and had left my script in London until I realised no-one cared.

Neighbourhood supermarkets caught on in Rome in the late 1990s. I knew I had been in Rome a long time on the morning when I woke up excited because it was the opening of the first local supermarket. I had spent my whole life shopping in supermarkets in Australia. *Every* Saturday morning for the decade before I left was spent shopping at a supermarket. But I had lived in Rome seven years by then, shopping at *l'alimentare*, the local grocers, and a supermarket was a big thing.

L'alimentare is a quaint and wondrous part of Italian daily life. It is a mix between a grocery shop and a delicatessen. Most of them require you to walk down the one aisle with a shopping trolley. They sell canned and packeted goods, personal hygiene and cleaning goods, fresh bread, salami, hams, cheeses and a wonderful assortment of dried tomatoes, olives, anchovies, baked eggplant and peppers in oil, pickled seafood and smoked salmon. I love getting one hundred grams of everything. That was until one day, while I was at the checkout, Gianni the checkout guy produced a slip of paper from his pocket and told me to read it when I got home. It was a sensual, romantic, tender poem about me. A beautifully written declaration of love. I was so embarrassed I always found it hard to shop there forever after.

Which was actually rather hard, as this *alimentare* was at the bottom of my previous apartment building. In fact, all the shops were. Almost every apartment block has its own collection of daily living foodshops. Italians don't like to go far to do anything and they like to shop everyday. That is another reason why supermarkets have been slow movers here. Why do a weekly shop and stick it all in the freezer? What would you do for the rest of the week? Who would you talk to? Every purchase is a social interaction. What you had for dinner last night, where you are going on holidays, the latest chat show topic and, of course, the football scores (although people often keep away from those, as it can lead to blows and ruin a good morning's shopping).

These are all topics for discussion before, during and after the purchase. There is no such thing as a rush. I found it infuriating until I adjusted to the pace, and realised the mental and physical benefits of not trying to do one hundred things in an hour. How pleasant life is when a simple task becomes one to do slowly and with relish. How much more is your sense of satisfaction in life when every task is noticed, and noted, when accomplished.

The Italians certainly know how to live life. They don't know how to build apartment blocks, though. The first apartment block I moved into in Rome, in the apartment I shared with Elish, was on a lean. A quite significant, Leaning Tower of Pisa, have-to-sleep-with-your-head-up-the-right-end, feel-a-little-tipsy-until-you-get-used-to-it type of lean.

During the 1960s housing boom in Rome, scores of apartment blocks were erected in our area. It is quite close to the centre, only about a fifteen-minute drive and still quite green, so it was a popular area. However, the land was not adequately surveyed. No-one can quite tell me why, but suffice to say it appeared the land had been surveyed – Romans come from quite a good stock of builders after all – when it hadn't. For further clarification, I refer you to the aforementioned observations on the Italian relationship to numbers, and the functioning of the Italian State.

Soon after being built, the buildings started to sink, lean and generally move. That is also why we had a number of nice parks around us, all about the size of apartment blocks. The area is well-known in Rome, I discovered. My new Italian friends would always laugh at me when I told them where I lived. 'Oh, the place with the leaning apartments of Pisa!' they would say.

I come from a family of architects and engineers. My father won't step out onto a balcony he hasn't built, as he knows how easy they are to get wrong. I also have a number of friends in those professions who told me after visiting that the apartment would definitely collapse and that it was just a matter of time. I was justifiably concerned. I had paid my huge bond though, and the rent for this apartment was very, very cheap. The block was full of families who had lived there since it was built. Nobody else seemed to worry about it, so I just put it out of mind. Until the day of the earthquake.

Italy regularly hosts earthquakes, some highly destructive and well-known, such as the 1980 earthquake in Naples and the 2009 earthquake in L'Aquila. In between and since, there have been regular, low-level earthquakes in Rome and its surroundings. Earthquakes in Rome, although not high on the rictor scale, result in a lot of damage and are dangerous. This is due to the age of the buildings (2000-year old ruins), the fact that they are all high-rise and the bad condition of the relatively new ones, like ours. Even the smallest of tremours can cause gas explosions to badly maintained apartment blocks, collapsing of buildings due to unsurveyed or unapproved renovations, and fatal cracking or structural damage. I have trembled through many such small earthquakes in my seventeen years here, all safely, but the first one I ever experienced happened to be the biggest, and I was living in a leaning building.

On the day of *the* earthquake in 1994, I had just come back from a run and was doing some stretches out on the balcony. In fact, I was doing some leg stretches against the furthest edge of the balcony, the part where the lean is the most pronounced and faces the concrete drive six storeys below, when I felt the building begin to wobble. 'Wobble' is the only word I can use to describe what I felt. The building actually and very definitely wobbled, for what seemed like minutes.

This was my first earthquake ever, and it is scarier than waking up and finding a tarantula on your face. There is nowhere to go, nowhere to run, nowhere to hide, nowhere to *get away from it*. I didn't actually know what it was. I didn't know it was an earthquake or that Italy could have earthquakes. What I did know was that I was in a building which was on a lean, that was doomed to fall, and that it was wobbling.

I ran out the front door, and my worst fears were confirmed as I saw my ashen-faced neighbour huddled with all his children in his doorway. *You fool!* I thought. *That is what you do in an earthquake? It is not going to help you if the building is falling down, is it?*

I thought all of this in the split second it took me to run from my front door to the stairs. *Lucky I have my running shoes on and not my usual three-inch heel Italian streetwear*, I also thought.

I bounded for my life down the stairs. I expected that at any minute the stairwell would probably go and I would have to jump from floor to floor, as I knew it would be a few seconds before they would cave in too. I was prepared. The one thing I knew was not going to happen was that I was going to be squashed to death by rubble in a badly made apartment building in Rome.

When I reached the bottom floor, having rushed past five floors of ashen-faced Italians cowering in doorways looking incredulously at me leaping down the stairs, I began to realise the building was probably not going to fall. At least, not today. I did not stop, though. I rushed right out the main front door and stood at the bottom of the leaning building, at the wrong side of the lean. I knew I should have kept running as, logically, I was in the direct path of the falling building. But something made me stop. It might have been the old man from the *bar* next door who met me grinning at the front door and asked me with an air of excitement if I had 'felt it'.

'Err, yes,' I said. 'I felt it. Amazing, wasn't it?'

He buzzed upstairs for his wife to open the main door. I realised I had left my keys in the apartment and asked if he wouldn't mind letting me in, too. I climbed the stairs, shame-faced, looking at all the families still with their doors open, who were now mostly on the telephone.

The whole place was abuzz with excitement. Everyone stopped talking and turned to stare at me when I reached my floor. My front door was wide open.

'You know,' said a small child of seven, one of my neighbour's kids, 'running down the stairs during an earthquake is probably the most dangerous thing you can do.'

In comparison, a trip to *la frutteria* was always easier after that.

Chapter 23

Long live the piazza!

I never get sick of doing the same things in Rome. I can go for walks to the same piazzas three times a day, have coffee in the same *bar* three times a day, walk the same walk, see the same shops, and it always seems like a fresh, new, exciting experience for me.

Today is Saturday, and time for a trip to the market that used to be my local before I swapped the inner city for Garbatella. It is one of the most colourful, certainly one of the oldest, in Rome. Held in the beautiful piazza of Campo dei Fiori, it is also one of the things I never get sick of doing. I walk to it along my old street, which resembles a narrow corridor. Its sides are ancient buildings, which stop the light from reaching down to the pavement. I turn into Via dei Cappelle (street of the hat makers) which is wide enough for a car and pedestrians, but no-one would be mad enough to try and get a car down there.

It is a street full of antique furniture makers (it used to be hats, hence the name) and more of their produce is actually on the street than in the shops. Men are planing and sanding, staining and talking, smoking and standing together. A red plastic bucket and mop lean against a wall next to a fountain. The water runs continually from these 'pedestrian' fountains, set up by an emperor to ensure that Roman citizens always had clean, fresh water to drink and wash with. Now they use it to mop floors. A solitary sock hangs from a washing line strung between two windows.

I keep my head down as I pass a rather large group of men. In the

Italian code of behaviour between the sexes, this signifies that I'm not interested in talking, meeting them, or anything else they might have in mind. Even so, they crane their necks as one to ogle me as I pass, not losing the rhythm of their conversation.

I am naturally blonde and have blue eyes. By now my gait, expression and clothes don't single me out from any other Italian woman, but I feel that my hair and eyes are like a shining beacon, a loudspeaker to announce my foreignness and hence my availability, vulnerability and difference from all the other women they ogle in the course of a day.

The market in the piazza of Campo dei Fiori hits me full in the face as I turn the corner and enter it. Fruit and vegetable stalls are crammed up against the walls of the piazza, obscuring vision and narrowing it to the pile of carrots and peppers in front of you. Past that heap is another and another, until at last you seem to break out into a clear space. This space is something that passes as a road for cars, although it is mostly covered in flower stalls. In this space is a raggedy old man, shouting at passers-by through the cigarette perched on his lip and pointing to a bucket at his feet. On top of the bucket, neatly laid out, their skins gleaming in the dull light, are kippers. They are beautiful. I look furtively at them but I am too scared to buy any. I don't know if he will clean them or not and I am sure I wouldn't have time to ask him before they'd be bound up in newspaper and thrust into my arms.

I need minestrone mix. It is the first thing I see on the stall to my right after the fish man. I am elated. I find it all too intense some mornings, the sights, sounds, smells, the vibe.

In fact, in order to deal with the vegetables in my face, the vendors screaming in my ear, the pickpockets jostling me and the bags pulling my arm joints out, I had already braced myself with a stop at my usual café, the Gran Café.

This little piece of pastry heaven is off the main piazza. It is on the corner of another, more sedate and slightly grander piazza, made so by the fact that the impressive Michelangelo-designed French Embassy is in it. Like everything French, it demands to be adored in quietness and grandeur.

The Gran Café is not just any old café; it is also a *pasticceria*, which means it makes its own pastries, tarts, biscuits and croissants right there on the premises. This means three things: the products are often hot, they are always fresh and they are always good. As they are made there, it cannot be blamed on the supplier if anyone complains.

It is usually an extremely busy café but today I was lucky, as the weather was bad so no-one was sitting outside. I was greeted by the woman at the till, who screamed, '*Buongiorno, bella!*' at me, a term she uses with everyone female, in between swearing at the electric cash register. I ordered, which was then repeated in shouts to the men working behind the counter next to her. She gave me my change and screamed, '*Via, via!*' (go, go) then, '*Si, dimmi!*' (yes, tell me) to the next person.

I made my way to the crowded counter and repeated my order, screaming. They screamed it back at me. Other people were screaming their orders. Italian cafés are to be exalted for their coffee and pastries, but not for their relaxing atmosphere.

* * *

Getting the minestrone is easy, as the man serving me is considerate. He waits until I have made up my mind which fruit and vegetables I want instead of making me hurry up by screaming the names of every fruit and vegetable under the sun in an apparent attempt to jog my memory. This method never jogs my memory – it just confuses me more.

The first time I ever went to the markets in Rome I came home sweating, crying and empty-handed, and vowed never to go again no matter how cheap everything was. As I sobbed in the arms of my then flatmate, she assured me that we would just go to the supermarket from then on, and that it was a good experience but we didn't ever have to do it again. I miss her so much.

The minute you stop to look at anything, the vendors scream, '*Dimmi, signora!*' (tell me, Mrs) at you and then stand impatiently scrunching paper bags in front of you. Then, when you suggest something, you have a kilo of it before you can blink. Then they scream, '*Poi, poi?*' (then, then) at you and you have to scream back, '*Basta cosi!*' (that's enough), at which stage they tell you how cheap the tomatoes are this week, and you have a bag half-full of them as well.

You have to think quick in another language, so it's no wonder it has taken me many years to be able to do this. I have also learnt to scream, '*No, sto soltanto guardando!*' (I am only looking).

I glide past the fish stalls. I usually stop to admire them, even though the vendors scream at me. There are glistening pink salmon cut into steaks, buckets of still-alive and crawling creatures, all imaginable shapes and sizes of shells containing tiny, delectable creatures, slippery eels and fish shimmery in their silver skins.

The displays are stacked on ice or swimming in buckets, and most creatures there I have never seen before. The men behind the stalls are fishermen with weather-beaten faces. If you point at a fish they have it gutted in front of you in the blink of an eye with a razor-sharp knife, and the insides slip into a bloody bucket at your feet.

Next to the fish is a small stall with half a lamb hanging up and some chicken pieces on display. It is in front of a monument which is in the middle of the square and a resting spot for tourists. Several of them are looking with disbelief at this store; there is no refrigeration, no packaging, just raw meat hanging up on display. I don't think they mean it, but their faces are full of revulsion.

I head for the cheese and salami caravan. I buy ricotta and some salami; small, thickly sliced and chewy, with big globules of fat. There is a family of tourists standing behind me nervously deciding what to get. They are consulting their guidebooks and watching me. They seem disappointed that I speak Italian and understand the barked commands of the *signora* serving me. The *signora* ignores them and begins talking to two elderly ladies that have just arrived. She serves them some ham to taste and they feed it to each other, all the while talking. I turn to go and smile apologetically at the family, wishing them luck. *Maybe I should offer to help*, I think, but I am gone before I finish the thought.

The bread shop, which is actually a permanent shop in the piazza, is not as crowded as usual, it being already late in the morning, and I only have to queue for about five minutes. The greatest fun is getting out once you have made your way to the counter and bought your bread. You turn and face a sea of people, smiling apologetically, holding your bread up high over your head like a prize and laugh. Everybody laughs. It is the only way to deal with the fact that just getting your daily (albeit extremely good) bread is a ridiculously stressing experience.

The five men serving behind the counter seem to know automatically who is next and there is never any complaining or undue pushing. There is never any bread on the shelves either, as it sells too quickly. So you already have to know what you want.

I usually get *pizza bianca* (white pizza bread) which is like a flat white focaccia; crispy on the outside, a bit oily, definitely salty and called 'white' because it isn't painted with tomato paste. It is always hot and I usually eat it all on the way home. Sometimes I buy sweet buns for Sunday breakfast. Italian bread comes in so many glorious shapes, sizes and flavours.

Bread never comes sliced, even from the bakery. When I first discovered this, my concern was how I was going to slice my bread thin enough to fit in the toaster. Then I discovered that toasters didn't exist either, which solved the whole problem and made me realise I would have to eat *cornetti* every morning for breakfast like everyone else. It was an early, but important, letting go of what was and embracing what is.

I have completed a full circuit of the piazza now and I'm am back in front of the first pile of carrots and peppers I started from. I am looking for *rughetta*. I ask an ancient-looking woman, who only has two teeth on the upper left side of her mouth and who is wearing a black plastic garbage bag as an apron over a full-length skirt. She yells to another, just as ancient woman, who is peeling something and then, as the answer is in the affirmative, yells at a young woman, who comes to serve me.

I stare in amazement at these two elderly women as I wait for the *rughetta*. They look as though they were here a hundred years ago and maybe stayed too long.

I lie. I tell the young woman I am a photographer from Australia for a magazine and ask if I can take their photo. I ask her because I am too afraid to ask the women themselves. They have a look that suggests they are rooted to the earth and nothing fazes them. The young woman replies that everyone wants to take photos of them and many do and it annoys them a lot, but if I ask they might say yes.

The young woman asks them for me, and the one with few teeth grins and says triumphantly that her photograph has appeared in magazines all over the world, so what is one more?

'All over the world, haven't we been?' she says to her friend, who stops peeling and swaggers over to me.

'Yes, that's right', she agrees. 'Come back next Tuesday morning at 8am and we can do a photo shoot then.'

Crossing the square, I duck in to the *salumeria*. I say 'duck' because you have to duck your head as you enter, otherwise it is clanked against the dozens of parma hams hanging from the roof. Salamis hanging in a line make a curtain from behind which the men at the counter ask you what you want. Sausages are coiled in long loops from the roof and the counter. The room is filled with cuts of pork, shish kebabs, livers and more salamis. I order *prosciutto*, a hundred grams, and go out into the sunlight again.

* * *

I go back later in the day to Campo dei Fiori. At 6.30pm I enter an entirely different piazza. Gone are the stalls of fruit and vegetables. In fact, not even a vegetable scrap on the ground remains. In the place where the fish stalls had been not even a faint smell lingers. The piazza is clear, wide and spacious, occupied only by the central statue of Giordano Bruno. Around the sides of the piazza are several restaurants that hadn't even attempted to try and show their faces this morning. Tables covered with red checked tablecloths or white linen ones stand under large umbrellas. A newspaper stand is there but besides that the piazza is empty, a great sweeping space, washed clean by rain and road sweepers, an unimaginable sight only a few hours before.

I walk slowly through the quiet space towards the cinema and the *alimentare* on the other side, checking the faces at the *vineria*, the wine bar, for familiarity. A large fountain bubbles away, which had been completely hidden this morning. A dog bounds around and a small child plays football with his father on what I suppose is his version of an oval. The piazza had served as my shopping mall this morning. This afternoon, the same piazza is my leisure park, my place to meet friends, relax and wind down. Long live the piazza!

WINTER

Chapter 24

Yes, Rome gets cold

It is winter! Snowy, icy, freezing winter. It is a time to store up cold freshness, enough to last you through the long, hot summer. It is sometimes hard to tell that it is winter in Rome. The days are often bathed in brilliant sunshine, bright and clear as a spring or summer day. The only difference is the colours. It is a lemony sunshine, sometimes even as pale as almond flesh. It may be bright and strong – if bathed in it you can feel the warmth of the spring to come – but it is not the full, deep, banana custard yellow sunshine that you get at other times of the year. The sun glitters like a cold crystal. You can look at it and get its measure, unlike the fiery orb it becomes in the summer, the one that threatens to destroy your retinas if you dare to look it full in the face.

The sky is a brilliant blue. The soft sun brings out the full hue of the Mediterranean blue in the Mediterranean sky; there is no strong sunshine to compete with its colouring, to dilute it. It is there in its full, overarching glory, clear and cloudless, and it can fool the unsuspecting with its hints of summer delights.

We had some friends from Berlin staying with us last weekend, in December. The sunshine was brilliant on their first morning out. They gaily walked out into the air, minus several layers that they would usually wear, including some that most Romans were wearing. They were brought back by midday, crying and shivering, to be doused with hot water in order to restore their body temperature to that of the living.

It is cold, very, very cold. I know some countries are much colder, but I think zero degrees Celsius qualifies a place to be called cold. The air bites at you. You see your breath in front of you and exercise is harder on your lungs due to the freshness of the air. It is harder to build up a sweat doing anything, and so much energy is required just to keep warm. Ear lobes, fingers, noses, foreheads and toes are all liable to become painful without the proper attire. Gloves, hats, scarves and good woollen coats are a necessity, not an option.

The outlines of those things that were clear in autumn go hazy again, like in summer, surrounded by the cold, frosty air. Where the sun touches during the day warmth can be felt, but the moment it moves on its warm kiss leaves no trace. It is quiet. The air is still. The leaves have mostly gone, and reduced the trees and bushes to stick-like figures of their former selves. There is nothing to rustle through, even if there is wind. Dampness holds most of the flowers and grasses in place, sodden and unmoving. The rains come occasionally but they don't lash at you like in autumn or spring.

For most of winter, Romans are recovering from the overindulgences of Christmas and New Year. It is reported that most Italians put on an average of three kilos each over Christmas. Many of them go to work it off on the ski slopes for a Settimana Bianca (literally translated as 'White Week', although it is probably something like 'skiing holiday' in English). It is a tradition as sacred as the annual summer holiday, and I suspect one of the reasons that the average Italian gets five weeks holiday a year – four weeks summer holiday and one for the Settimana Bianca. This is apart from supplementary holidays, such as two weeks for your honeymoon, which by law cannot be taken out of your annual leave.

The Romans who remain in Rome bask in the quietness of post-Christmas festivities and leave most of the carnivaling up to the Venetians. February, too, is quite peaceful. It is too cold to spend much time outside so the streets are quieter, the rains have washed away the rubbish so they are cleaner, and the cool temperatures serve to keep smells and noises at a distance. Bathed in winter sunshine, Rome is sparkling and at rest. Even the tourists are fewer. Those who come for Christmas and New Year leave quickly afterwards, and most restaurants and hotels close for the rest of January.

Once Christmas has passed winter is a cool, quiet and peaceful season. Things hunker down – plants, birds and humans – and wait for the awakening that is spring. Large amounts of carbohydrates serve to keep up winter warmth and provide the calories required to keep warm. Beans, polenta, rice, barley, lentils, pasta and red meats feature almost exclusively in winter menus. Lentils that come in a variety of colours and sizes, as well as a myriad of grains that I have never seen before, appear in soups and accompany meats. Root vegetables such as potatoes, turnips, white beetroot and carrots are everywhere, as well as many types of broccoli (Sicilian, Roman, Calabrian), cauliflower and a thing that looks like a cross between the two and is called *broccolo*.

Indoors it is always warm and cosy in winter. Rome may not do air-conditioning well, but it does heating very well. I have never, ever been cold indoors in Rome. Heating is seen as a serious business and therefore seriously attended to. The fear of a change of temperature and exposure to cold air, leading to influenza or fever and sudden death, is never far from most Italian minds. It is therefore imperative to keep inside temperatures warm and constant. All Roman apartments are heated in every room, including bathrooms and corridors. Thick walls and the inherent design of apartment blocks keeps in the heat, as it does in the summer, so that loose, light and comfortable clothing can be worn indoors.

Winter is the time for visiting and lingering in a *vineria*. These are the Italian equivalent of a wine bar, and are one of the best inventions ever. An authentic *vineria* is always dark, crowded and very small. It is essentially a place to sample wine by the glass, as much as you want and mostly whenever you want. Being an Italian institution, it will come fully-equipped with the possibility of eating something, sitting down and feasting your eyes on the aesthetic array of wines stacked up around the walls, from floor to ceiling. If you go to a *vineria* that is sleek, spacious and offers you a written menu, then leave.

A typical *vineria* is run like the taverns of ancient Rome. Wines available are written up in chalk, on the wall or in tome-like volumes that take more than one person to carry and are taken from table to table by the proprietor, if you ask. Food is what you see on the counter, or written up on the wall. Traditionally, the food consists of a plate of cheeses or salamis and hams, a mixture of both, or sometimes small appetisers, such as smoked salmon wrapped around olives or tiny stuffed tomatoes.

Winter evenings are a delight to spend in a place like this. Deep reds from the north and south of the country warm the cockles of your heart as you imbibe. They serve in clearing out the arteries of the pungent cheeses and the juices of the succulent salamis and other cured meats, some of which are in fact just slices of fat. I love living in a country where lard is a respected food group.

A *vineria* is not the place for a romantic date or a quiet catch-up with friends, unless you go at the unsociable hour of 6pm on a Monday evening, and even then you may not be in luck. They are popular at any time of the evening and are usually filled to standing room only. Jostling is a sign of a great *vineria*. If you leave one feeling like you have been continually jostled throughout your evening, you have been at a good one. Those who are lucky enough get a seat or a table; those who come later stand, often right up against the table.

The proprietor and one or two staff members must continually wend their way through this crowd carrying plates of cheeses and salamis, and you often have to go and ask yourself at the counter for your wine. If you want something that is not written in chalk on the wall you will be handed the tome, inside which you will find almost every wine known to mankind, and some known only to the Medicis. You will find wines from all over Italy, and nowhere else, ranging from the usual 11 to 15 euro, to your whole month's paycheque. It is best to come with someone with whom you don't want to have an in-depth conversation, as it is hard to keep your eyes off the floor-to-ceiling stacks of labels, bottles, boxes, books and other wine paraphernalia. It is also hard to concentrate or listen while the effects of the gorgeous wine, the deep cheeses and the succulent salamis are being felt. It is better to give yourself over to the gourmet delights and just groan, nod, sip and watch.

Coming out into a bitter winter night is the only way to counteract the glasses of wine and plates of cheeses and salamis. If it was summer you would probably collapse. Somehow, the winter nights allow such indulgences and your waistline doesn't seem to get any bigger. Gulping in fresh lungfuls of air, seeing your breath steam out in front of you, crunching along clean, wet sidewalks in the dark and in the low temperatures, is a great way of sobering up. It takes a surprisingly short distance before you realise you are ready for another round.

Chapter 25

A Roman New Year's

The lentils are simmering, the seafood is glistening, the champagne is chilling and all the windows are clean. We have invited eight people for a relaxed, intimate New Year's Eve. All evening I have watched people stream in through the gate to our apartment block, carrying plastic bags and big paper bags clinking and crammed with goodies.

New Year's Eve is a big thing in Rome – in all of Italy – and there are precise rules and traditions which are mostly always followed. It is quite proscriptive. There are always lentils, which represent prosperity, so you are therefore supposed to eat as many as possible in order to become rich the following year. The lentils accompany a pig's trotter or a *cotechino*, a rather slimy but delicious pork sausage. We don't know what that represents. Seafood is always served for *antipasto*. Dessert is always a *pannetone* or *pandoro*, the traditional Christmas cakes, and there is Prosecco at midnight and lots of wine, pasta and cooked meats thrown in for good measure.

The windows are clean, as we want to take in that other Roman tradition on New Year's Eve: fireworks. They start two or three days before New Year's Eve if you're lucky, otherwise you may be hearing crackers let off for up to a month beforehand. These are the small ones that aren't anything to look at but make a noise like gunshot, very loudly. The aesthetic ones usually start going off at about 11.30pm and go for at least an hour. They are let off from every spare space available: sidewalks, small piazzas, parking lots, rooftops and balconies. They are sold to everyone and anyone. The best ones are made illegally in Naples and every year there are news items of police raids to factories where hoards of illegal firecrackers are being made and sold. This year's toll of serious injuries is just five hundred people and no mortalities, for a change.

Our guests arrive, amazed at the amount of car spaces available in our street and in the small piazza at the end of it. You usually have to circle at least three times before finding something semi-legal to park in.

We break with tradition and drink Prosecco from the beginning. Our feasting begins with marinated squid, soaked in olive oil and parsley; rich, white and chewy. Then we have smoked salmon on brown bread with butter, cheeses and salami from Milan, and smoked ham, or speck, from much further north in the cold, Germanic regions of Italy. The lentils and pork sausage are next. The plain, wholesome flavour of the lentils, which have been lightly stewed with garlic and fresh olive oil from my colleague's olive grove, perfectly complement the tangy, fleshy, unmistakeably porky flavour of the sausage. It is divine; pink, grisly, full of flavour and eaten only on New Year's Eve.

It is nearing midnight and the clean windows are about to be used. Little did we know when we accepted to rent this apartment that one of its qualities would be the ability to watch fireworks from every window. From our windows and balcony it is possible to watch fireworks in the south, west and north of the city. However, our guests are so entertained by the ones being let off from the roof opposite that they fail to notice that the piazza, where there were so many car spaces earlier in the night, is also a place for major firework letting-off. And I'm not talking about the large sparkler type suitable for back gardens; I'm talking major Catherine wheels, rocket shooters and ones that light up the whole sky.

It seems the whole city is alight, as every second the skies are lit up from close by and far away, in every direction and from many different balconies. Soon the rooftops are hidden by clouds of smoke and nothing can be seen except the fireworks once they go off. And they do, for a full hour. It is too dangerous to go down into the street to check our cars – every now and then we hear an almighty clap and see smoke billowing from the direction of the piazza. It is a good idea we have started the Prosecco early, as it takes the edge off.

Although exciting, for me it is tame after having witnessed a New Year's Eve in the very south of Italy. At 5pm all the shops began shutting, which was early as usually stores are open until 7.30pm. But it was not their usual shutting and bolting. To my great consternation, shop fronts were being boarded up by the harried shopkeepers with nails, hammers and pieces of wood, in a hurry, with furtive looks over shoulders.

'What's happening?' I had asked Alfredo.

'Ah, it's just how we do New Year's Eve here,' he said.

'But what is going to happen?' I ventured. 'Why do they need to board up the windows?'

'Oh, it's in case of *bombe*, you know, the homemade fireworks that people let off on New Year's Eve?' he said.

Well, now I did know. Shortly afterwards, my husband drove our car out of the city and walked back in. It took him an hour. The whole city was walking back in. The streets, usually triple-parked with cars, were deserted. I had never, in all my ten years of visiting this southern city, seen the streets without cars.

'Is that because of the 'bombs', too?' I had asked.

'Yes,' Alfredo said. 'And also the things people throw over their balconies at midnight to celebrate.'

'Like what?' I said, imagining things like rubbish, paper cups and streamers.

'Like whitegoods, televisions, electrical appliances; anything they don't want anymore,' he said. 'It's symbolic – out with the old. It's an old tradition and not many people do it anymore but you don't want to be near that one washing machine when it falls from the sixth floor.'

The worst was yet to come. After finishing our romantic seafood dinner, just the two of us, it was time to go out onto the balcony and enjoy the view of the fireworks. Except that the balcony opposite us, on the other side of a very narrow, one-way street, was letting them off. The balcony was very small and closed over at the top, so when lighting firecrackers they couldn't be aimed up. They had to be aimed out, at us. After a few lucky misses we hurriedly went inside, lowered our heavy wooden external blinds and watched the rest on television.

* * *

It sounds like a war scene outside our apartment in Garbatella, and I am reminded of another, rather unsuccessful New Year's Eve in my first year of living in Rome. I had hosted two young men who were refugees from the war in Bosnia. My flatmate and I had met them sleeping in a car and often had them over for a hot meal and to take a wash. They had been drafted into the Bosnian army, and after three years of fighting had fled to Italy in order to escape another three years in the army. One of them was sixteen when he had first been trained as a sniper.

As soon as the firecrackers started going off on New Year's Eve they were both under the dining table, petrified. No-one really enjoyed themselves after that, so I try to avoid inviting guests that have had actual experiences of war.

All night, as I am filling champagne flutes full of Prosecco and champagne, I am also receiving constant knockbacks as guests say things like, 'Oh, no thanks, I'm doing water for this round,' or 'No thanks, I'm alternating; one water, one champagne.'

I hazily think, *But why would you want to drink water when the champers is so nice and really not necessary to dilute with water if you drink in moderation, like I'm doing.*

* * *

The next morning I wake with a champagne headache and hangover that I am really too old for. It is like I am in my late teens again and all that 'drinking wisdom' that you earn from hard experience has just been forgotten. I marvel at my ability to regress into a teenager just because it was New Year's Eve and I was at home so could have as much as I liked.

I can barely move my head and, as on all such occasions when I have overindulged, visions of steaming plates of pasta dance in my head. Eating pasta and headache tablets always makes me feel better. It's the getting to the pasta so I can take a tablet that is the hard bit.

'Where can we go?' I lament to my husband, assuming that on New Year's Day all will be closed in the country that doesn't know what a convenience store is.

'Well, we could always go over there,' he says, pointing at *Er Timoniere* whose door is miraculously open. The Hallelujah chorus goes off in my head as I struggle on a pair of trousers, wash my face and don my coat.

We are surrounded by *case populare*, or State-owned housing blocks. They can never be sold and tenants never leave, hence generation after generation of families live here, and many people live within eyesight of their extended families, if not in the same apartment block. It is sometimes still 'colourful', like the other day when a woman got out of her car, stood at the bottom of a five-storey building and proceeded to loudly ask the *puttana* (slut) who knew who she was, to please come out and explain herself. The shouting went on for about twenty minutes while the whole neighbourhood watched and a distraught man tried to unsuccessfully drag her back into the car. The *puttana* wisely never showed her face.

One of the best reasons to live here, besides its proximity to the centre of Rome, its quiet traditional lifestyle, its friendly and truly 'Roman' population (Roman is the only dialect spoken in this suburb) is the food. The tiny, family-run *trattorie* have no signs, are in no guidebooks, have no menus, don't take bookings and make the best traditional Roman food around. Lunchtimes they are packed, as those in the know come from all over to sample a traditional Roman lunch, and the locals who work in the area don't go home for lunch. Dinnertimes they cater more for 'tourists' to Garbatella or foreign residents like me who are delighted they only have to walk across the street to go out for dinner.

The menus in *trattorie* are not huge and consist of what ingredients are available that day. There are staples, such as the local way to cook zucchini, liver, offal, lamb, pasta with tomato sauce, minestrone with beans, as well as in-season local Roman vegetables, such as *brocoletti*, *puntarelli*, *cicoria* and artichokes.

The restaurant is not very busy when we go in at around 2pm. I order my usual *rigatoni amatriciana*. I am usually not a big fan of tomato-based pasta dishes, but as my head is pounding I feel the need for tomato warmth, and my stomach craves the salty *guanciale* the sauce is based around.

We drink naturally carbonated water. After not too long out comes the pasta, both my husband's dish (carbonara with zucchini) and mine. They are carried separately by two different women, on two mismatched plates. They carry each dish as though it is a work of art, which it is. They have lavished care and attention on each individual type of pasta and accompanying sauce, to create a unique dish. The way they carry it tenderly and how they lovingly place it in front of you, with a flourish and a wipe of their hands on their already stained aprons, makes you realise you are eating something special.

After only a few mouthfuls my headache abates, as my body fills with steamy, oily tomato and *guanciale* sauce. I can taste a hint of *peperoncino*. It is dripping down my chin but I don't care. Each mouthful is a sensation that revives me. The sauce is bringing me back to life, soothing my aching head, energising my tired body and cranking my few brain cells up. It takes me ages to eat, as the plate is huge, my movements today are slow and I want to savour every mouthful.

We finish with *puntarelle* and *broccoletti*. *Puntarelle* are the ends (literally 'little ends') of a green leafy vegetable that I don't know the name of and have never heard of before. Apparently, you only eat the points. They curl up when cut into strips, and are crisp and juicy like celery but much better tasting. They are eaten soaked in oil and with a hint of anchovy. The *broccoletti* are made up of dark green leaves and tiny broccoli flower stems, which explains why this plant is literally called 'little broccoli'. It is quickly boiled, then put in a frying pan with oil and garlic. It grows wild and only in the winter, as does the *puntarelle* plant.

It is New Year's Day, my favourite day of the year. It is a chance to wipe the slate clean and begin again, and I walk into it with wonder. Equipped with a cautionary headache but armed with the delights of *Er Timoniere*, I know this will be a good year.

Chapter 26

Ghetto diving

It is Saturday morning and instead of our usual routine of shopping, chores and resting, we decide to throw caution to the wind and get out into the streets of Rome to enjoy the magnificent winter sunshine. There is always this pull when you actually live in a place; the pull between tourist and resident. At some stage the resident just takes over and you could be living anywhere. It is not my experience, but I have heard it enough to know it is the majority of foreigners' experiences once they settle in Rome. I vowed it would never be mine.

You must get out of your apartment to enjoy it. So we are on a bus heading into the centre of town to meander, wander, take in the sights and go wherever the wind or our fancy takes us.

The city of Rome can be divided into a number of sections, all linking up, but quite discreetly. As a resident, you say you are going to the Coliseum, Campo dei Fiori, or the Piazza di Spagna area and you spend most of the day there, eating, drinking, shopping and looking, utterly content and full-up with things to see and do. This is the difference between a resident and a tourist.

Tourists do everything and mix it up, rushing through one area to another, scraping the surface and never quite getting the essence. An example is what they do with the food: eating pizza and pasta at the same sitting, or ordering a pizza with too many toppings, or a *cappuccino* after dinner, or complaining that there isn't enough sauce on their pasta dish. They miss the fact that Rome has layers. Layers that become more subtle and yet more satisfying the longer you sink into them.

The pasta is a good example. Outside of Italy you get used to pasta sauces that cover the pasta, allow it to swim in it, and can pretty much be eaten on their own whether there is pasta in the dish or not. Inside of Italy, the pasta reigns supreme. The pasta is the point of the dish, not the accompaniment to it. You order pasta in order to eat the pasta. It is gently flavoured by its sauce, but only in as much as to add to the experience of eating the pasta, not to lead it. Therefore, many sauces are scant, subtle in flavour or barely there. At first it may feel rather boring eating pasta dishes in Italy, but once you get used to the subtle layers of flavour then the pasta begins to sing its low, sweet song until you want to hear it again and again. And you can only hear it when the sauce is quiet.

I scoffed, along with the rest of my ex-patriot friends, when I first heard that not only do certain types of pasta only go with certain sauces, but that certain *sizes* of pasta, in particular spaghetti, can only be paired with certain sauces. It is at this point you begin to understand that the world of pasta is a lot more complex than originally presented. And now, having been here so long myself, I too crave the soft, sweet song of pasta and for it not to be drowned out by the sauce. I now shudder in horror at a cream sauce being served with unribbed pasta, and will absolutely not stand for spaghetti number 6 being served with *vongole.*

Today, as our bus pulls up at Piazza Venezia, the central pivot of modern Rome, my husband looks out of the window and says, 'Let's walk around the ghetto today,' as his choice of which section of Rome he would like to spend the day in. When I first heard someone talk about 'the ghetto' in Rome I was intrigued. *Wow,* I thought, *Rome has a ghetto.* I couldn't wait to see what lower socio-economic Romans looked like. Did they have a special dialect that was different from the Roman dialect? Did they have their own intricate relationships of kinship, bartering and social survival like other ghettos? And how would they be different from the surrounding Roman ones?

I didn't think I had ever seen a lower socio-economic Roman before. Even the supermarket shelf stockers wore labels, had groovy sunglasses and nice shoes. Even if they only had one set of clothes it seemed that no-one wanted to advertise the fact they had no money, so did their best to look like everybody else. Rich and poor alike had the same routines, the same lifestyle and the same kind of dwelling, to me. The differences were subtle, like where you went on holiday (but everyone still went), how many changes of clothes/bags/shoes you had, where your apartment was (but not how big it was) and how much jewellery you wore (but everyone wore some).

In answer to my original, many-years-ago-now question, I was even more surprised to be told that it was a Jewish ghetto. Once again, I tried to imagine the lifestyle differences and unique markings of an Italian Jewish lower socio-economic type and couldn't wait to go and have a look. Upon further questioning I was disappointed, however, as I found out that the ghetto hadn't really been in operation for nearly four hundred years. How typically Roman to be calling an area the thing it had been in the 1600s as though it was yesterday.

The ghetto is hidden away between the market square of Campo dei Fiori at one end and the huge Vittorio Emmanuelle monument at the other, flanked by the river and a couple of major streets in Rome. It was in this part of Rome that Jews living in the 1600s were herded into and forced to stay, rather than freely live anywhere in the city as they pleased. At one stage there were gates which were locked at night, so movement was only freely allowed to the outside of the area during the day.

Jews were originally brought to Rome as slaves by various emperors, as spoils of war after the Romans decimated Jerusalem and other Jewish cities. They integrated, like all the other nationalities and types of slaves brought to Rome, and were subsequently persecuted by various Popes and made to live in a high-walled and unhealthy part of town.

It is an area that you can dive into from any one of the major and busy streets that surround it. In it you find calm and tranquillity. Surrounded by streets of blaring horns, speeding buses, horse-drawn carriages and general chaos, the ghetto is like a quiet 1600s oasis. What easily made it a prison then makes it cut-off and peaceful now, even while being in the very heart of Rome. On the map it looks small, easily missed. It is so easy to stride along with your guidebook, looking up to the Renaissance Capitoline Hill or down the shopping street of Via del Corso, wedged in with other tourists all trying to stride along on the same tiny sidewalk inches from the cars whizzing down. 'Look down there,' I want to say, 'Look down there.'

The streets of the ghetto come winding out onto these main thoroughfares. They look quiet and still, like they lead to another land. It is hard to see down some of them, and they would have made easy thoroughfares to gate up. You can't ever see into the ghetto; you have to go inside it to see it. It opens up a little at a time. It is not taken in, in one swoop like many of Rome's grander piazzas, or seen from one length to the other like some of Rome's more famous vistas. And it is one of those places that is far bigger on the inside than it appears on a map. I know that this is a physical impossibility. But I have found this the case in many cities, particularly in Rome. Spend a morning and half an afternoon wandering around, then come out of it and look at where it is on the map. It is difficult to believe that it can take that much time to see the place as it is indicated on the map.

We enter at Piazza Campitelli and marvel at the huge stone square medieval building that is the Irish Embassy. We snoop around the courtyard a bit and look at fountains and statues. Most mornings the courtyards of all buildings are open; it is public space for visitors, businesspeople and residents alike. Most of these buildings have impressive internal courtyards where once carriages and horses stood, and where now Fiats and Mazdas are parked. I wonder at how the Irish scored such a great building to house their embassy in. How great must it be as an Irish person in Rome going to get a document at such a building as this? Australians got given an old bank downtown, with bars on the windows and ancient (not in a good way) green carpet throughout. Visiting our embassy was not an enriching experience. Several years ago Australians procured a better one on the outskirts of the Roman centre, but in terms of embassy buildings it's nothing to get excited about.

Piazza Campitelli, with its magnificent medieval buildings and impressive churches, is like the grand entrance or foyer to the ghetto. After this, the streets are narrow, cobblestoned and lined with intriguing places to eat. The ghetto is not a shopping area, although there are still many traditional material shops, tailors, shirt makers, linen and bedspreads to be found. I once had the task of finding a type of cloth that was only made commercially in the USA and for certain types of parachutes. I found it by going to the material shops in the ghetto. Huge, cavernous and mostly underground, they stock everything and anything, and understand even the strangest types of material.

We get to the Turtle Fountain in the Turtle Piazza fairly quickly. I often have flashbacks to when I was a young backpacker in Rome with a lot more time and energy. There are places I went back then that I have never found again, or wanted to. It feels like another life now, and I have been here so long I have mostly forgotten them. But every now and then I will come across a place (usually a bar) that stimulates a long forgotten memory. The Turtle Bar was the kind of bar where you had to wear their costumes to get in, such as feather boas, and you often ended up singing and doing other unanticipated theatrical performances there.

I'm not sure if it still exists. Once was enough, and I never returned when it was open. Rome is like that. Certain places open at times that are completely unknown to anyone but the proprietors and are difficult to work out. If you ask them they will say things like, 'My daughter used to have a dentist appointment every Tuesday afternoon so I had to shut the shop, and now I just keep it that way,' or 'I only open when the guy across the road opens.' This is also why if you find a good place to eat, shop, drink or lie down in, you should do it immediately and not think you can come back and expect it to still be there. In some cases the entire location will have changed. Like the lands at the top of the Faraway Tree, places in Rome only stay fixed for so long and then they move on.

Further down the road is an interesting eatery, small with a handwritten menu and very cheap. Unfortunately, it isn't quite lunchtime and the fresh cream-filled pastry and coffee I had for breakfast is still tiding me over nicely. Romans don't do much with fresh cream; it is not really part of their desserts or their cooking. It is so hot most of the year and refrigeration is so low that cream doesn't keep. I love cream. It is one of the things I miss a lot. Double cream, clotted cream and pouring cream is something I drool over in Australian supermarkets. Here it is possible to buy, but it is only the thin pouring type so needs to be whipped to be used for most things.

My local *bar* excels in fresh cream management. They know how to whip it, serve it, maintain it and fill any pastry to the brim with it. So every Saturday morning in winter (you can tell that winter has begun in Rome because the fresh cream appears) I have my usual fresh pastry, which is much like a croissant, opened up and layered and lathered with as much cream as can be piled in there. Half of it goes in my coffee, the other half in my husband's coffee, half of it down my face and the other half I eat along with my *cornetto*. It is heaven.

I sometimes think we live in a ghetto. We live in a suburb that is small, in a close-knit community which is fiercely proud of their Roman working-class roots. Most people are related to someone else in the same suburb and many have been born there. Roman dialect is spoken, hardship and scraping by is part of daily life. We recognise most people at our *bar* and they recognise us. We nod to some and generally only chat to the *barista* and friends that I know from work who wander past. We have a few local characters that are hard not to notice. One of them is Pasquale.

He came up to us once when we first started having our Saturday morning coffees outside on the sidewalk with everyone else. He looked us both right in the eye and said, 'There is only one thing you can have faith in in this world, and that is your own integrity. Not family, not State, not church, just your own integrity,' and walked off. My husband sat quietly, nodding his head and with a contemplative look.

Since then, Pasquale always approaches us when we have our coffee. Sometimes it is just to wave from a distance as he marches up and down the sidewalk. Sometimes it is to look at us once again in the eye and say things like, 'Wherever you are at this moment, it is the right place to be; everyone has their own place in the universe.' My husband thinks he is a minor prophet.

Today he said to me, 'You had better get as far away from Italians as you can. To be Italian is to be Mafia. It taints everything.'

He has never introduced himself to us or asked our names or made small talk. He chats to everyone and everyone chats back and knows his name. I don't know who looks after him or where he goes; he is always alone. But he lives here somewhere in this community, is part of it and is treated kindly and considerately by all those around him.

* * *

We continue our wanderings in the ghetto, along tiny cobblestoned streets that have no sidewalks and wind up and down like we are traversing small foothills. Maybe this is why it feels like we are covering more ground than it looks on a map. The buildings are all painted dirty yellow, burnt ochre, and with dust. Marble columns and iron gates form part of walls. There are no street signs and paths meander off in all directions. It appears that the streets came about as a result of the buildings and not the other way around; where there were spaces between buildings, a walkway appeared. Some are big enough for cars, others not. It is wonderful being in a pedestrian world.

No wonder the Romans refer to this place as a ghetto even four hundred years later, as inside you are still in the 1600s. There is no evidence of the twenty-first century in some corners of this place, and it is a special historical treat as a result.

We spill out into a wider space, which is newer and has been redone to make a piazza. Cafés with chairs take up space on the newly cobbled area. A dull alarm goes off and poles rise from the ground to fence the area off from cars; nothing can drive in or out. It is an urban control tactic, also used in the city of London, to stop car bombs and other activities where vehicles might be used for anti-social activities. We are behind the synagogue, which is always guarded by armed police against terrorist activities.

It is also where some of Rome's most famous restaurants are, which combine traditional Roman and Jewish cooking. It is also where two shops are located that both my husband and I have seen once but never again, and have spent years trying to understand the opening hours of in order to be able to go there again.

Today they are both open and have their opening hours painted on their windows. It is like a small revolution has occurred since New Year's Eve. The first shop is a Viennese bakery. This is important, as

Rome is not quite a centre of multiculturalism. Therefore, if you want a chocolate brownie or a muffin, you have to go to the UK. They are not available in Rome, or at least they have only recently appeared, are in select locations and are generally poor copies of the original, as only one company makes them and distributes them to bakeries throughout Rome, mostly in tourist areas. No decent Roman bakery would bother making a muffin.

This bakery is one of the only places in Rome that does such things, along with sachertorte, carrot cake and other Viennese delights. Now you know why we have never given up our search. We have not found it open any other time we have come here over the past four years.

I spy the opening hours. Firstly, the hours are made public. Secondly, they are now open during many of the times that we had been here previously. Thirdly, they have obviously succumbed to that pesky factor of business – client demand.

The opening hours are partly a result of Roman businesses leaving the client part of the business out. If you come from a land that has client service as a principle then you will be shocked and amazed at your treatment in a Roman (or Italian) business. You, the client, are having a favour done by being allowed to access this service. If you understand that, the fact that the service is hardly ever there, or lacks quality, or is performed by someone who is also on the phone to their friend and smoking at the same time, will not phase you.

Sometimes you just have to wait until the bank teller has finished their game of solitaire before being allowed to access your money. You are lucky they let you leave it there. Sometimes you just have to wait until the jeweller comes back from his coffee break (which he takes in front of you) before he will look at your watch. Sometimes you just have to wait until the previous client has finished chatting with the hairdresser, even if your appointment started half an hour ago. Sometimes there are just too many customers in a shop at one time and you will all be told to get out and come back another time. Sometimes you have to wait until the post office clerk has finished chatting with her colleague about her holiday, even if you are standing at the window waiting.

I had patiently noted over the years that the only time the Viennese bakery was open had nothing to do with demand. Or that our demand had to fit in with their supply. It works because, in any big city, the demand is mostly higher than the supply. You can't go elsewhere and if you don't like it, plenty more customers will come in your place. It is also a legacy of a socialist State system, where there is only one supply.

So a minor capitalist revolution had occurred and it was now open all day (no closing down for four hours over lunch) plus on Sundays. That was another thing. When do you most feel like going to a bakery? Was it:

a.   between the hours of 9am and 1pm
b.   between the hours of 4.30pm and 8pm
c.   anytime in the day, but particularly in the afternoon

I never understood the point of closing down for four hours if you were a place people would go to while the shops and offices were closed to have a cup of tea. And Sundays. Most of Rome was still as the grave on Sundays. It was formal Sunday lunch restaurant or nothing.

Now there is a *bar* open. Now that we know there is a commitment to opening hours, we feel safe to gaze and then come back.

The second place that I know about but have never found open, and had struck off as an urban myth, is also open. A huge, cavernous underground china and glassware store. It goes for miles, and as well as beautiful china dinner sets and glasses, it houses cookware and electrical goods. I sate myself and make up for ten years of missed browsing. Even my husband gets into it. It is lunchtime on a Saturday, a time I had often passed by here before and never found the place open.

There are no opening times on the door and I know I won't get a sensible answer, so I just thank my lucky stars and leave, preparing myself for the next ten years of Coventry. At least I know it exists and can now join in those conversations my friends often have about the products in 'that place under the synagogue'.

Now the cream pastry is wearing off, so we head to the small eatery with the handwritten menu. It is tiny inside. Behind a bench two men proudly show off their pre-prepared wares and indicate the microwave they have. At 2pm we have just beaten the Roman Saturday rush hour and watch while people file in and try to find seats

We choose *pasta a la Norma*, big folds of pasta sheets interspersed sparsely with eggplant, tomato and fresh grated sheep's cheese. I have tiny homemade pork sausages and beans with unleavened flatbread and an artichoke. On the menu is also liver, cabbage rolls, spirals of pasta with pesto, polenta with tomato sauce and sausage, and various types of wild Roman greens sautéed in oil and garlic. The sausages are small and piquant, the tomato and oily sauce holding the beans. The whole combination makes me feel warm and wholesome inside.

As the sun starts to lose its faint wintery warmth we load up on Viennese pastries and take the bus home, content in our knowledge that we have enjoyed one of the reasons we live here. The city of Rome and all its hidden, secret layers, the places and experiences that only occasionally appear to sate you, but when they do and you happen to catch them it is all worth it.

Chapter 27

Giorno di San Valentino, Valentine's Day

Winter is the time for getting away, for being peaceful, for curling up inside and watching the rain fall, or for just keeping warm. It is the time for bean soups and heavy meat pasta dishes. It is the time for losing Christmas kilos and the time to put them all back on again, by eating special sweets that are available only in February for a few weeks, to celebrate the *Carnevale*. It is the time for getting into the sun as often as possible by skiing in the Alps or walking in the countryside whenever the weather permits. If you can brave the cold it is also the time for bracing walks, low hotel prices and good weekend getaway deals. It is February, and in February there is also something else to celebrate.

Italy is a country that celebrates every Saint. Almost every week you can honour one. Father's Day in Italy is celebrated on *Il giorno di San Giuseppe*, Saint Joseph's Day, which falls in March. Most people have names which also correspond to a Saint's name and so receive gifts, greetings and endless phone calls on their Saint's name days. So if, for example, your name is Vincenzo, you will receive phone calls from friends and family on the fifth of April, which is *Il giorno di San Vincenzo*. Depending on your age you could even experience a mini birthday-type event, with gifts and a special dinner or treat.

My husband's *onomastico*, or name day, is the fourteenth of August, *San Alfredo*. When we became a couple and he mentioned this fact shortly before the fourteenth of August, I responded with a 'that's very interesting, thanks for telling me' type of comment. I was completely caught off-guard when his phone started ringing at 8am and didn't stop all day, and even more so when his friends started asking me what I was doing for his *onomastico* and what had I bought him. It seemed a little unfair to spring a second birthday-type celebration on me with no notice.

This was especially as I have always loved birthdays and do them so well, both mine and his. So I was a bit peeved that I had somehow missed out on the significance of this event and had come up completely lacking. Nowadays, of course, I count down to the event and plan special celebrations that go on for days, informing all and sundry that it is my husband's name day. I wish I had one.

Although every Saint is celebrated in Italy, no Saint is better celebrated than *San Valentino*, Saint Valentine, on the fourteenth of February. Then the whole country rallies, whether or not your name is Valentina/o. Every second person in the street can be seen carrying flowers and even flower pots. Elderly women carry them around with them all day, wearing floor-length fur coats and holding little pots of roses. They seem to say, 'I may be old but I am not forgotten, look at me.' Young men on bicycles can be seen carrying huge bunches of roses as they peddle along. Big women, ugly women, spotty boys, fragile old men, they all carry flowers around on Saint Valentine's Day, giving and receiving them with no sign of chagrin or embarrassment.

It is all over the news and television, restaurants start advertising special meals weeks beforehand, hotels put on special weekend deals and prices, as every city and every province gears up to celebrate the God of romance, Saint Valentine. We are in Italy after all, and these people take their romance seriously, studiously and applied with full force.

* * *

This year we decide to go to Florence for the weekend to spend our

Saint Valentine's Day there. In almost every hotel there is a special offer on for that weekend, but there is one in particular we have wanted to go to for a long time. It is luxurious, small and full of character. It has been around for over two hundred years and is situated in the very centre of Florence. It has now been restored to its original décor, when it housed many of Britain and Europe's young artists and aristocratic travellers as they did their 'grand tours' in the eighteenth and nineteenth centuries.

Alfredo and I have both been to Florence many times. This is my fifth. The first two times were with girlfriends. One was an architect, the other a student of Classical sculpture. As a student of the study of human beings, I was far more interested in them than the buildings or art. However, I was thoroughly schooled in both by my two old school friends, who took it upon themselves to educate me as a matter of course. I have therefore seen every sculpture of Michelangelo's in the city (and there are many), every Renaissance painting, every church, every Renaissance painting in every church, every Renaissance and medieval building, and every painting inside every Renaissance and medieval building. One of these visits was done in a day.

On that occasion, during the train trip to Florence, a two-hour journey, my girlfriend listed every single one of Michelangelo's sculptures, drawings or possible creations and marked their locations on a map. She had mentioned that there were a few things she really wanted to see and I only appreciated how seriously she wanted to see them as the trip went on. I spent the trip smoking, sipping coffee and babbling on about my love life while an intricate, timed breakdown of our day was occurring before my eyes.

I will never forget being dragged all over Florence without so much as a coffee stop, from 10am until 8pm that evening when our train left again. But I am ever so grateful, because now I never have to see them again. I got it all over with in one day and I now know more about Michelangelo than anyone else I know, and can regularly impress people with that. More importantly, I am now free to just watch people every time I go back to Florence.

Florence is also a place to go with lovers. I have been with every one of mine, and so has Alfredo. We have been there together though, when we were just young lovers ourselves. We don't talk about the other times.

So Alfredo and I decide to journey by train to Florence, for old time's sake, and also because it is a scenic trip, quite quick and there is nowhere to park a car in Florence. My previous trips have consisted of rattling along in spacious carriages, trains that stopped at every station and being served breakfast. Now we have less time and more money, so we take the fast train that doesn't stop at all between Rome and Florence. It is plush, packed and, although the speed of it is a feat of modern engineering, it still doesn't have doors that close properly.

Early into the trip the sliding door from the carriage to the ante-carriage (where the toilets and outside doors are) breaks down. It begins opening and shutting by itself every five seconds or so, letting in blasts of freezing air and just annoying us, as we are sitting opposite it. We inform the conductor, who goes into the bathroom, puts some liquid soap in his hands and pours it out onto the door rail on the floor. The doors shut.

Florence is of course magnificent, especially the food. Because we have both been here several times each we are really only interested in eating, sleeping and having the occasional walk around to see something nice. It is therefore lucky that Florence is quite small and every main sight is within a ten-minute walking distance. And there is a lot to see. Even without going inside anything, everywhere we look there is beautiful stonework to gaze at; marble carvings and mosaics, murals and paintings on city walls and buildings, statues, tiny cobbled streets and wide impressive squares. The river runs through the middle of the town and the bridge over the river, which is so full of ancient shops that it looks like another street, is also wonderful to see, as are the markets and the fact that there are barely any cars. Most of Florence is now a pedestrian only zone and it makes for leisurely, peaceful walking while gazing up or ahead at the nearest building, monument or square.

About five centuries ago the inhabitants of the city of Florence were largely responsible for the re-awakening of Western art, science, literature and philosophy after a long period where the Western world did nothing much but grow crops, burn people at the stake and go to bed early. This re-awakening was called the Renaissance, a Latin word meaning 'new birth'.

The city of Florence became the centre for all these things, helped along by a healthy business and banking industry that financed much of the arts. It became a city where there was a huge concentration of artists, sculptors, painters, poets, thinkers and astronomers. It was a place that influenced the rest of the Western world in much the same way that the Romans had in their time, four centuries beforehand. It was also the capital of Italy for some time. So it is like going back in time to see what the centre of the universe looked like in 1550. Even now it is still spectacular, especially the food, although that would have changed a lot since the Renaissance.

Florence is famous for the *bisteca fiorentina*, a gigantic, Fred Flintstone-style cut of meat, usually the height of a small child and spilling over the sides of an oversized plate. It is served fairly raw and melts in your mouth. But as both Alfredo and I have eaten this several times before in our previous visits, we feel no compulsion to explode our stomachs again with this gigantic morsel, and settle instead for the more mature and delicate tastes that Florence has to offer. These include its salamis, in particular its salami with *finnochio*, fennel;

crostini Toscana, little pieces of toast piled with mashed chicken liver and potato; and *ribollita*, a thick soup of beans, bread and oil. And its pasta dishes, mostly thick egg-based pasta with heavy meat sauces of venison, boar and pheasant.

Our first stop for lunch on Friday is the covered market in the centre of Florence, where a fast trade is done in *ribollita*, *crostini Toscana* and various plates of the day at one of the open-air market stalls. Whatever the dishes of day are you can be sure, being in the centre of the fresh produce market, that they are made up of the freshest ingredients around. Florence is freezing today, around two degrees Celsius, and the market is essentially outside. This means you need to eat wearing your coat, hat and gloves.

Being a market stall, there isn't anywhere guaranteed to sit. However, opposite the stall a series of long tables and many chairs have been set up. People come and go with their trays of steaming *ribollita*, sitting where they can, packed in together and enduring the cold to gulp down some of the city's best and freshest fare. I am wedged in alongside bankers, beauticians, pensioners and tourists. All have come to sample these wares, and no wonder.

My *crostini Toscana* are fragrantly hot mounds that evoke memories of other lives that I had never had; ones where I lived underground close to dark, pungent things and to the source of life. My *ribollita* is sweet, the white beans nestled around thick Tuscan bread, soaking up their juices, garnished with piquant new green olive oil. My husband has sausages and kale, a dark green leafy winter vegetable that he would normally not go near, except it has been doused in so much olive oil and salt that it is heavenly.

It is tempting to think about a glass of hearty red to go with this, especially as it is so cold. Chianti wine, along with other heavy reds, are Florence's speciality but we know we have many meals to come. Instead we resist and buoy ourselves up with the thought of a hot chocolate at the famous Café Rivoire, almost as much of an institution in Florence as Michelangelo himself.

We amble through the city after lunch, admiring the stalls full of leather bags, coats, belts and books; anything that can be made, covered or stuck onto leather is, in Florence.

We whisk ourselves into the Duomo for a quick look. Although we have seen it dozens of times, it is one of those monuments that demands homage paid to it every time you are in the city. When it was completed a couple of centuries ago, its dome was the biggest unsupported roof in the modern world (the Romans had done it seven hundred years beforehand but no-one since – too busy planting crops, burning people at the stake and going to bed early) and was admired across Western civilisation. The Duomo was back then a version of the eight-star hotel in Dubai that is shaped like a wave and has a tennis court hanging out of its side, miles above the ground. Filippo Brunelleschi, one of Florence's hottest young artists, designed and built the Duomo, along with several others in Rome. He also painted a number of masterpieces hanging in art galleries today, and contributed quite a few of the city's amazing sculptures. Just your average Renaissance man.

We finally arrive at the Café Rivoire, my favourite in Florence and not only because it is now owned by Gianfranco Cavalli, the greatest fashion designer in history, although you do have to like animal print and all its derivatives to enjoy his designs. The Café Rivoire is situated right opposite one of Florence's most amazing buildings, *La Vecchia*, a medieval castle, the home of Florence's first family during the Renaissance and for many years its government building. It is situated in one of Florence's most beautiful squares.

It is the perfect place for people-watching and pretending you come from the previous century. Everything is luxurious. Small tables covered in white linen are packed together around gilt chairs that often face not each other but the crowd, so you can really be looked at. Waiters in bow ties carrying drinks on silver trays, marble topped counters, and the soft hum of coffees and teas being made all complete the picture. It evokes another time, when things were slower, when you didn't have to fit in the whole of the Renaissance in one day or sample all of Florence's wine and *bistecca* in one weekend.

It is also my favourite because it was first opened by a chocolate maker, a royal chocolate maker no less, to provide the everyday person with the best hot chocolate available. Now, that really is a gift to humanity.

We stumble in from the cold and take our place at the window, facing it to watch out, and sip our hot chocolates. They are lusty and full. They reach out to warm even my fingertips from the inside and soothe all my aches and pains. It is deep and not overly sweet, thick and only really drinkable due to the fresh cream melting all through it and making it remotely like a liquid.

I watch a couple by the wall. Their backs are to it and they are sitting next to each other but facing out into the room full of other patrons. She is beautifully made-up, her silver hair coiled up behind her head, wearing pearls and a simple sweater. He is wearing a jacket and tie. They have water in crystal glasses, a whole bottle of olive oil on their table, and are delicately picking at their *bresaola*, parmesan and *rughetta* salads with silver forks. They look like they have been there since 1940. It is a leisurely half-hour that passes, sheltered from the cold, listening to the strains of Portugese, French, Italian and Japanese being spoken at tables near us.

We come to this café again on Sunday morning and it is a cacophony of sound and movement. There are no tables and even to take a coffee standing up at the counter takes waiting. It is packed to the gills with elderly women in floor-length fur coats wearing their sunglasses indoors, with bright lipstick and baubles of gold on their arms. They are the post-war generation that survived and flourished; the first one to do so in a long time. Their joi de vivre is always evident, out loud and proud. Not for them the political correctness or self-actualising of the generations since. They know what privation and suffering is and they enjoy its lack as often as they can.

Sunday morning, this café is claimed back from the tourists and becomes uniquely Florentine. It is theirs. It is an institution and a requisite stop on Sunday morning after a stroll around the piazza, after church and before lunch.

I speak with a talkative, white haired lady on my left who carries a shopping bag. We are at the counter sipping our *cappuccini* together. 'I come here every Sunday,' she tells me, 'every single Sunday I pop in, on my way back to the house, just to have a quick coffee at the Rivoire. What days do you come here?'

* * *

Saturday night we venture out to further sample some Tuscan delights. We go to an *enoteca*, well-recommended, to further test our aptitude for Florentine tastes. It is a large cavernous place a little out of the central part of town. It has recently been renovated and opened, and has a great reputation. As Florence is famous for its wines, salamis, cheeses and heavy pasta dishes, an *enoteca*, which specialises in these dishes only, seems the perfect place to go.

We have a plate of salami, among which is the salami flavoured with fennel. Fennel grows all over the country, but for some reason it is not put into salami unless the salami is made in Tuscany. And then it is not imported outside of Tuscany. So to sample my favourite salami I must go to Tuscany. I don't mind, really. Except when I taste it, then I get the familiar feeling of frustration, and the question 'why' on my lips. Why can't they have this in Rome? Don't go there, warn my husband's eyes over his Tuscan *prosciutto* and *capa cotto*, salami made from the insides of an animal's head. The bread is soft and without any salt, another native of Tuscany. This makes the flavour of the salami stand out even further. The *prosciutto* is sliced so thinly that you can see through it. It tastes salty and pink and delicious.

The wine is even better. I know nothing about wine except to say 'yes' to whatever my husband orders. He has never had any training either, but has an innate Italian ability to pick the best one from the menu and I am never disappointed. Each time it is a new sensation and each time I can't remember what I've drunk, but it has been unlike anything I have ever tasted before. This time is it deep and full-bodied, almost chocolaty in its depth of character, and compliments the salamis and other cured meats perfectly. The fennel in the pork salami bursts out of it and is part of it all at the same time, like chocolate added to milk. I feel the flavour in my nose and it makes me want to put my head down and snuffle it like a pig at a trough. I explain to my husband that if only they had this salami in Rome then I wouldn't feel the need to inhale it, but he doesn't let me do it just the same.

Our pasta comes and mine is light and cheesy, a potato-filled ravioli sprinkled with thyme, while Alfredo's is a spirally pasta called *fusilli* sprinkled with sausage and onions. We are dining in an early Renaissance palace, beautifully restored but still very rustic. Gigantically high ceilings, stone floors and walls, huge wrought iron chandeliers and different sized tables spread far apart from each other. It is full and very buzzy, but not noisy or crowded. There is a genteel hum as the mostly-Italian diners work their way through the magnificent Tuscan fare.

To get to the bathrooms, which are underground, you have to go via a lift and keep your finger pressed on the button the whole time.

As you do it moves you down a slim stone shaft that connects the ground floor within the cavernous underground realms of the ancient palace. Another girl and I giggle the whole way down to conceal our panic of being stuck in a stone elevator shaft or trapped underground while peeing.

* * *

The next day we wing it for lunch. Having slavishly followed recommendations up until now with very good success, we think we have a pretty good gist of the city's good restaurants and their characteristics, enough to be able to spot one ourselves. We have eaten hearty pastries and drunk delicate *cappuccini* every day for breakfast in two different cafés without being disappointed. We have eaten wonderful pasta and steak along with delicious wine at our hotel. We are confident that we are in a city where it is difficult to eat badly.

On Sunday afternoon we head back to the same district we ate in the night before at the *enoteca*, having passed several good-looking *osterie* along the way. An *osteria* is an even more local, and therefore unknown, type of Italian eating establishment. It is usually very small and serves those who live within a 100-metre radius of it, with some provision for the odd passer-by. It is not fine dining and usually doesn't have a menu. The waiters tell you what has been cooked for the day, and often a small but extremely homemade and good selection is available. It is just what we feel like after two days of more upmarket dining. I have a hankering for salami with fennel, which I know will be made even more painful by having to say goodbye to it, but I just have to try it anyway.

There are some tips for being able to spot a good place to eat in Italy. Firstly, do not eat anywhere that has no Italians dining in it. Peer through the windows, poke aside the blinds, do what you have to do, but do not sit down in an establishment where you can see no obvious Italians, and they are mostly obvious. Secondly, do not eat anywhere that does not have an Italian in the kitchen, at least supervising. Italians can tell if pasta is cooked al dente, or how long it has to go, just by looking at it.

Also, if you can see any type of Italian worker eating at a restaurant then try and get into it. The more blue-collar looking the worker the better. The cooks in these establishments are competing with these workers' mothers and wives, who have mostly been raised to cook. These people are used to the highest level of Italian home cooking, and therefore if they eat out it has to compare. If it is a Sunday and they have the clear choice of eating at home or going out, and are eating out, then try at all costs to get into this establishment.

Lastly, if they cannot fit you in without a reservation then you know you are at a good place to eat. This is little consolation as you are going out the door, but good if you can go back there. One trick to get around this conundrum is to come early. Many good places will have a couple of tables not booked. Sometimes it is just because they are not full, and sometimes they do it on purpose to make room for any regulars that may turn up. If you come a little earlier than the Italian lunch hour you are more likely to find these types of tables.

My husband and I are in luck. We spot a little *osteria* close to the one we ate at last night that looks rather authentic, and is not advertising itself too grandly. Nearing it, we see a group of men, postal workers, at a table by the window. We go inside and are given one of the three tables not yet booked. In a short period, we know why.

The salamis and wine are well up to standard, the *crostini* melts in my mouth, but the ravioli with sausage causes us both to order a second one immediately. We had attempted to share. Laughing, the waiter brings us another bowl, telling us in dialect that we really look as though we are hating it. We agree as the meat sauce runs down our faces. Afterwards, we ask about a large, low dish covered in a creamy substance that had caught both our eyes as we entered. Could it be a homemade tiramisu? Yes. So our meal is finished off in a haze of mascarpone delight.

On our way back to the hotel after lunch the streets are deserted. It is grey, cold and windy. Sunday just after lunchtime means that every single Italian will be dozing or recuperating from the lunch hour in some restful way. Taking the measure of the streets, we wonder what impact it will have on the queues outside some of Florence's best art galleries. As suspected, it has had a drastic affect.

We enter the Accademia, Florence's second-best gallery after the Uffizi, and the home of Michelangelo's first, and some say best, statue – the one that established him as a major talent. It is the statue of David. It is huge and sits in a part of the gallery built especially for it. It is worth seeing more than once. David is naked, and I note that most of the women are sitting or standing behind him. I also walk behind the statue, and then understand why so many women have chosen to stop and sit there. Explaining this to Alfredo, he wonders aloud why we aren't all in the front then. 'Women are not so literal,' I reply.

The bottom of David, if I may say, is stunning. It looks like two soft, ripe peaches dangling just so from a tree. It is indented in the sides but fully rounded at the bottom. It is square and projects masculinity, yet in its hint of fleshy softness expresses just enough femininity to be completely sensual.

I'd had my salami with fennel, my deep red Chianti wine, my creamy tiramisu and my fill of bottoms for the weekend, both David's and Alfredo's. I was sated and ready to go home.

Chapter 28

Winter blues

I have the Winter Blues. Living in Italy does not exempt you from these, no matter how lovely the city of Rome, or indeed the whole country, is. The Blues come on here as well, and ever so quickly. It doesn't take much. I blame the sun. It is so rare for it not to be present, that even a day or two of greyness can cause the Blues. I reflect on how much my capacity for handling cold, grey weather has been reduced because of this consistence of sunlight and that, after seventeen years in Rome, I have next to no stamina for bad weather.

On cloudy or cold days I want to stay in bed, staring at the wall, waiting for spring to come back. Or, if I do get up, I want to have dinner and go to bed by 5.30pm when it starts to get dark. The thought that I was still sweltering at that time just a few months back, and longing for the evening cool, does nothing to enliven me. It is dark. It is cold. It is hard to enjoy any of the things that I love about Rome. Rome is not a winter city. All there is to do in winter is eat, and go to the Opera. If you don't like Opera, or have seen all of them three times each and are trying to lose weight, a Roman winter is a long and boring ordeal. This is why I need weekends away, though I have had just one and so have to struggle through the rest of February without this hope.

Today also started badly. I had to go to the post office, a scary errand at the best of times due to the long waits of over an hour, the frayed tempers of both staff and clients, and the general frustration at having to wait while you watch the postal workers talk about their holidays. In addition to this unwelcome task it was raining heavily, the wind blowing so badly that it was impossible to even use an umbrella. Oh, and there was a transport strike. This has one of two effects, neither of which can be known until the day. Either it means that Rome is stalemated with traffic and everyone sits in their cars for up to three hours to get to work, or they don't even bother and half the city closes down. The same effect can be seen when it is raining. When it is raining and there is a transport strike as a result, it is quite clear what the outcome will be.

My neighbourhood was a ghost town this morning; quiet on the streets and quiet in the shops, those that were open. And, miracle of miracles, it was quiet at the post office. Most people had decided that today was a day for staying at home. For the first time in seventeen years I got served within minutes of entering. I then needed to get back in time for the fridge repair man, who was coming any time between 9.30am and 3pm, possibly today.

Italy is still a country where any kind of delivery or service man (and they are all men) requires you to wait at home, sometimes over a period of days, for them to arrive. They will not give you a specific time or make an appointment. The closest you will get is a five-hour timeframe on a given day but it is not guaranteed, and although you may assume that you will be top of the list in the next five-hour timeframe, somehow you never are. Then a completely different day, sometimes a week later, will be given as the next available appointment. I was incredulous when this first happened to me.

'But I work,' I stammered. 'I get paid by the day. If I have to stay home half a day that means I miss out on half a day's pay, and you can't guarantee that you will even come during that time.'

'Can't your mother be there?' they asked me.

'No,' I said.

'Can't your aunty be there?'

'No.'

'Mother-in-law?'

'Not married.'

'How can you be in this country without any family?' they asked. 'Who will look after your children? How come you get paid by the day, isn't that illegal? Why don't you have a contract for life like all Italians, where you are entitled to stay at home and get paid while waiting for an electrician?'

I was beginning to see that I was a fish out of water a lot more than I had initially supposed.

I am not just a foreigner because of my nationality; I have imported with me a foreign lifestyle. It is one of independence and where relationships are based on economic exchanges, or choice. You come and fix my fridge because I pay you. Because I pay you, you come when it is convenient for me, not you. I have you in my life or live near you/ with you because I want to, not only because you are related and we are dependent on each other for our livelihoods to function.

Because of this I mostly end up living a hybrid life. I need others to help me much more than I would in my own country, so neighbours and friends take the place of family. I arrange to work from home so I can still get paid, and be available to get packages and repairmen. But being at home means I am still accountable to deliver certain things and can't accept invitations to while away an afternoon having coffee with my neighbour or doing the washing.

My entreaties to the fridge repair company that I have to meet with a Swedish diplomat for a work-related appointment at a certain time falls on deaf ears. My explanation that my husband has gone away for the weekend without me and I am therefore alone is met with disbelief. My claim that I have no cash in the house because, unlike most Italians, I use my credit card to live on is met with anger by the repairman. He expects to be paid a lot of cash right now for something that was not agreed on and done without asking me. He was here to fix the fridge (which is under guarantee) but has ended up fixing the electric socket.

I am left shaken and furious by our exchange as he berates me for not paying, believing that I just do not want to pay, rather than the fact that I do not have the cash on me. I ask him to leave and threaten him with calling the police, and my neighbours, if he doesn't leave immediately. He tells me that he is friends with the police and doesn't care if I ring them, thereby insinuating that his personal relationship with them will overrule their civic duty towards me.

The encounter frightened me because I knew I was helpless. I can yell in Italian and gesticulate as well as the next person, but in the end I was at a social disadvantage, in a country that is governed by advantages formed through social relationships. I was a woman alone, and a foreigner. It was an opportunity for certain types of people to take advantage, to assume I would pay whatever I was asked, to be treated without respect, and to get away with it. None of the usual barriers were there: a husband, a mother, a sister, a father, a professional look (I was wearing a tracksuit), dark hair (being fair meant I was probably Eastern European and therefore at a great disadvantage on a social scale to an Italian). A penis.

Sometimes it is tiring, and difficult, pretending to be an Italian when you are not. Like when I arrive back to my apartment block after a long and hard day's work at 7pm, meet my neighbours hanging around outside who have all been home for hours, and are walking their dogs and want to stop and chat. Even though my legs are so sore I can hardly stand up, I have to stand up a little longer making small talk, ask them about their days as they will ask me about mine, and exchange pleasantries so we can keep our relationships as neighbours intact. Sometimes I am incredibly jealous of women who, even at my age, get to go home and have their mothers cook them dinner, or who can wake up in the morning, see it is raining and not bother going in, knowing they will be paid anyway. When I am tired, hot, cold or in a bad mood, I resent having to jolly along the person providing me with a service, knowing that unless I do their bad temper and suffering will win out over mine. I am the client, the one wanting the service, and the customer is always last in Italy.

And although I revel at times in the lawlessness that abounds here, the personal relationships that supersede the rules, at other times I am frightened because what if I have no personal relationships that can help? What if the tradesman waits outside my apartment? What if he does know the police and their personal relationship with him is closer than their professional one towards me? I have a husband, a family, and some friends as well, who would all easily threaten to gun someone down on my behalf. But they do not live in my neighbourhood or in my apartment building.

As I am spluttering about my fear and anger to my husband over the phone, including the fact that I am not sure the fridge is actually fixed, he assures me that if the repairman has to come back he will invite Antonello to be there as well.

This calms me a little. Antonello is a huge, surly lawyer. He is also licensed to carry a gun, which he often does on account of the fact that he is a criminal court judge. I think of Gianni, the husband of Antonella, our downstairs neighbours who sports an earring and tattoos and would look menacing on my behalf if I needed it. I think of my girlfriend Katrin who lives in the building next door, who is always fiery and intrepid despite her lack of language skills.

She once went into a hardware store and told them that Mickey Mouse was on her balcony and that she wanted to kill him. Could they sell her anything to help accomplish this? She didn't know the word for mouse and so approximated what it might be. Unfortunately, her choice of word referred to only one mouse in particular.

It still does not quite change my malaise. Despite everything, at the end of the day it is still winter. It is still grey, grey, grey outside, and windy. It means it is not pleasant to go walking, and even if you did there would not be anything interesting to do or look at. All Romans would be indoors. Bracing, physical walks which would serve to flush out the Blues are curtailed due to the freezing temperatures, rain and darkness. My *cappuccino* runs are sporadic and I am loosing contact with the *barista* and owner of the *bar*, as my appearance there is not to be relied upon.

And then out of nowhere, in typical Italian fashion, wanting to make a big entrance, an unforgettable spectacle, just at the very last minute, the sun appears. It appears and immediately begins setting as though it has already done too much. Its golden light appears on the wall of my home office where I am working and causes me to look up and admire it. The scene I behold looks like something Biblical. Strong rays of light stream upwards, illuminating the blue, blue sky that has recovered from the overcast moodiness of the day. I stop and sit and watch it slowly set, its glow getting further and further away, but still promising me that one day soon there will be more to come.

Now the scene looks like an upside down desert. The clouds have come together to block out the blue sky and the sun's light is turning them into an undulating surface of golden sand. Then they turn pumpkin orange and start to strata, leaving long, streaky purple shapes. I think of my deep red Chianti that can only be drunk when it is cold and dark, waiting patiently for me until the end of the day. I think of the chewy egg pasta only eaten in winter and the pungent parmesan, oil and basil I will throw over it tonight. I think of eating it in warm, cosy surroundings, and then I forgive winter for not being spring.

Chapter 29

In hibernation and hiding

Winter here is about hiding. Hiding from the outdoors, bundled up inside stone villas in front of fireplaces. Hiding your skin under multiple layers of clothing, knowing that as soon as the weather warms up most of your flesh and that of others will be exposed. It is a time of hunkering down in soft warm layers of wool, pasta, olive oil and bedcovers stuffed with duck down. It is a time that nature hides under the sodden earth. A time that delicate foliage hides from the lashing rain and the chill of frost. It is because of this you can notice immediately when winter begins to lose its hold.

It doesn't take much. The first sunny day that offers a hint of warmth in its rays brings out blossom, even though it is still bitterly cold. Snowdrops show their heads overnight and tiny shoots of green grass begin to cover the wet earth. The sun produces its warmth in a visual way; the rays are not quite strong enough to dissolve the mist but exist with it, casting sunlit vapours over everything, making you feel like you can walk into it. Everywhere there is the promise of spring, the physical evidence that it is just around the corner in spite of the cold and the dark nights. But there is still time for hiding, for snuggling deep down into your duck down coats as well as bed coverings.

Last Saturday night we did exactly that. We hid, about sixty of us, to surprise Francesca for her sixtieth birthday. Almost the whole population of the apartment block where she used to live made the two-hour trek down to her new place by the sea. We brought with us food and cheer. We huddled together in her lounge room in the dark, waiting for the moment when she would open the door to be greeted by her daughter, and we shouted, 'Surprise!' And she was.

There were brothers, sisters, uncles, nieces and nephews, her boss, her best friends, her old friends from where she used to live and her new friends, namely my husband and I. In a daze she walked through the crowd, hugging and kissing each of us. Luckily her daughter had encouraged her to dress up and make herself up for the shopping trip her brother had just taken her on. Francesca cares about her appearance and to be 'surprised' in her tracksuit, or worse her pyjamas and bed hair, would not have suited her at all.

In true Italian style we had arrived and waited around for two hours before she came back home, without eating or drinking anything even though the table was laden. Alcohol is not usually served before a meal, or without anything to eat. And everyone must wait for the whole attendance of the party to be present before starting to eat anything. As a foreigner I knew I would not be subject to the same amount of judgement as others and so had been helping myself steadily to the cheese puffs for about an hour. There was no wine on the table or I would have been into that too.

This is quite a strictly observed social rule. In spite of the abundance of food generally, it is only consumed in quite regulated and tightly adhered to circumstances. Even for the children, most of whom were staring at me in open longing and wonder while I held fistfuls of cheese puffs. Their hands were smacked away whenever they tried it themselves.

'But why can the lady eat?' I heard them ask.

'She isn't from here,' was the response. 'She is a foreigner.' It covers a multitude of sins and allows me licence that would not be given to another Italian, nor in my own country most of the time.

The 'she is a foreigner' statement is made without any tone of judgement, just an acknowledgement that I am outside the circle of Italian social rules and I am therefore ignorant of what is required in my behaviour (even though I know very well) and that I am governed by my own set of social rules, which must be just as important and valuable. The idea that I come from a culture that doesn't actually have any social etiquette would not be something that would occur to them.

In order to stave off their own hunger and boredom, most of the Italians had been smoking nonstop for the past two hours. It is something I have learnt but often forget to do, that is, to not go to an Italian event hungry. It is likely that the meal will start anywhere up to five hours later than scheduled, but usually at least two. As it is usually a marathon event and you are expected to participate until the finish line. It is also not wise to be too hungry, as this makes you eat a lot during the first two courses, which makes the following four quite difficult to get through. Usually they go for hours so you get a bit of time to digest in between courses, but digesting *antipasto* and pasta, if overeaten, can take days. It is better to attend any of these events mildly hungry but not too hungry, and to be able to smoke if necessary.

Once Francesca arrives and kisses everyone and has opened presents, we are allowed to start eating. All food has been provided by family members or close friends, enough for sixty people, along with supplements from guests. We have brought a quiche, known to Italians as a *torta rustica*, or 'home-cooked tart'. A quiche is something that never fails to amaze my Italian friends or my husband, who encourages me to make them at every opportunity. It also helps that it is quite a common dish in Australia and one that I grew up knowing how to make. Italians love this authenticity and the fact that it is like something they have but, according to them, much, much better.

My quiche is on the table with all the other *antipasti*. This is when a *torta rustica* would be eaten, before the pasta and before the *secondo*, the main dish. It is next to two other Italian-style *torte rustici*, which are similar to a Spanish frittata. They are made without a pastry base and usually have potato, cheese and are always vegetarian. This is a conservative crowd of traditional Roman eaters and I am steeling myself to have to take most of my quiche home with me, as has often happened when I donate a dish that is not strictly Italian. I slice it, as I feel that might make it more attractive.

The paper plates are handed out and sixty people head towards the meal, which is introduced by the three *torte rustici* and followed by plates of chips, peanuts and cheese puffs (those that are left). It is the *antipasti* of the economically challenged. I dive in, take a piece of my quiche as I am interested to taste it, prefer it to the other *torte rustici* and tell myself that at least it will look like one person has taken a slice.

All of a sudden there is a ruckus and what looks like a swarm of people all trying to get to the same place at the same time. People are transfixed and sounds of gastronomic delight are coming from their mouths as their neighbours are asking them desperately what it is. Instead of answering them, they are cutting more pieces and passing them over their heads to their nearest and dearest, determined that they should participate in this experience as well, before the person next to them gets to have a slice. There is a rush of activity, a storm of voices acclaiming the food and encouraging those further out to hurry up, and then it is over.

A quietness reigns. The crowd parts and I see my empty quiche dish in the middle of it, next to the two other full *torte rustici*. My husband's eyes are shining with pride. Stories are already being told about what it was, who ate it and who missed out, and everyone wants to know where it came from and how I made it. I am carried shoulder-high on the acclaim of every woman present who probably can hardly believe that the foreign woman who ate most of the cheese puffs in front of the starving children could possibly be cultured enough to create a culinary sensation.

And so I begin. I have the floor and in my okay Italian I give a twenty-minute presentation on how to make a quiche. I am interrupted constantly, as is the Italian discussion style, to check facts, to ask quantities and to clarify instructions. My husband hovers at my shoulder ready to help with translation, like when I tell them I used 'fountain cheese' instead of the more commonly known 'Fontana cheese'. The women dismiss him when he tries to correct me, claiming they knew what I meant and would he stop interrupting the flow of the lesson. At the end of this discourse I am a fully-fledged member of the party, to be respected as much as any other Italian, and unfortunately now probably expected to abide by the same social rules.

They now know the sum of me. I can cook and I can speak Italian well; I am one of them. By the end of the evening I too have learnt to make a few more dishes, as each Italian woman offers her recipe of the evening to me. It calms me down completely.

As a foreigner and a career woman without children working in an international environment, I often feel out of place with my neighbours, who are postal workers, office cleaners, mothers and seamstresses. I needn't worry, as we are all equal when it comes to the kitchen, it seems. I have demonstrated my prowess and opened up the sacred corridors of Italian womanhood for myself. I will be spoken to as one of them. The men will eye me with awe and respect. My husband is drinking it in and exchanging knowing looks with the other husbands. They look at him wistfully and understand that he is getting something different, more than in the bedroom. He is now also more relatable to them; he married a woman who can cook.

We follow the *antipasto* with two gigantic foil containers of lasagne, a dripping hot mozzarella cheese and béchamel mix with clumps of tangy tomato, minced beef and chewy blankets of pasta. It is served by the eldest man present and he looks like a priest giving communion wafers. Each of us line up reverently with our plastic plates held with both hands at chest level as he deftly cuts and serves the squares. Swooning faces turn around once they have reached the top of the queue and the lasagne is worshipped in silence.

This is almost the only time Italians stop talking. The silence is equal to the meal. A silence of sixty excitable relatives on a Saturday night is a deep mark of respect for the chef. Francesca's sister-in-law is responsible for this. It is her husband who is serving. But unlike the frenzied activity after my dish, based on surprise and the unexpected, this is a well-known and long-anticipated dish. Her reputation precedes her and there is more than enough for everyone, so the activity is leisurely and savoured.

Quite some time after this the *secondo* is served. This has been prepared by Francesca's other sister-in-law. She carries high over her head a huge platter laden with crumbed chicken fillets and slices of roast veal in gravy. Another bowl contains peas and yet another roast potatoes cut into tiny pieces. The wine is also flowing by this stage, a local red bought by the ten-gallon-drum-load.

As I have now been properly introduced and quantified by the Italians, I become their after-dinner entertainment. Everyone is full and sleepy – they need stimulation before the dessert and coffee – and in true Italian style they are curious about foreign cultures, countries and ways of life. I find most Italians to be this way. They may be very traditional and remain close to their own cultural traditions, but this doesn't mean they are closed. It is usually the opposite, maybe because they hail their own traditions so much they assume that everyone has their own and are eager to learn what they are, to compare them, to long for them and to feel content for the ones they ascertain are better. In a competition with Australia, they are mostly wistful and long to have my traditions for their own. They would throw away their Roman heritage, the Coliseum and the Vatican for our beaches, our wildlife, our carefree way of living, our economic wealth, job opportunities and houses.

I try to warn them about being so far away from everyone else in the world and these people, who live right in the middle of the Western world, take no heed. I try to deter them with stories of flies, poisonous spiders, sharks and snakes, and their eyes light up with the adventure of it all. I try to drill into them the lack of tradition in family life and cuisine, and they roll their eyes at me, telling me they would find a way to bear it all. In the end I laughingly give up and tell them that yes, it is a beautiful and great place to be, but for me this is my adventure, right here in Rome. This is my experience of a lifetime. But I sort of understand their point of view, as I realise that for this I have exchanged closeness with my family, fish and chips, Aussie humour and being able to see the horizon, all of which I miss every day. What we have in common is our willingness to sacrifice in order to live our most sought-after experiences.

The conversation moves on to lighter things. From across the room Silvio, our neighbour, shouts out, 'Is it true that Italians are always talking about food, that we spend one mealtime talking about what we will eat next?'

We all laugh and we all know the answer.

Dessert is served to the sound of much groaning. A tiramisu, again in a huge foil baking dish, is served, along with a plate of *bigne di San Giuseppe* and a birthday cake, which is a custard and fruit tart. The *bigne* cause a sensation, as they are an example of the kind of food I have referred to previously: they exist for a few short weeks in February and March to celebrate *San Giuseppe* (Saint Joseph's Day, also Father's Day in Italy) and then they disappear, never to be eaten, spoken about or made until the same time next year. As such a fuss is being made and the *bigne* is being divided into ever-smaller portions to make sure everyone gets a piece, I wonder aloud what would happen if they were made at another time, say in April. No-one would eat them in April, is the response.

Only after the final coffees and glasses of grappa are served is it possible to leave. Which we do, clutching our stomachs, with my husband talking nonstop about what a hit I was with the quiche.

Chapter 30

Emerging

It is time. The clocks have gone forward, the air is warmer and the blossom has taken over. I somewhat reluctantly say goodbye to winter. I do not cast it out carelessly, running into the arms of the coming season, as I do with all other seasons. Winter is short here in Rome, the shortest of all seasons, even though I know that isn't logical. It is barely cold here for a month or two, it barely rains and it seems that these few short months of darkness are scant time to recover and prepare for the onslaught of continuous sunshine and heat for the other ten months of the year.

I therefore enjoy the short days and dark, stormy nights. I enjoy roasting myself by a fire, exhaling frost and eating as many beans soaked in dark tomato sauces and accompanied by deep, full-bodied reds as I can. It is something I look forward to every year and say goodbye to with reluctance, knowing that too much sunshine, *spaghetti alle vongole*, pinot grigio and gelati is just as bad as not enough.

Winter is for rejuvenating, for hiding and taking care of all those little, secret projects you have been saving for a rainy day. Winter is home-based and full of fleshy comforts, such as warm nights cuddled up on the couch, lusty ragus on egg-based noodles, chocolate so dark it tastes like it has been dug out of the ground, and soft woollen layers that cover up all your sins. Over the next ten months the peeling off will occur, until even being naked is not comfortable and there is far too much of everyone else's flesh on display.

The twilights are long, lingering and cool rather than cold. They call me out onto my balcony to hear the birdsong, to watch the sun set over the blue domed church in the distance and to fill my nostrils with the scent of gin. I know I have limited time left to enjoy the inside of my apartment, so on Saturday morning when I wake I know what I must do.

Most Saturdays begin at our local *bar*, the hub of Italian social life and where the conversations are about food, football, politics, food, football, politics, food, football, politics, food. It is our ritual on a Saturday morning (though it can occur after noon) to slowly wake up to the world over an unrushed *cappuccino* and fresh *cornetto* – the quintessential Italian breakfast. As I have the quintessential foreigner's breakfast every other day – a rushed bowl of cereal eaten while putting on make-up and getting files ready for the day – it is a particular treat to sit down and leisurely enjoy my very good coffee and indulgent pastry.

Alfredo and I sip and stare into space, processing the week's frantic work experiences, occasionally speaking but mostly not, and observing, sometimes for hours, the people traffic and antics around us. It slowly brings me into the present and disassociates me from work, this ritual, and it is particularly sacred and necessary. It is also particularly necessary that I am uninterrupted during this processing.

It is therefore to my dismay that I discover there are no spare chairs and tables outside this morning. I cannot bear to be inside, as I have been inside since the beginning of the year, so I ask an elderly woman if I can share her table.

'Of course,' she says. 'It's only me, you are welcome to sit down.'

She has blonde, well-cut hair, large glasses and a huge new red wool coat on, which matches her lipstick. I later find out that she is ninety-one. My husband comes out with his coffee and goes back inside to bring mine.

'Is the waiter coming out?' the woman asks hopefully.

'No,' my husband replies, 'what is it that you want, *signora*?'

'No, don't worry,' she says, 'I'll get the coffee myself.'

'Stay where you are,' Alfredo says, 'I'll order it for you.'

The elderly are reverently respected in Italy and, like each child is treated as your own, each elderly person is treated as though they are your own parents. There is a kind of unwritten rule about this in Italy. It is as though there is a social pact throughout the land with all adults, that if they treat the elderly as reverently as they would their own parents, then somewhere else someone will do the same for their parents. It is a lovely pact that I see enforced over and over again.

Our table companion begins to talk. My only reluctance in asking if I could join her was this. I know that a request to join someone means a request for conversation and interaction, unlike in Australia. In Italy it is an invitation to make a new friend and it would be incredibly rude to sit together and not speak. Luckily I have dark glasses on, so can nod occasionally while thinking my own thoughts and staring into space. I also have my husband here. He seems to be a magnet for Italian women, even if I say so myself, and particularly, but not confined to, older women.

Italian women are, in general, susceptible to Italian men in a much greater way than I have observed their northern European cousins to be. Whenever I need a favour and it's a woman I have to ask, I always send Alfredo. The way their faces open up, their eyes become more sparkly, their bodies more enigmatic and their smiles wider never fails to amaze me. And I take it as a deep compliment and am even more grateful that he chose me, a person who hardly let him hold my hand in public for the first three years of our relationship, who drew up a list of how chores were to be divided when he moved in and told him in no uncertain terms that a uterus was not a translation device for the instructions on how to operate the washing machine.

I listen while the elderly woman politely tells us how she had moved to the area in 1964, just as the first modern apartment blocks were being built in among the fields and open spaces that were here to begin with. Her husband worked on the railway and his office was nearby. She has now been without him for fifteen years, she tells us, and my heart breaks as it always does when I hear stories like this. They were married when she was eighteen and he twenty-two; they were each other's first and only loves. It is obvious she still misses him and their life together.

My husband and I share a suppressed laugh when she tells us that he was such a great husband that he took her out every Sunday to see Roma. At first I thought she meant that he took her out to walk around and visit Rome every Sunday, which to me would have been the definition of a lovely husband. But no, she meant to see Roma, the football team. He took her to see them play every Sunday for thirty years and for that she is still grateful.

She is also the quintessential elderly Italian woman in that her son lives with her, in fact has never not lived with her. She tells us he is forty-five.

'He has never found the right woman,' she tells us, with a hint of sadness and hesitation, which usually means he probably found at least one but he cheated on her and she didn't accept it, so she left him. The 'right' woman would have welcomed him back and understood. Italian mothers are endless in their defences of their sons.

These men are a well-documented social group in Italy. They are commonly referred to as *mamone*, or 'mummy's boys'. They never leave home and are cooked for and cared for by their mothers until they die. They are almost always single. No-one could ever compete and why bother when you would have to understand the washing machine instructions for yourself? Some of the first questions I asked Alfredo when I met him was, 'Do you live at home?' and, 'At what age did you leave?' These are standard questions you should ask Italian men if you are even remotely interested in one of them. If the answer to the first question is 'yes' or the answer to the second question is 'thirty-five' then leave and don't look back. It is, under no circumstances, worth it.

The week slowly fades away and the weekend embraces me while I listen to the story of a woman's life unfold. The story of Rome, fifty years ago and more. The sunshine is lapping my back for the first time in many months. I am outside enjoying my coffee instead of inside and I begin to appreciate the end of winter. The morning is moving on and, as much as I am enjoying listening and enjoying the woman's obvious joy at being listened to by somebody new, we need to buy vegetables. We respectfully wave goodbye, her giving us all the tips she knows about Garbatella's market stalls, such as who has the best produce at the best price, which is her compensation for the fact that we paid for her coffee. She makes us promise to find her at her usual coffee spot near the market where she goes every day.

Our vegetable shop is opposite the *bar* where we are sitting, which means we often end up having a coffee with our fruit and vegetable seller or waiting while he finishes his coffee. He is one of the few vendors left in Rome that actually sells their own produce. He has a market garden at the end of the suburb, just across the large main road that separates us from San Giovanni, the next suburb. It means his produce is zinging with freshness, always seasonal and that he has pumpkins. It is not a big staple of the Roman diet – I went for years without my favourite vegetable when I first came to Rome.

Fruit and vegetable sellers also provide service, as it is generally not acceptable to touch the produce yourself. You state what you want and how much and the vendor does it for you. This is the old-fashioned, lazy person's ideal produce shopping. I much prefer it to picking my own, bagging it, weighing it and standing in line to do each of these activities. On a Saturday morning when my brain is still scrambled from the week, it is enough for me to look and point.

I am also particularly open to suggestion. When my fruit and vegetable vendor says to me, 'Here, try this,' and shoves a piece of fruit into my mouth it always works, much to the annoyance of Alfredo, who thinks I am constantly taken as a soft-touch by all the wily Roman shopkeepers. It is helpful for me to be able to ask how to cook something though, to have a constant supply of home-grown pumpkins from October to March, to be able to buy one potato instead of a kilo and to get free herbs with every purchase.

Our fruit and vegetable man and his wife live next door to their shop. They also have a number of dried herbs from their own garden, and they collect various greens that grow wild in the parks and embankments of Rome. One such herb is called *ortiche* and is actually known as a nettle in English, though not the stinging kind. It looks like a rough version of spinach and is used in much the same way. It constantly amazes me that the shopkeeper has a variety of wooden crates filled with 'salad' or 'herbs' that are long-lost relatives of our common lettuces and greens, which grow wild all over Rome.

Everything is seasonal and I have given up asking for things that are not in season. For one, I can't stand the looks and responses I get, as though I am a crazy person.

'What?! Strawberries in February? They don't grow in February! There's no way you can get strawberries in February, what are you saying?'

And it continues. It took a number of years of this kind of verbal bashing for me to understand what fruits and vegetables were in season when, and every time I waited with baited breath to see if I would be called out like a fool, or whether they would say, 'I just sold out but I can have them for you tomorrow.'

Coming from a country that imports everything all year round, or freezes it for use later, I had completely lost touch with the meaning of 'seasonal'. At first, it seemed incredibly antiquated and restrictive.

What do you mean I can't eat strawberries in the middle of winter if I want to? I would think.

Now it feels like each season has its offerings and I look forward to the ebb and flow of produce, treating each one with excitement and as though it is special.

Our fruit and vegetable shop also sells eggs fresh from a farm, homemade *mozzarella di bufala* (the very best kind) and lately, *ricotta di bufala*. As our vendor is always trying to suggest produce to me and Alfredo is always trying to get him to stop, I had gone for about a year without trying any of these cheeses. Then one day I went there without Alfredo, and we wanted mozzarella for dinner. That night, as we were rolling around our dining table in ecstasy, having eaten double the serve we intended, I revealed that I had gotten the mozzarella from our fruit and vegetable guy, the one who was always suggesting we try it. There was no hint of chagrin whatsoever on my husband's face, but he never raised an eyebrow again when my hand dipped into the bowl full of milky white water to receive my weekly supply of *mozzarella di bufala*.

Last week Vincenzo suggested I try the ricotta. It came in a small pat, like butter, neatly wrapped in one sheet of paper, soft and slightly wet. He recommended to eat it with some jam. That evening, I ate almost the whole thing while I was cooking dinner. It was so soft and creamy, and also light. It tasted like a creamy cloud of compressed yoghurt. It had that slightly bitter aftertaste that comes from the buffalo cow. I thought it couldn't get any better until I tried it the next morning on toast with a slight layer of strawberry jam. More visions of heaven opened up to my tastebuds and I sang the praises of Vincenzo once more.

I tell him this on Saturday while he is bagging our goods. He responds by opening his wallet and giving his wife ten euro. He then proceeds to tell us the story of when his son was born and how he didn't eat for twenty-four hours but wasn't hungry, because just prior and in preparation he had eaten two large slices of homemade bread with *ricotta di bufala* and jam. His wife smiles and explains that he repeats this story so often (and many others) that she makes him pay her ten euro every time he does.

* * *

My husband and I go out once it is dark and head to our engagement of the evening, Rome's most famous jazz club, Alexanderplatz. Four of Italy's greats have gathered tonight to play their respective instruments – bass guitar, drums, piano and the double bass. It is small and crowded, as a jazz club should be. The service is erratic but is based on tables, so it feels quite civilised to be able to order a cocktail from our table and be served it there. It does take most of the concert for this to happen, but is nice when it does.

The crowd is hushed as the musicians begin to play, and they take my breath away. As my mind wanders and my heart opens to new possibilities, as my fingers tap and my head nods, I thank my husband, who introduced me to the experience of jazz. I had no interest in it whatsoever prior to meeting him and had to be enticed into listening to it before I understood how good it could be. I still know barely anything about it but I like the chaos, the flow, the way the music has a life of its own and sometimes just takes over, and that the musicians let it.

It takes a particularly brave person to allow that to happen time and time again, to create new spaces and flows, and to not mind exactly where you will end up.

Lightning Source UK Ltd.
Milton Keynes UK
UKHW010755211021
392589UK00004B/453